Listen deeply,

Listen deeply

IAD PRESS

et these stories in

Kathleen Kemarre Wallace
with Judy Lovell

Map of Places, 2007,
acrylic on canvas, 15 x 20 cm

This book is dedicated to the old people of Therirrerte, Uyetye, and Atnetarrkwe: teachers, healers, storytellers, parents, grandparents and custodians from the past. Their teachings give us the knowledge in this book.

Contents

Awelye akerte, Arrernte cultural life 1
Wantyeye-wantyeye-akerte 15
Travelling dance 17

Altyerre 21
Keringke Rockhole 32

Tyenge artweye akerte, My family, my country 35
Arelhe Arrentye 41
Evil spirit woman 44

Apmeraltye, People of one land 47
Arlewarrere Atherre-akerte 50
Whirly winds 51

Uyetye 55
Awele-awele Uyetyele Aneme 58
Bush tomatoes 61

Kwatye, Water 63
Ant lion sisters 69

Ngangkere, Traditional healer 75

Ahurratye, Drought 85
Artwe Anyente Mpwernikwe
Akweke-akerte Uyetyele 92
Brothers-in-law 94

Ltyentye Apurte community, Santa Teresa mission 97
Seven Sisters 101

Awenke arle aneme, Growing into a young woman 107
Arelhe Anyente Therirrertele 110
Desert flower spirits 111
Kwerralye Purle 112
Morning Star and Evening Star 115

Audio CD with Arrernte stories inside back cover

Amangkelhe-ileme, Growing up a big family 119
Tyangkertangkerte 121
Mother tree 124

Akngartiweme, What's happening now? 129
Alantye-akerte 134
Giant 137

Therirrerte 141
Apmere Arturte-akerte 145
Bat ancestors 148
Antethe-akerte Therirrertele Itwe 150
Young woman 152

Itelarentye, Knowing our culture 155
Evil spirit eagles 156
Tapping stick song 162

Akangkwirreme, Listen deeply 169
Emu man ancestor 171

About *Listen deeply* 177
About the paintings 179
Acknowledgements 180

Spirits and Skin Names, 2006, acrylic on ceramic, 42 cm diameter

Kathleen and grandchildren Luke Wallace, Jacob Doolan and Maureen Ellis.

The stories I'm sharing with you in this book and on the CD don't belong to me alone. They were told to me by my grandparents, mainly Atyelpe Therirrerte-arenye and Louisa Riley, and by some of my aunties and uncles – Agnes Abbott, Lena Hayes, Alan Drover, Urlampe-arenye – and other elders too, such as my husband Douglas Wallace and his father Bruce Wallace (Wallis). There were many of our people living here in the old days and these stories come from all of them, from their ancestors and before that from the *altyerrenge*, the time when the first beings created Arrernte people and our world. They're stories from my grandparents' country, our homelands – Arturte, Therirrerte, Uyetye, Mparnwenge (Hayes Springs), Irlkerteye (Salt Springs), Keringke, Itnewerrenge (Marion Springs), Antewerle, Atyenhenge Atherre, Ltyentye Apurte (Santa Teresa), Alherrulyeme and Tyelkempwe – from all those places, and other places around there. The stories I'll tell you are about some of these places, the ancestor days, the spirits of those places, and something of my life as I grew up.

Many of the people who taught me have passed away now, including my husband. I don't speak his name aloud anymore because it reminds me that he is gone, and that makes me feel sad. Arrernte people show respect to a deceased person and to the grief of their living relatives by leaving their name unspoken for some period of time. Like many other Aboriginal groups we use a special word,

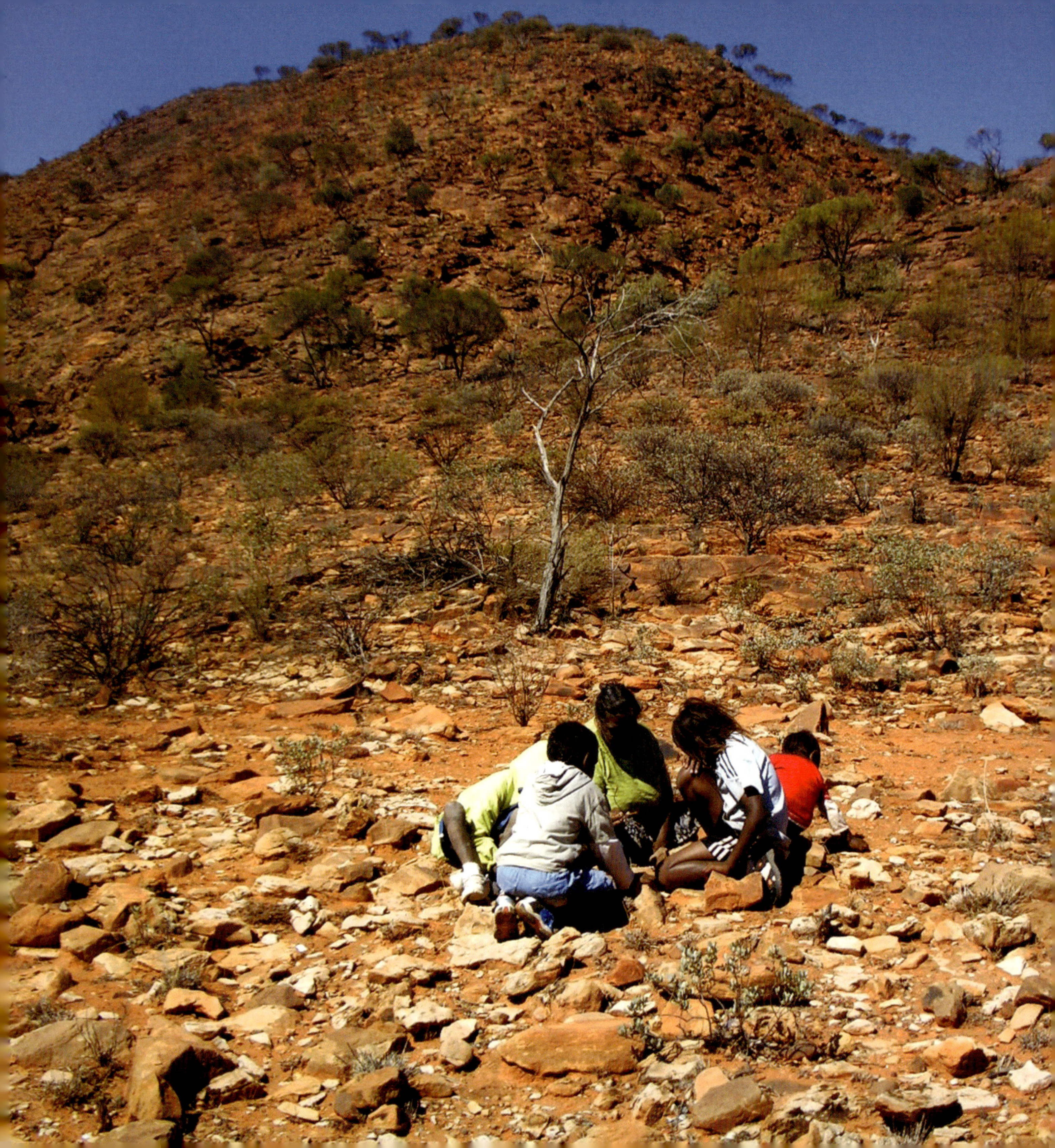

kwementyaye, instead of saying the name of the person who has passed away. We also use *kwementyaye* for all the people still alive who share the name of someone who's gone.

The stories in this book are for learning from and they are for sharing. When I first learnt them from my grandparents I had to work for the reward of a story – I hunted for lizards and collected bush food for the old people to earn my place to listen. Old people sometimes sang when they would tell a story – that's how they taught me – they showed me and sang to me in our own language. Originally, my people spoke a different language than the Arrernte we speak today. I think that old language is now lost, except in some of the song verses. It was similar to the Arrernte we speak today, but it wasn't quite the same. One old lady said to me just before she died in the 1990s that the language we had originally spoken was called Ingwarenye – it's like "midnight language" when you translate it. It's also called that because our old people kept to themselves, they were not well known to other language groups, so they were *ingwarenye* – separate, unknown. In the old days we never had books but the stories we told were often sung and danced. I have forgotten how to sing some of those old songs, in that old language, because when I first came into the mission I had to learn other things – a lot of other things – and I didn't hear those songs often at the mission.

We were only allowed to speak in English and I almost lost my language, but it is important not to forget our Arrernte knowledge. We need to speak and understand our languages so we can keep our knowledge.

As time went on and whenever I had the opportunity, I listened to a lot of the stories and I remembered many of them – I let those stories come into me. I thought really hard about them. They taught me many things. They stayed with me when I was living out bush as a young person, they kept me going, surviving, and knowing my own family and culture. The stories taught me about myself too. When we lost our bush life, they held me together through all the changes. In those days Auntie Aggie used to sing some of them and this helped me to survive when I was first at the mission. I can't sing anymore because now my voice is no good, and we don't dance as often, but we do still sit down together and sing and tell stories. I can remember my grandmothers and also Atyelpe, but Werirrte passed away when I was very small. I've been taught the stories for his country by my uncles and aunties. Some of them you can listen to on the CD.

OPPOSITE: Kathleen shows her grandchildren Bart Doolan, Maureen Ellis, Jacob Doolan and Luke Wallace the carved grinding stones.

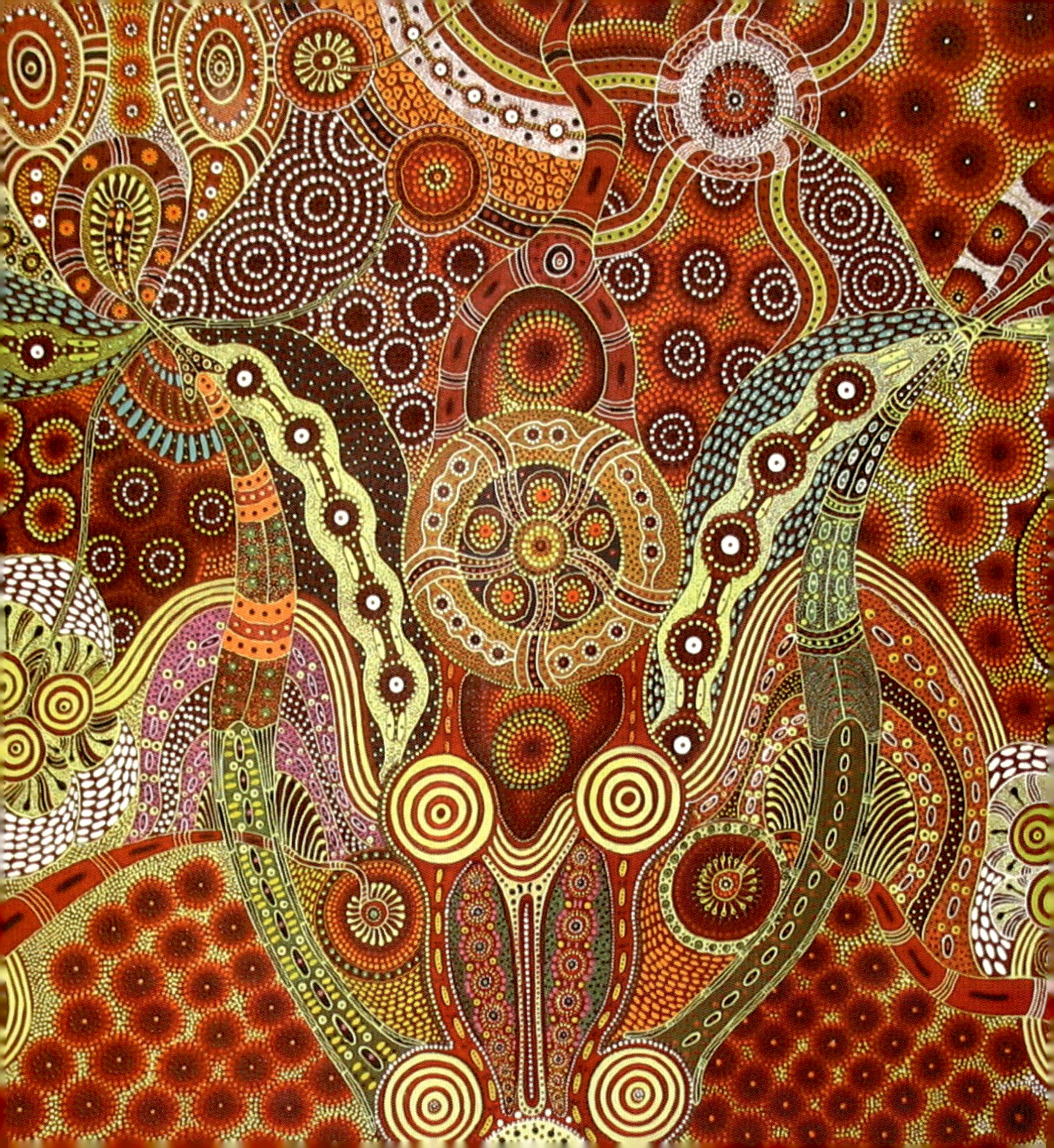

Awelye akerte, Arrernte cultural life

My people come from the *apmere*, land, which includes many places of great importance to us – they're the special places that come from our ancestors. They're places where our ancestors emerged in their country during the *altyerrenge*. In the early days, through dreams, these *altyerre* beings taught our human ancestors. They showed our ancestors ceremonies and taught them how to behave correctly using the skin system, a system of kinship and relationship; they gave them songs and dances and taught them how to paint and how to relate to the spirits.

We lived in this land that we have come from – all our food, medicine, clothing, decorations, weapons, tools, songs, stories – everything we needed – came from this country. There were many reasons to move around our homelands: to search for food and water, keep up with seasonal bush foods, clear and clean waterholes; to undertake ceremonies and other special activities like men's business, hunting, women's business, marriage and trade. It was important to know your country, it meant you could survive there and also that you knew how to travel into other places safely, respectfully. Things are different now, but the richness of our culture is still present, and the stories of these places are still important to learn – it's important to know what place you are a part of.

Living in this way was always hard work, but it got much harder when white men moved into our land because, since then, our

OPPOSITE: *Wantyeye-wantyeye*, 2004, acrylic on linen, 90 x 150cm (detail)

lifestyle has changed so much. These days our elders will sometimes finish up without sharing all of their knowledge with us younger ones. Sometimes we miss out on being taught by our old people because our families have been moved apart, but many Aboriginal people still learn and respect the ways of our *apmere*, its laws and business. Our elders take their

Altyerre Beings, 2003, acrylic on ceramic, 20 x 20 cm

wisdom from the *altyerrenge* and the spirits of *apmere*, and from them they understand what to teach the younger ones. These days we walk more in two worlds. We have to know how to make decisions and live with many other people, different cultures and religions, but we need our elders to grow us and our country up to be strong and to survive, to know our own world too. Aboriginal people have a lot of knowledge – we know country. Sharing this knowledge benefits everyone. All young people should learn the right way to survive in a community and how to share with and protect one another because most of all we need to learn how to look after the country together, learn how to survive with it.

Now I'm an elder. I want my children and other young people to learn from these stories. I want everyone to share the stories and learn about the land, and life and survival. That is why we decided to make this book – I'm going to use the book to tell you about some of the stories I was told, and about myself, and about some of the places that were homelands for my ancestors and that are still sites of importance for us today. These are the places where whole families of people lived, moving around our country, from one place to another. Sometimes they also contain *altyerrenge* sites or stories. It is important to make this book to teach others. There is plenty to teach – what my elders taught me I will pass on through the stories, the writing and the pictures in this book, so that you can also understand something about *altyerrenge*, and our homelands, before and now.

All the springs across my homelands are significant sites. Many of them have some petroglyphs, rock carvings, or *urlpe*, ochre paintings. Those rocks have been carved or painted, over and over. They were still being painted by the old men in the 40s and 50s

Spirits Who Give Knowledge, 2005, acrylic on canvas, 16 x 12 cm

LEFT TO RIGHT: Grinding and testing ochre from Tyelkempwe Creek in preparation for dancing.

when I was a child; then still in the 60s, even after the mission life began, some old men kept on looking after those paintings. I paint on canvas because it is a modern way to keep the stories alive and offer this knowledge to other people. Many old people have passed away now, and the younger ones don't seem to think about repainting the old sites anymore. I think the traditional owners should keep painting them, fix them again. They should all know the stories about their places – the springs and rockholes, the ancestors' sites and the features. It is still the men's job to look after those rock paintings.

I remember the paintings in different caves and at the springs. I used to watch sometimes while the men were painting them, renewing the stories. That was exciting for me because every time there was a ceremony, it was time to mix up *urlpe* with fat or with water and to paint it on people. The red ochre on the caves was usually mixed with kangaroo fat. The white and yellow were mixed with water. For brushes the men used to use sticks. They made a stick very straight, heating it in the fire and straightening it to make the handle. Those brushes gave really good lines. Painting out bush was linked to very important activities and times when the larger family groups all came together. In those times I learnt how to find, grind, mix and use *urlpe*. I still know the body paint designs using the right colours and shapes.

That *urlpe* the men used in ceremonies needed to be taken from the right place, and prepared with the correct men involved and with the appropriate singing and other activities. The body paint designs had to be the right ones too. These jobs are all shared out according to a man's position in his family and their relationship to the country where they are making the ceremony.

The places we camped at, lived in and visited often had rock art which had been painted and carved over many hundreds of years. It is the hands of my ancestors speaking to us from the country, telling us about the *altyerrenge*, the days of our ancestors, our laws and business, the creation of our homelands and the spirits who still inhabit them. I learnt many things from those paintings and from listening respectfully to their stories. They spoke to me deeply. Through all my life those stories have guided me and strengthened me.

Years after I had learnt to paint body designs for ceremony, I learnt to use acrylic paints and shop brushes, and then I made cultural designs, and painted the stories I had learnt and remembered from my elders. This kind of contemporary painting is a good way to teach other people about us, our culture, our country, our stories. We still have to be very careful with using those cultural things because we also have to respect the ownership and appropriate access to knowledge from our elders.

OVERLEAF LEFT: Rock carving of hunters from the *altyerre*.

OVERLEAF RIGHT: *Tyepetye*, sand drawing of hunter from *altyerre*.

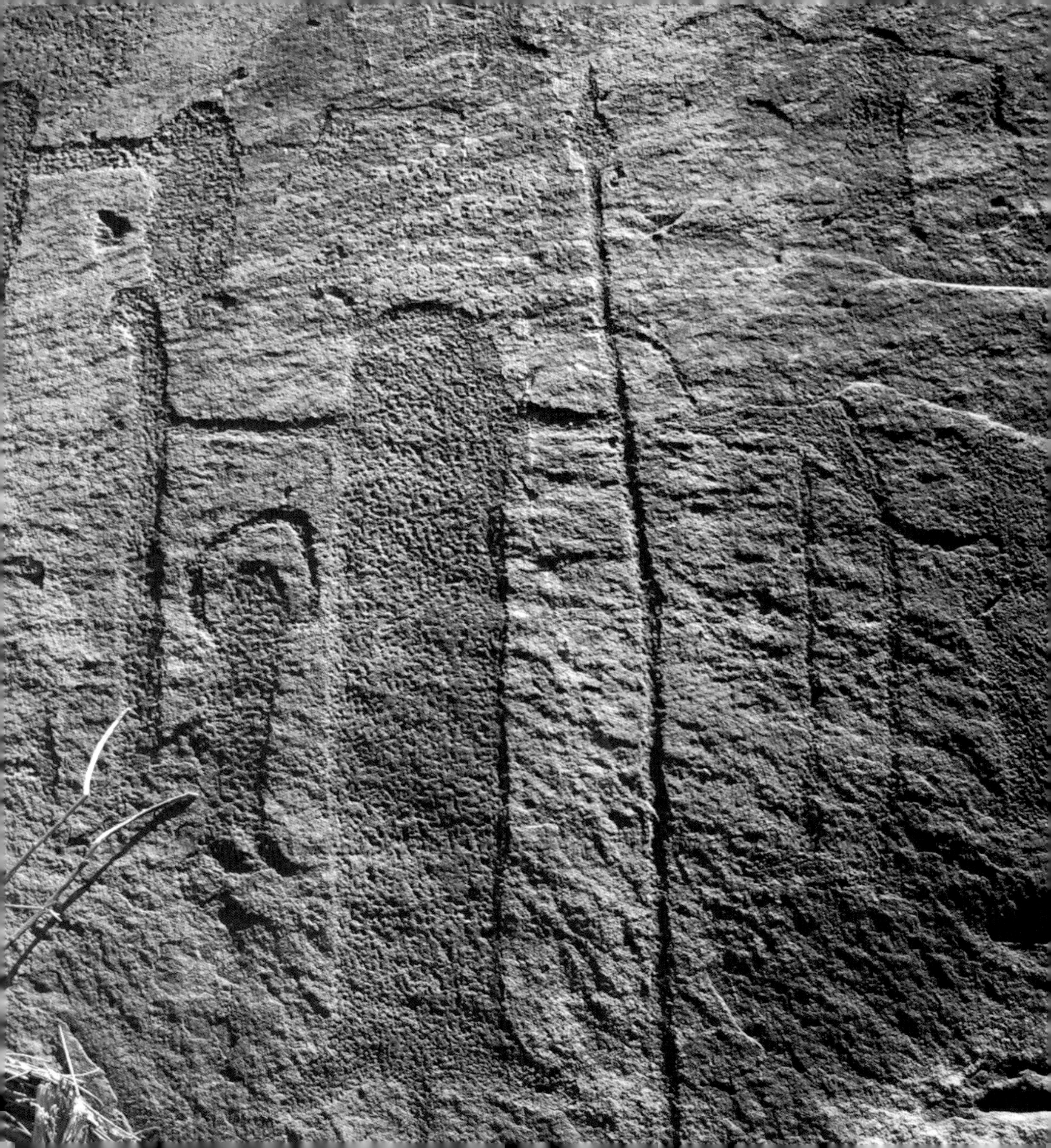

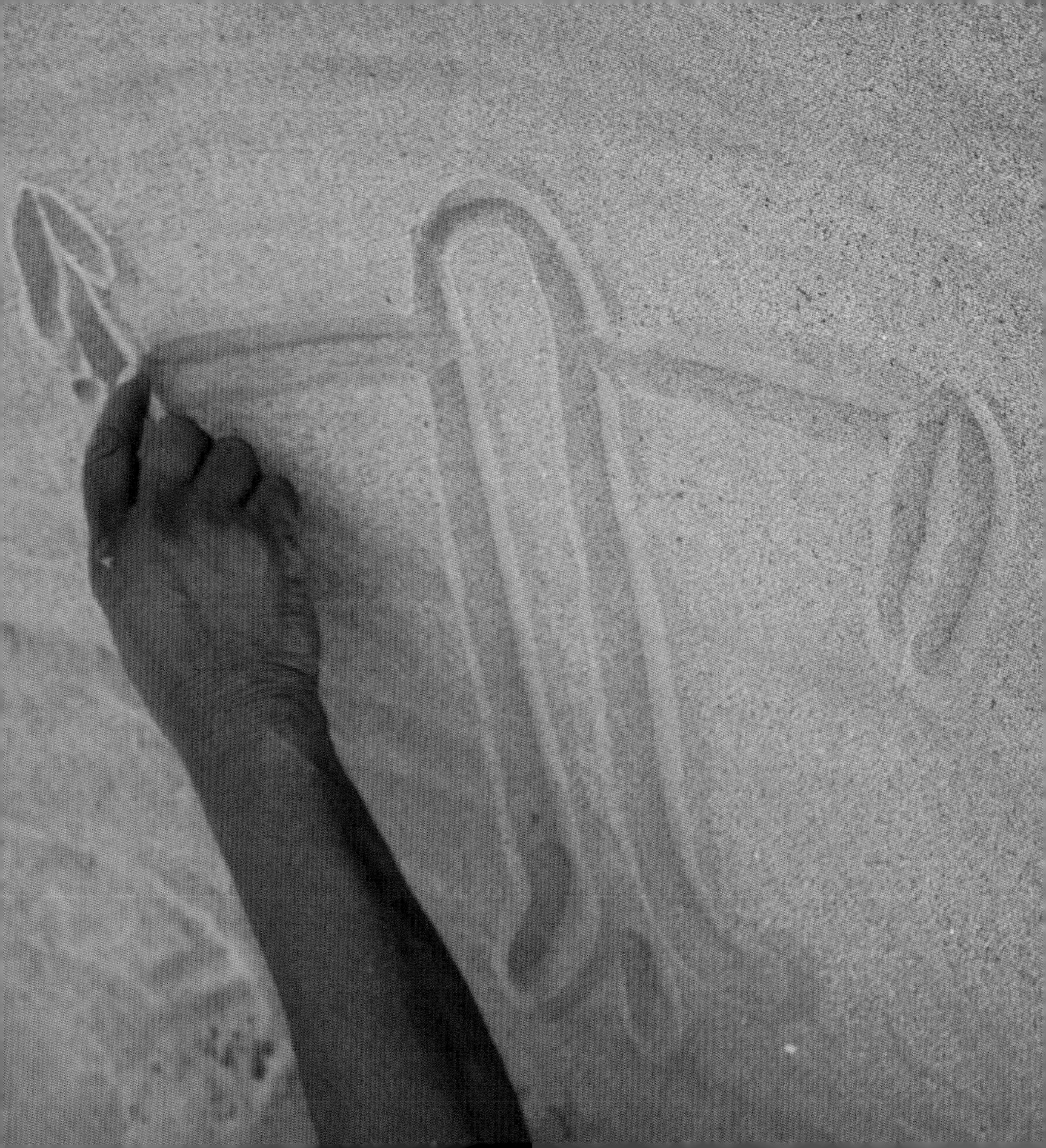

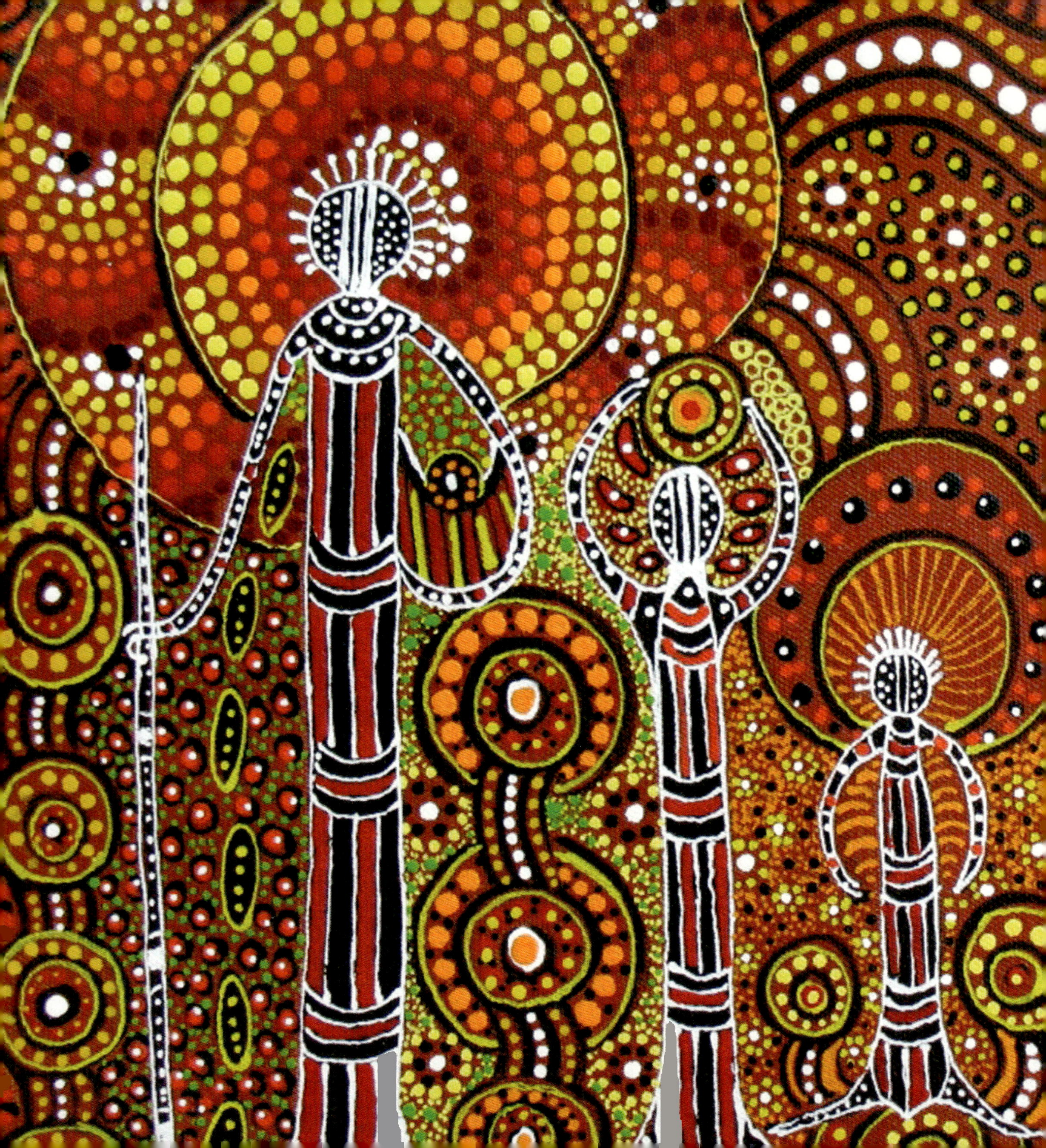

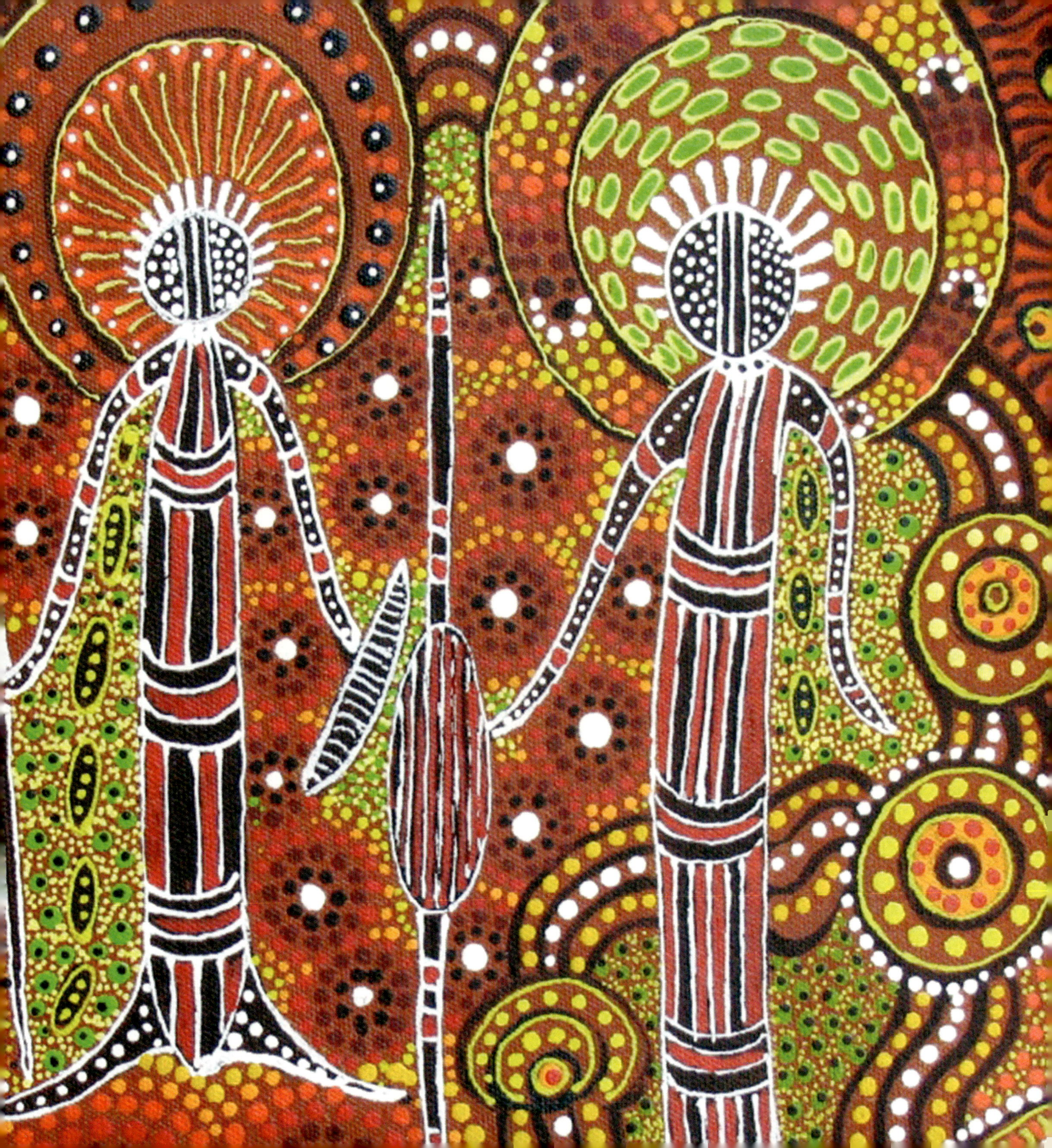

PREVIOUS: *Ancestors of Therirrerte*, 2008, acrylic on linen, 34 x 24 cm (detail)

We still have to look after the knowledge and pass it on in the right ways. Painting is a vital way of telling a story for me, and for all Aboriginal people.

I was already painting before my grandfather Atyelpe died. I had asked his permission to use designs from our country in my paintings after I realised that we needed to turn to our cultural knowledge and to preserve that and teach it to the younger ones. He gave permission to me. At the time, I was living at Ltyentye Apurte, Santa Teresa, and painting landscapes with fabric paint onto clothes. Some of the other women I was painting with wanted to do their own thing too; they were thinking about their old stuff, the cultural designs they used to do. We were thinking about doing those in a different kind of paint, acrylic paint. But first we had to ask permission from the old people.

Even though I had permission to use figures and designs from rock carvings, that didn't mean I knew all the stories. There are some carved *altyerre* beings from my homeland, carved into the rock at a place near the Simpson Desert. The figures are very old – belonging to our ancestors. Even though my grandfather gave me his permission to use the figures and other carvings in my own painting, to carry forward the stories and designs from the old people, they have no story for me. I was never told about them in detail.

I asked Atyelpe, my grandfather, and he said, "it's all right for you to do this". Different people were told differently by their elders. You see, some of the women were frightened to paint circles, because circles are special things, powerful things. The men used to paint and carve circles out in the caves and on the rocks and the women were very concerned about breaching any laws, or making themselves or the country sick. In the past it was the men who did the circles, that's why I had to ask my grandfather's permission. Then I had to make them a bit differently, to show things in my way.

We have songs for many places and things, which teach us too. Sometimes those are sacred and secret things. We don't share those things because they might be dangerous, bring sickness or damage to our ancestors or our country. Those things are taken care of through Aboriginal law and business. Songs can come from the country and be especially for a certain place, but we also have songs for telling stories, for teaching, for healing, for passing messages over long distances, and for other things concerning our spirit world. The power of songs is also used by *ngangkere* for their business, too. *Ngangkere* are our traditional healers, whose special abilities have kept us well for many generations.

Before, there was a lot of singing and dancing that brought people together, all

Ancestors of Therirrerte, 2008, acrylic on linen, 34 x 24 cm
My grandfather's spirit and those of our old people before him still reside in this place.

painted up. We had a lot of happy times, plenty of *urnterrirreke*, celebrations, where everyone joined in, dancing and singing together. We still have *urnterrirreke* where the families bring their children and we all share dances and songs together, learning. These are public ceremonies, for everyone. These dances are when we spend time with our family, the ancestors, the spirits and our *apmere*, too.

Before dancing the ground is cleared enough for bare feet or else we have to wear shoes. Sometimes dancers used to use big long, decorated sticks. The dancers stood these up or held on to them, maybe even swinging the stick right around. In some dances they used a big stick, painted with ochre, but with feathers put on top. All the different coloured ochres, plus the white lime and the black charcoal,

LEFT: *Dancing Woman*, 2005, acrylic on canvas, 16 x 12 cm

RIGHT: *Dancing Spirit Women*, 2005, acrylic on canvas, 16 x 12 cm

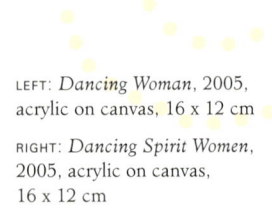

were used to represent particular designs. The designs and the colours of the design belong to the person, the ceremony and the place. There are many combinations of colour and design – many of them represent a totem or ancestor, a ceremony and place. This is what we have to know about before we paint the body designs onto the dancers, or decorate the poles or dancing sticks.

Dancing sticks were made especially for certain people and certain ceremonies. When we finished the ceremony it was important to put the stick back somewhere special until next time. As children, we had our own little dancing sticks and bunches of leaves made for us, then after the dance we could leave behind these little sticks and leaves – ours didn't matter.

Arrernte people used to keep the dancing sticks in a safe place, always choosing the right dancing stick for the ceremony, or making a fresh one if needed. Many of the important objects that were used by the men were not for the eyes of the women and children, and these things were also kept very safe in special places. As young women growing up, it was something we had to learn, places to avoid because of their significance to the men's business. When we were considered old enough to look after ourselves we were sent out to show our learning. This was a hard journey, we must travel always knowing which way to go, and gather the food available in any one place without being told by our elders. We could do this together, or even with family, but we had to

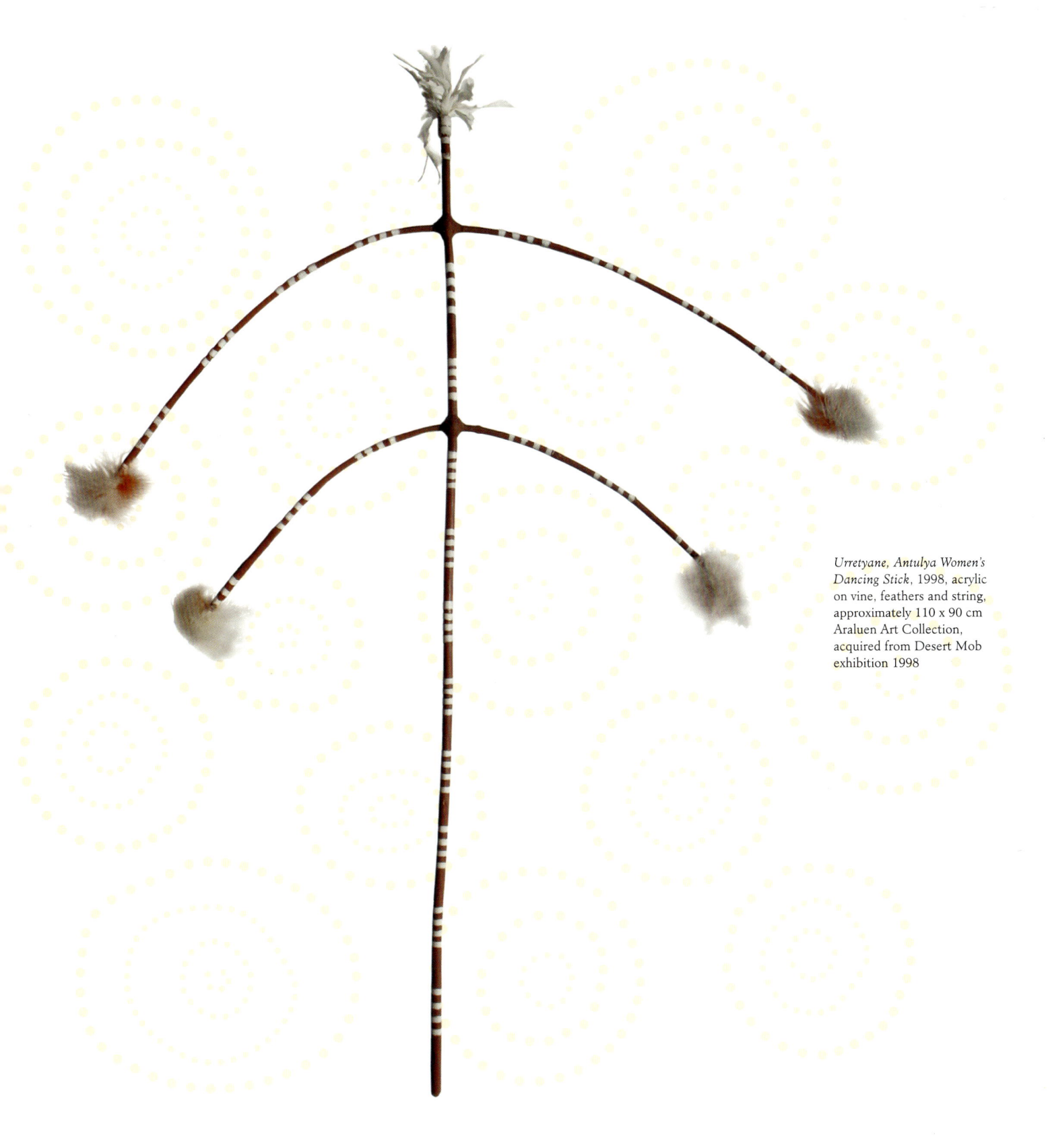

Urretyane, Antulya Women's Dancing Stick, 1998, acrylic on vine, feathers and string, approximately 110 x 90 cm
Araluen Art Collection, acquired from Desert Mob exhibition 1998

show that we had learnt everything in the years we had been taught. When we could do this well we were considered to be grown women. This is how it was in the days before. I had to learn this way, a lot of us were taught like this.

We still paint our dancers up with their special designs using *urlpe*. Women have their own special designs, colours and ceremonies too. I was told by my grandparents that, in the early days, our ancestors did not know what to do with the *urlpe*. We understand that when consciousness was just beginning, before our ancestors had learnt very much, people would paint themselves any old way, without a design. *Altyerrenge* beings gave us knowledge about the colours including designs to use in ceremonies. "Why don't you paint yourselves like this for ceremonies? You can use the charcoal and the red, yellow ochre and white lime," they said. Since then, we've learned what the old people taught us, which was what they learnt originally in the *altyerrenge*, from the ancestors. They showed us that the colours are for the ceremony, and the design is for the kin group you are with and the ceremony you are dancing in. Through dreams, *altyerre* beings showed people where to go to find *urlpe*. That is how our ancestors came to know how to use them. That's still happening, too. Spirits are still teaching our people through their dreams.

When we all dance together, the whole family, we paint up for ceremony to make everyone feel happy, but also to make sure we look similar to *irrernte-arenye*, our spirit ancestors. They are the incarnate spirits of the *altyerre* beings who reside within us until we pass away, and they join in when we dance. Dancing in ceremonies helps to look after our land, our culture and spirits, and that's why *irrernte-arenye* join in when we dance.

I was at Uyetye with my grandparents when I was old enough to walk. I lived in the *alwekere*, or women's camp. I didn't live with my parents; I slept and lived with the group of women. This is how we had all lived out bush for a long time before the mission. We would listen to stories and join in the dancing. We girls, single women and older women slept in the *alwekere* and the single men and boys slept in the *arnkentye* – there were plenty of times when we all got together to sing and dance. I remember we did a lot of dancing at Todd River Station, later on – every night we would dance.

Wantyeye-wantyeye-akerte

Wantyeye-wantyeye the areke ayenge akweke-arle anerlenge, Apmere Alyathengeke. Itne-arle akwetethe urnterrirretyarte. Atningke rarle apetyetyarte apmere arrpanenhe-ntyele. Awelye atningke anthurre re itne: Antulye-arenyeke, Therirrerte-arenyeke, Arlkwete-arenye awelye, ane Wantyeye-wantyeye yanhe ikwere, itne urnterrirretyarte. Yanhe itnenhe ingkerreke, ampe mape-arlke urnterrirretyarte. Arelhe akngerre mape angwerre-angwerre arne mpwaretyarte, intelhe-iletyeke arne mape urrtyane-arlke mpwaretyarte. Urrtyane apele arne urntentye akngerre nhenge itne akngernelhe-iletyarte amekerre tnemele, Antulye-arenye mape-kenhe. Penangke mape-kenhe ane Angale-kenhe. Therirrerte-arenye arne arlpennge akweke ware. Arlkwete-arenye awelye-kenhe arne arlpennge kine.

Wantyeye-wantyeye arlpennge ulkere aneke. Arne akngerre-apenhe re itnekenhe aneke, anteke ulkere. Atherrame itne ngkernetyarte, artepeke-atherre. Ampe-arle the aretyarte. Arelhe-arlke, ingkerreke anthurre-arle apetyeke. Arrpenhe-arle apmerele anetyeke arrangkwe. Ingkerreke anthurre-arle apetyeke apmere urnterretyenhe ikwere-werne. Arrpenhe ingkerne apetye-alpetyeke arrangkwe! Arelhe mapenge anetye-alperle artwe apeke re ingkerne apetye-alperlenge. Alyentye akngerre mape akenhe akwintyele anerrirrerlenge arlenge. Ahelhe-arle atyete anthurre renhe itne mpwareke. Arne renhe-atherrenhe ngkernerle mpepeke, intelhentye atherre. Kele arelhe re imernte, artwe-arlke, urntetyemele-urntetyemele urnterrirremele. Kele imerte ikwere-iperre itne anemele aneme. Intelhentye itnekenhe aneke ane tyelarre itnekenhe akenhe mperlkere. Akenhe alte-nge mperlkere akweke artikwenge arlpere aneme. Artikwe apele akweke anthurre arlpe-arenye. Arlkwetyarte kere akweke itnenhe, tile atnyenerlenge urnteye-arle arrerneke arelhe mapeke alteke-alteke arlpere arrernemele. Akenhe irrketye akweke-akerte, anintyepintyeme. Tharle akwete renhe itelareme.

Akenhe artwe mape akenhe atyeyarte-akerte aneke, arlpennge akngerre. 1950s the areke, anyente-ngare ware the areke, utyaknge nhenge the arerle-iweke. Akenhe arnwere mwerre akngerre re aneke, Wantyeye-wantyeye nhenhe. Ayeye mape itne-arle ileme Wantyeye-wantyeye yanhe ikwere, iwenhe apeke re itne aneke? Awengkere

Wantyeye-wantyeye, 2005, lino cut on paper, 39 x 28 cm

apeke arelhe itne aneke anintyepintyemele. Arrkene-kwenhe-irrerreme ingwartentyele. Mape atningke re apetyewerretyarte apmere arrpanenhenge-ntyele Wantyeye-wantyeye ikwerele ane itne imerneke kine itneke-kenhe, ayeye itnekenhe. Mape akenhe nhenge akangkentye anthurre re. Arelhe mape intelhentye ware. Artwe mape intelhentye akine aneke.

Arrpenhe apeke inge arnpeme Wantyeye-wantyeye-iperre impatye rarle irlkerte-arle-irreme. Wantyeye-wantyeyeke artweye ante irlkngeme renhe.

Wantyeye-wantyeye-arteke itnekenhe kine aneke apmere arrpanenhe, urrwempele aneke. Ayeye itnekenhe imernerlte-apemele apmere arrpanenhe ikwere. Nhake-ampinye mape ante ware apeke apentirretyarte. Apmere Port Augusta-nge Arrernte mape apetyeke, Arrernte apmere Altyerrenge aneke. Yanhe ikwerenge Arrernte mape arrateke kwatyenge-ntyele, atyenge ileke-arle. Ampwe mape atyenge ileke; yanhe ikwerenge itne arrateke. Arelhe anyente arrateke. Ikwerengentyele mape atningke atnyenemele nhenhe ularre apetyemele angkentye arrpenheme anteme irreke. Awenhe-awenhe atyinhe, Werrirte-arenye, yanhe atyenge ileke.

Wantyeye-wantyeye, 2004, acrylic on linen, 90 x 150 cm

Travelling dance

I remember, when I was young, travelling with my family from Uyetye almost as far as Alice Springs. We were with a large group of other Arrernte people, and every night there was a different dance performed by the ones whose country we were in. I have painted a really big canvas about the dancing we did as we travelled. I'm not sure, but I think the dancing was part of the activity for a big ceremony and that it was the last time that big ceremony happened across our homeland – across that Arrernte country. It was probably about 1955. We were in a group which included women and children, but there were more dances and ceremonies happening around our camp than just the ones we saw each night. Once the dances had started people weren't allowed to come into the area; they either had to stay at home or at the performance. Those were strictly kept rules. This kind of dance cycle doesn't happen nowadays because the old people who knew the songs and the dances have passed away.

I think this big *urrwempele*, or travelling ceremony that we danced in, was called *Wantyeye-wantyeye* and men, women and children all performed in part of it together. It was about *apmere*, showing the stories of different places in our country. As we travelled, we connected the places and the people through the dances. Different country has different stories and that came through in each dance. The *altyerre* beings taught a dance to people through the dreams of our elders for each totem site, then people performed these dances in their *apmere*, country, showing the rest of us. This is still one way the spirits tell us ancestor stories and teach us dances and songs.

The *urrwempele* group travelled around through lots of language groups, like a long dance cycle connecting from one place to another. During the nights we shared songs and dances of our *apmere*, and then when we travelled, others showed their songs and dances to us, in their *apmere*.

Every place we stopped for the performances the ground was made smooth first. Sometimes dancers moved around on their knees, sometimes spinning around. This way they made particular little tracks in the sand and those footprints and tracks were part of the meaning, part of the performance, part of the dancing. I remember the dancers up on their feet dancing, then kneeling on the ground, they danced and moved towards the people singing.

Two poles stood up in the sand. They danced around and between them. The men and women worked together to cut the trees and make the poles, painting them with a little bit of red ochre, decorating them on the top with feathers. I remember white cockatoo feathers sticking up from the top of the poles.

The women elders wore hairstring headbands woven of their own hair, with *atirrkwe*, the tails of little marsupial rats, hanging at the sides. The hairbands had white, red and yellow ochre painted on them. This headdress was only worn by certain older women and we children had little headbands. It all looked beautiful – fire light, moon light, black arms and legs painted with ochre in special designs, the white tails on headbands, glowing.

This dancing happened a long time ago now. There's still dancing and singing of course, but not like the *Wantyeye-wantyeye*. It had started in the south originally, but it travelled all around to the area of Alice Springs then as far north as the Utopia mob. We were all peaceful people on this side, all really peaceful. This dance took place when summer was over and it wasn't too hot, but before the cold nights. We had big fires every night and all of us sat around them, watching, singing and dancing. It was really beautiful. There must still be a few living who remember it, but the last person who lived at Ltyentye Apurte and who danced has died – he was my grandmother's brother, Tim Riley.

Now days, everyone's too busy to follow the dances, and we aren't allowed on all that country anymore either, so mostly we just remember all that has passed.

Cultural Learning, 2007, acrylic on canvas, 55 x 35 cm

Tyepetye-ileme arrentye yaye, sand drawings from the Evil Spirit Woman story.

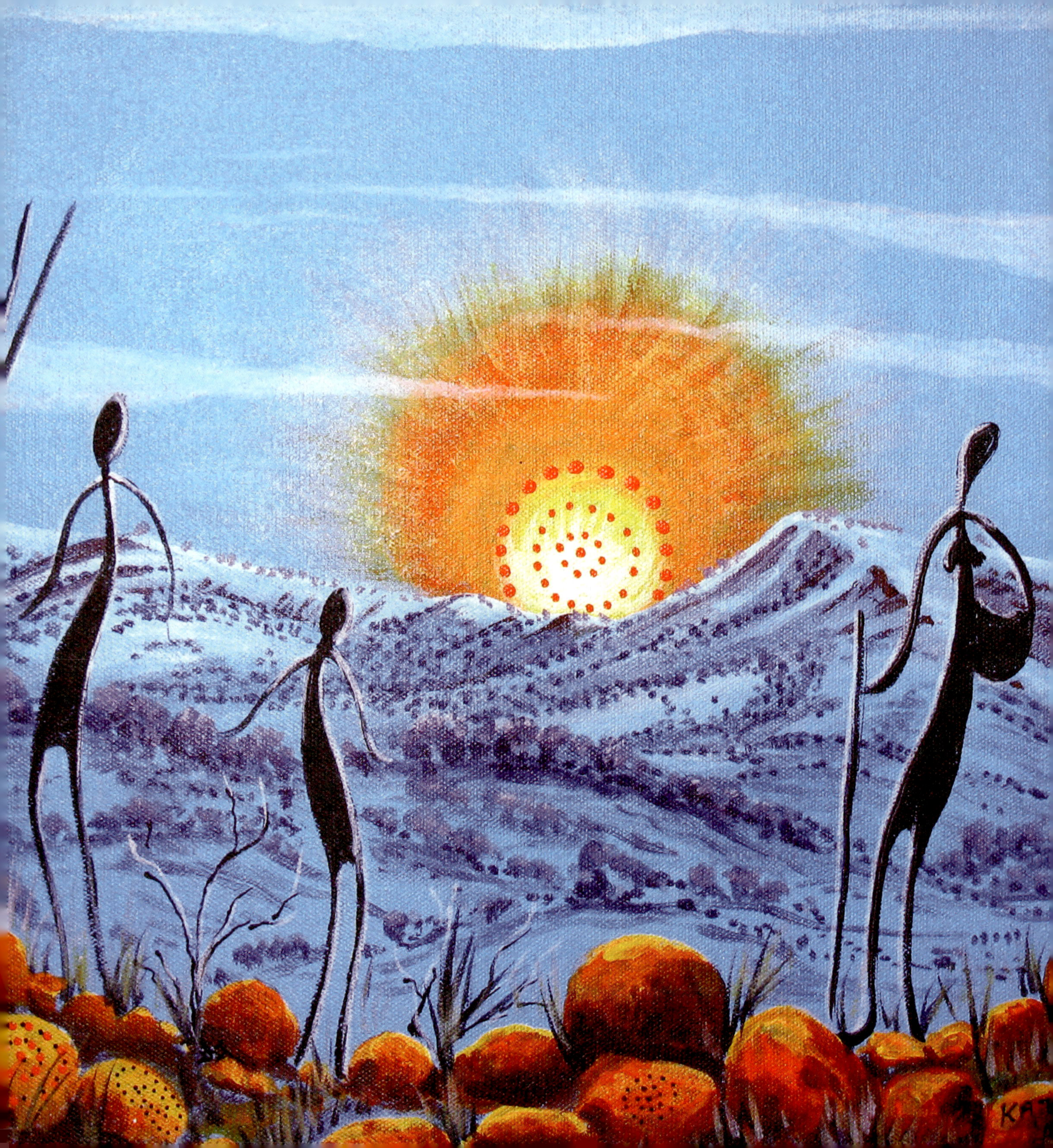

Altyerre

Arrernte people believe that there was a spirit long before anyone or anything existed and that this spirit made the earth first, then the stars, and then people. We call this *altyerrenge*; it's the time which was the beginning. Everything that exists today was first made in the *altyerrenge* – the grasses and earth, and seeds, the trees for shade and food – so that the country would have everything that Arrernte needed. The *altyerre* beings brought the earth into being and gave the Arrernte body and spirit so life could have a form. They were really happy to see their creation and the people in it. We remain connected to the *altyerrenge* through our totems and our incarnate spirits of this *apmere*. "We'll teach them everything," the *altyerre* beings said.

That's how our people learnt about how to go hunting, what seeds to gather, how to relate to one another, and how to keep their bodies and spirits strong through the healing arts and ceremonies.

In the *altyerrenge*, totemic beings appeared. They were capable of changing their form at will and moved around freely, travelling vast distances in any shape they chose. It was through these totemic ancestors, *altyerre* beings, that Arrernte were brought into life, given our skin groups, our totemic groups, our sacred sites and our spirits. Our spirits reflect our totem, and exist as a representative from our conception place. The totems we have are sometimes plants, animals or features of the land. I have the totem of my grandfather

ABOVE AND OPPOSITE (detail): *Keringke Spirits*, 2008, acrylic on linen, 30 x 46 cm

Werirrte – which is *alekapare*, the collared sparrowhawk. I also have the female totem of *aheyenenhe*, the sandhill python which was present at my conception site. My mother had the conception spirit of the *aherre*, red kangaroo, at Keringke.

We have many different spirits in our world who interact with us and our *apmere*, and who influence our lives – they too developed in the *altyerrenge*. Some spirits reveal themselves to certain people, or at certain times or in certain places, and might be helpful or tricky, depending on things we may not understand. Some of the spirits you'll hear about in these stories are *irrernte-arenye*, *arremparrenge*, *utnenge*, *arrentye* and *aleperentye*. *Irrernte-arenye* are incarnate spirits which enter a person at birth. After death, *irrernte-arenye* returns to the *apmere* to reside in their father's father country, at his conception site. *Arremparrenge* is a living spirit which exists in two parts. One of those parts resides within the living person, and the other resides at the person's totemic site – from there it may move around and show itself to others for any number of reasons. The part of the spirit which lives inside the person can also leave the body and move around independently when necessary. *Utnenge* is another living spirit. It is *utnenge* which may leave the body when it is sick. If it does leave the body when the body is sick, *utnenge* will usually hide away in cool holes in the ground. *Arrentye* are evil or malevolent spirits who can present themselves in the form of any thing. They can be extremely dangerous and evil, or fierce. They may even eat human flesh. *Aleperentye* is a woman assassin with spirit properties, sent to harm or kill a specific individual. She also exchanges her own spirit children for our real children sometimes.

If we had no living spirits, our life would be nothing to us. It is the spirit in us who makes us do things, move around and live life. Most of us have had the sensation that our spirit has left us at some time, and it makes us feel empty. Arrernte live with the awareness of spirits as an important and natural part of our existence. All of us have awareness of the spirits of our ancestors, our country and ourselves.

RIGHT: *Tyepetye-ileme*, sand drawings. Clockwise from left: design of kangaroo tracks; tracks of sandhill python; little birds' tracks.

OPPOSITE: *Irrernte-arenye*, 2006, reduction lino cut, 15 x 15 cm

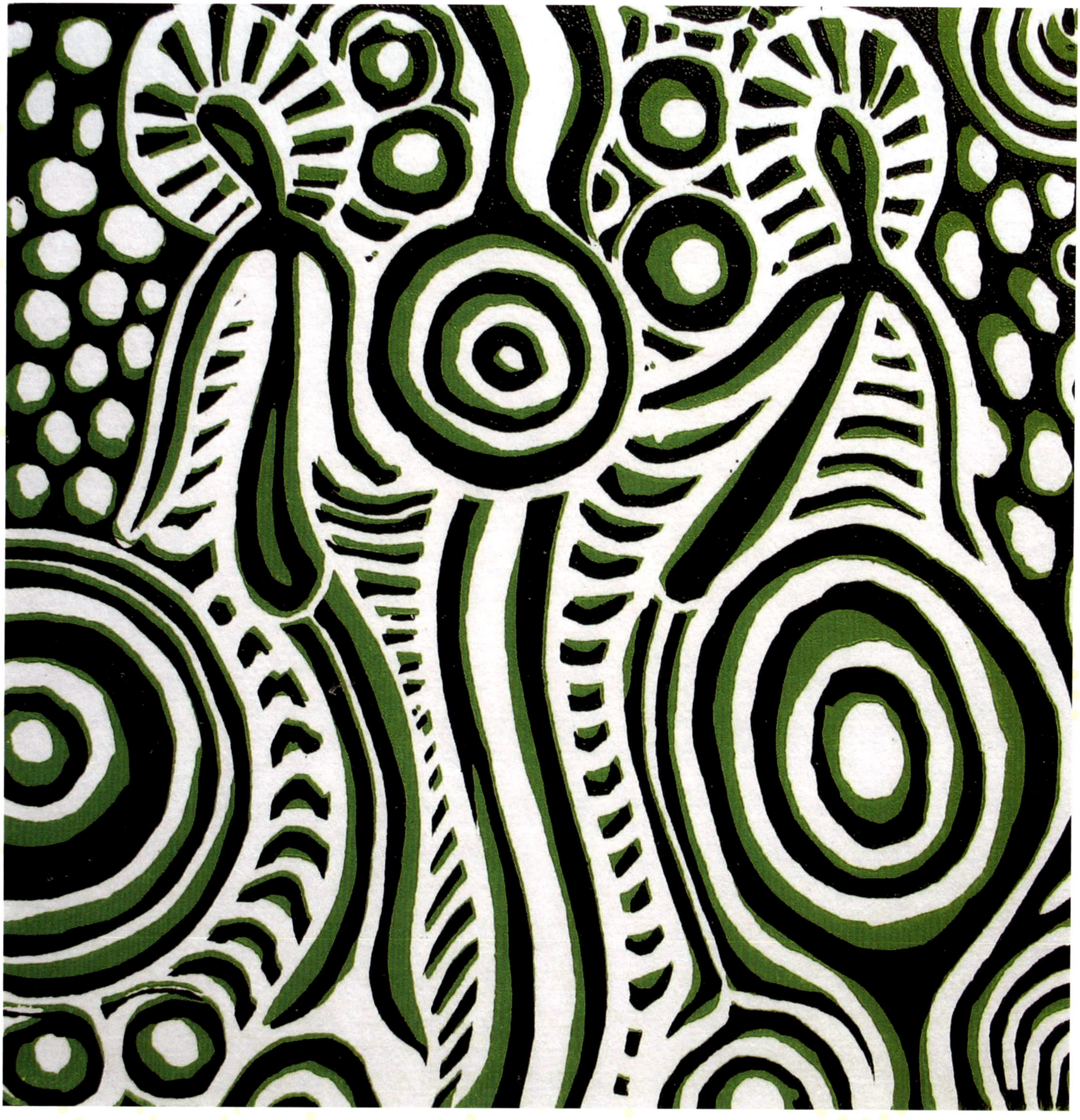

When a body grows tired and it cannot hold the spirit any longer, the person passes away. In times before the mission days, if someone passed away when they were far from home, people left the body wherever it lay. *Irrernte-arenye* strives to travel back to its *apmere* regardless of where the body lies. When somebody passed away near home we had a ceremony after they were buried which included dancing, singing and using kangaroo bone fragments on the burial site.

First, people painted themselves with lime and charcoal, only the white and the black. Then we smashed some left-over kangaroo bones into little fragments. We put the little bone pieces all over the grave. If one fell off the grave and went out of place it signified that one person was involved wrongfully in that death. If three or four pieces fell off, three or four were involved in that death. The way the bones fell off the grave showed us which direction those involved came from, making it possible to follow clues from the bones to find and punish those involved in the death. If the bones fell on top of the grave and nothing else – then the person had died naturally. To my knowledge this ceremony was undertaken only once after the mission was built at Santa Teresa. That was when my uncle passed away. Nobody does it anymore but in the early days at the mission my family still lived by their traditions. When my uncle passed away people covered their faces in ashes, and women added hair to their special hair rope.

After the ceremonies, the *ngangkere*, traditional healer, can help *irrernte-arenye* leave the body if it can't do so itself. After the death of a person *irrernte-arenye* will go back to their grandfather's country – their father's father's country. I will go back to Atnetarrkwe near Uyetye, where the totem of Werirrte-arenye, my grandfather, is. It is the same for all, *irrernte-arenye* go back to the father's father's country to reside in cool places, caves and under the ground.

In the *altyerrenge*, when our ancestors were still learning the first things about life, an ancestor passed away. This was a new experience for everyone. At first, the spirit thought that he had left his family behind for

Fragments of kangaroo bones.

LEFT TO RIGHT:

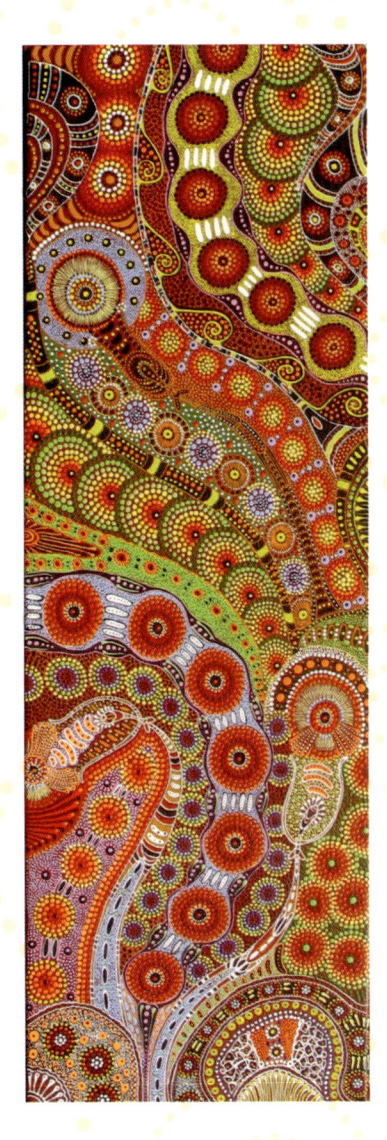

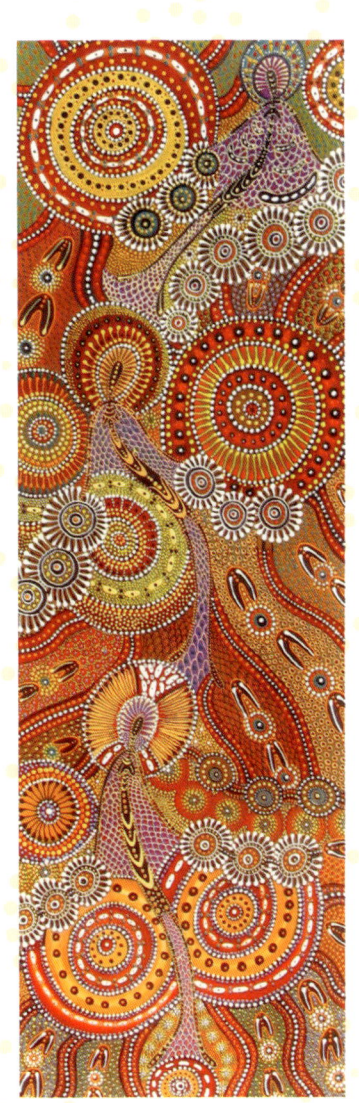

Spirits in the Landscape, 2003, acrylic on canvas, 90 x 30 cm

Ntyethe-spark, 1996, acrylic on canvas, 122 x 41 cm

Irrernte-arenye of Keringke, 2005, acrylic on canvas, 90 x 30 cm

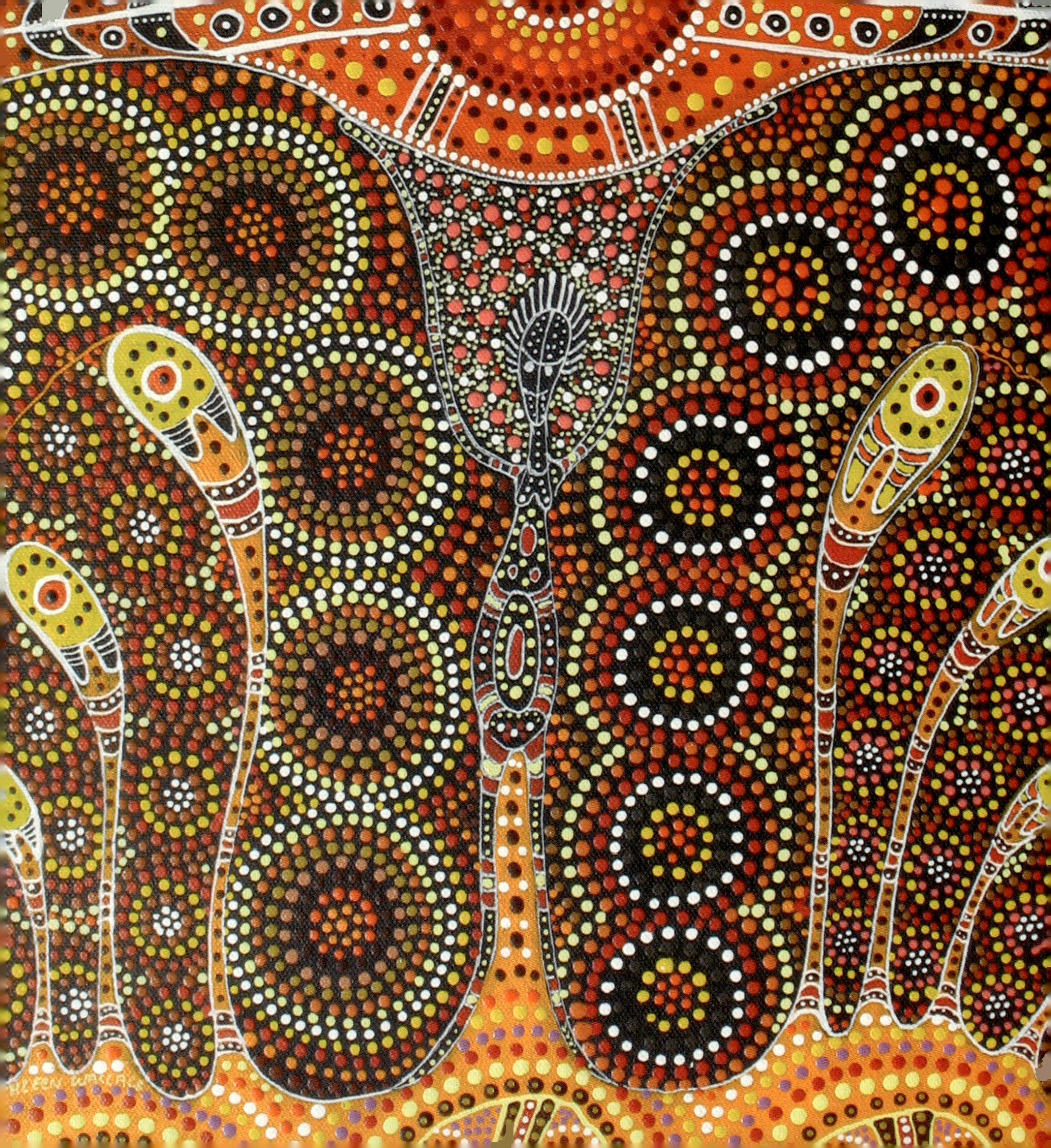

good. Where he was travelling was very dark so he couldn't see where he was going. Still, he travelled on, feeling his way. He hadn't travelled very far from the old body when he joined the spirit world where he would live in the cool dark of a cave. The spirit was *irrernte-arenye*. Turning around to look back to where he has left his body, he couldn't see his living family at all. He was walking slowly now, stumbling along and over rocks. As he cracked some rocks together under his feet, sparks lit up the darkness. He felt around on the ground wondering what made the sparks. He found the rocks and, by hitting them together and adding some grass, made a bright fire. In this way he made the first flames, which he gave back to his living family to create light and warmth. This is how our ancestor made the first fire for his living Arrernte family.

The *irrernte-arenye* are always present in country wherever our old people have lived. They like to live underground where it is cool and dark, and they watch over the country. If you travel somewhere unfamiliar, *irrernte-arenye* might not recognise you. Then they may play tricks with you. Sometimes they can make the ground appear to turn around so you won't know which way to go, or sometimes they will throw little things at you, making you jump. They can be tricky! *Irrernte-arenye* can also be good, and teach you, if you can listen. They can act as guides towards living the right way, and taking care of yourself and your responsibilities to others. *Irrernte-arenye* are also very important guides for *ngangkere*, who can also see them, and they will often try to keep us safe when we are in their country, even though we may not be able to see them. It is always best to respect the country you are in so the *irrernte-arenye* who watches you there will not take offence. Today you might feel they are watching as they keep an eye on you while they look after the *apmere*, land. *Irrernte-arenye* belong everywhere – not just Arrernte have them, all the land has them.

They are often referred to as little people, or as having long golden hair, but they are not always little and they do not always have long golden hair. There are little *irrernte-arenye*, babies who died, but then there are the bigger adults too. They were all living people – they are our ancestors.

I will tell you a story about some *irrernte-arenye* from Keringke Rockhole. Once, when we held a women's ceremony near Keringke Rockhole, as the women gathered and began getting ready to dance, a few of them walked away a little bit behind some trees to get ready. They were there when they felt someone looking at them. They peered around from the tree and saw a man and a few children standing out in the open. The women were looking from behind the tree and there he was, standing out in the open, with the children, none of them even hiding!

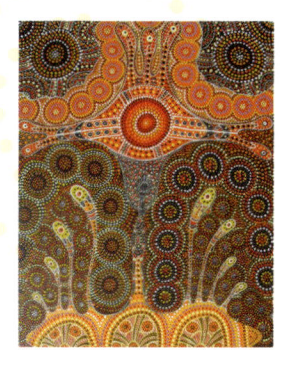

ABOVE AND OPPOSITE (detail): *Fire Spirits*, 1999, acrylic on canvas, 51.2 x 41 cm

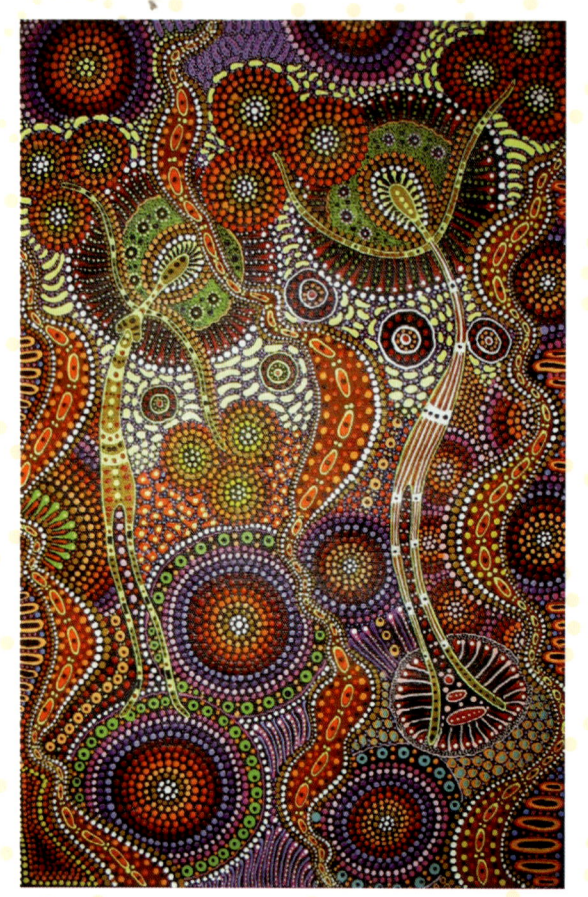

Keringke Irrernte-arenye, 2005, acrylic on canvas, 46 x 30 cm

The women were very surprised. They ran back to the ceremony ground, calling out to the others. "Hey, you mob!" they said. "We just saw a man and a few children standing over there in the open. They're not allowed to come up here, it's a women's ceremony. The men know better than this!"

Everyone rushed over to the tree from where the women had looked but there was nothing to see. They walked towards the exact place where the women said the man and children had stood but there was no sign at all. No sounds, no footprints, no marks of any sort. By then my auntie had figured it out. "That was a spirit of one of the ancestors from Keringke," she said. "He has come to see who was here, and the little children with him were the spirits of the children and babies from here who have died. They are *irrernte-arenye* who showed themselves to you."

Well, the other ladies who had first seen him said to my auntie, "but he was a really handsome man!" We laughed at them. "We want to see him again. He had long white hair, it was tied up just the right way and he had long spears!" Then my auntie had to remind them, "well, our men don't carry spears anymore, do they! Remember, those men are all gone." Then they knew! He was *irrernte-arenye* from that place – they had all fallen for *irrernte-arenye* at Keringke, a spirit man!

In my family some of us share the spirit of an animal that comes into us before we are born. This animal spirit is also our totem, and it helps make us a whole human. It first enters the mother's body at conception, when we are called into being inside her. The animal that helped my spirit was *aheyenenhe*, which is what we call the sandhill python. That snake came into the camp on the night when I was conceived and began to grow in my mother's body. The old women there knew when they saw the snake that I would grow in my mother. They killed the snake so that part of my spirit could come into being. Because *aheyenenhe* held part of my spirit in this way, I am not allowed to eat or kill those snakes. The *aheyenenhe* is a powerful women's totem.

This is how it was for my mother Kitty Hayes as well. She was helped in the same way by *aherre*, a big red kangaroo. After my grandfather Atyelpe killed a big kangaroo he fed it to my grandmother Louisa Riley. It made her sick! She said it tasted like bad meat. Then the old women knew that part of the spirit from the kangaroo would move into my mother, as she grew in her mother. I was told that when this happened Atyelpe and Louisa were camped in the Keringke Rockhole area. This area holds the story of important totemic ancestor kangaroos. It was a large site where many groups of people gathered for ceremonies over many years. We still find *athere*, or seed grindstones, *alyere*, or round grinding stones and *apwe*, or scraping stones, all over the camping area that people used when they camped here, but the cattle have broken a lot of them up.

Because it is my mother's conception site, and I am Kemarre, I am part of Keringke too. It is an important *altyerre* site for the *aherre*, the red kangaroo totem. Keringke is part of my spirit; it's a place I am connected to through the totemic ancestors, my skin name and my family. It is a place I look after, I am a custodian. Near Keringke Rockhole, in the creek bed, is a special site we call the *apethe*, joey's pouch. It's made of the rock along the creek between the camping area and the Keringke Rockhole. There is a little hollow in the river rock and you see where the outside has been smoothed. It was made like that to fit another piece of rock which acted as a lid.

Apethe, joey's pouch at Keringke Rockhole.

As children this was known to us as *apethe*. Inside, it held two very shiny, small, smooth stones. I remember looking in *apethe*, holding the precious stones, and putting them back carefully again when I was a young girl.

The joey stones didn't come from our country. They were different to any other stone I have ever seen. We were told that these stones represented both the young joeys of the ancestor kangaroos and that they signified the spirit of my mother. This was her conception site.

This *apethe* was made a long time ago. The stones had come from somewhere else. They were highly polished and shiny. They were very important to our family and many others. Both my grandfathers, Atyelpe and Werirrte, were strong in law and men's business. They were respected elders in the Aboriginal community and they both played a part in looking after the Keringke site. The *apethe* was a special part of that site, and it would have had other significance to them as men, which as a child I was never told.

When the Santa Teresa mission was built at Ltyentye Apurte many Aboriginal people moved to live here. After Mass on Sundays the people were free to go off together and have bush picnic camps. Of course people wanted to hunt, collect foods and so on. They used to walk along Yam Creek and dig the yams, set up their fire, make billy tea, cook damper and other food. From there, it is not far to Keringke Rockhole.

At some time after I began to live at the mission dormitory we found that the lid of the *apethe* was broken. Then it disappeared altogether, and then the stones disappeared too. We have asked quite a lot of archives and collections to look for these joey stones. I think this might have happened before the 1960s, because when TGH Strehlow went to Keringke the men told him the stones had already gone. At that time he was being given some of the men's sacred objects from their places above Keringke Rockhole, and other parts of our homelands, because they were not safe anymore in their special places. After that, the old men's business was finished. The men have not told me what happened to the stones either. I don't know where they went to, we can't find them. It makes us very sad because it was an important and sacred part of us.

RIGHT: Kathleen and her grandson Bart Doolan at *apethe*.

OPPOSITE: View down the gorge from Keringke Rockhole.

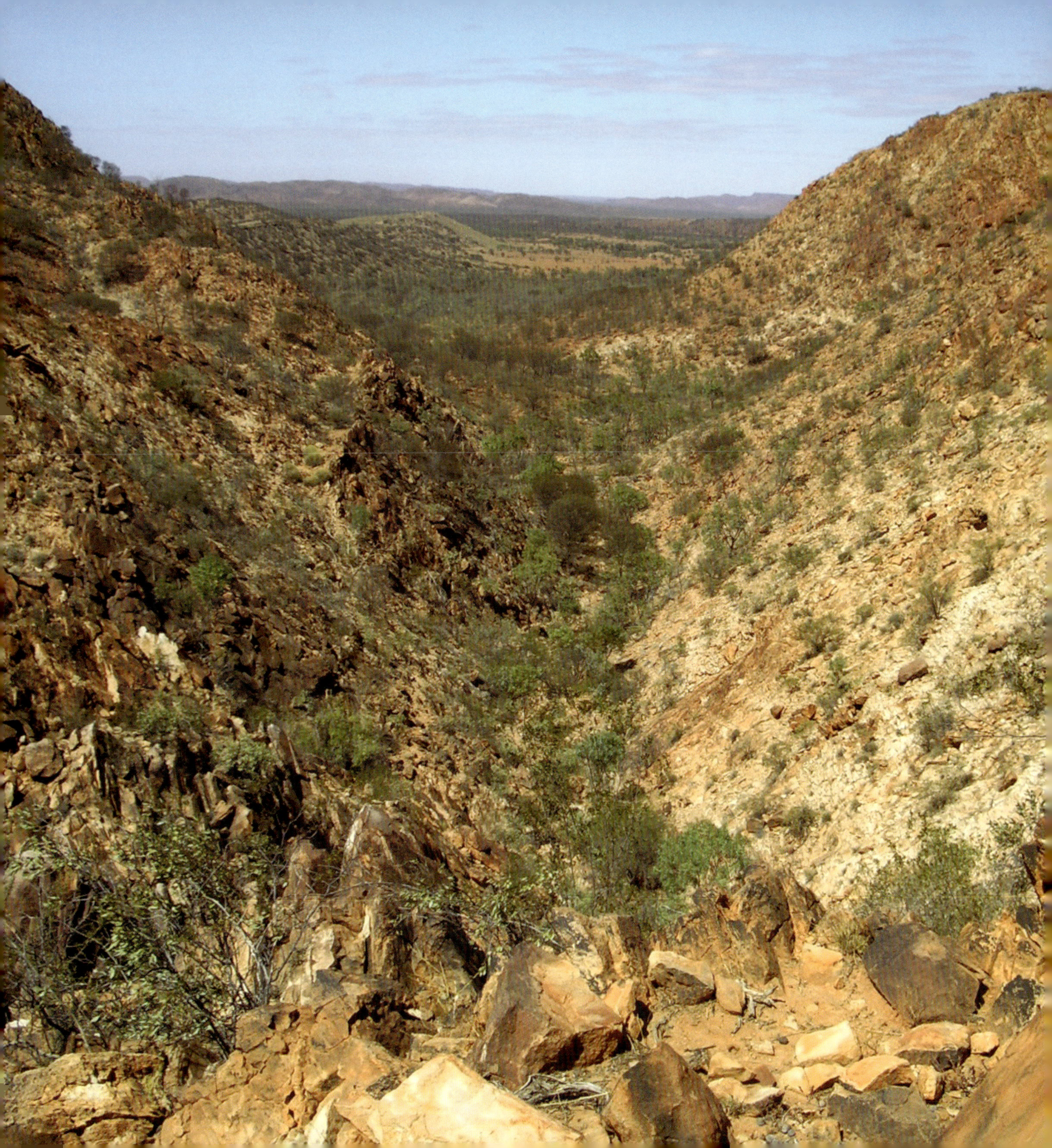

Keringke Rockhole

This is the story that we were taught by my grandparents. Keringke is a kangaroo site and this story is about how the rockhole here was made. The footprints in the rocks are from the totemic ancestor kangaroos who came through here in the *altyerrenge*, when *altyerre* beings were still shaping our country.

This big ancestor travelled as a kangaroo from the south-east, maybe from the desert. This ancestor kangaroo had a cousin around here, living on the other side of the valley. His name was Kwepalepale – *kwepalepale* is our name for bellbird. The ancestor kangaroo stayed with his cousin Kwepalepale, listening to his beautiful singing. It was a time of abundance; the country was green after the rain and there was enough food around for everyone and everything. There were many different grasses, plenty of other bush foods and *ayepe*. *Ayepe* is what kangaroos love to eat the most. At this particular time it was growing plentifully all along the creek and up into the gullies. As *ayepe* grows it spreads out across the ground with sticky little yellow creepers. They look like vines growing on the ground.

The time came for the ancestor kangaroo to go on his way. He moved off across the flats following the yam creek where grasses grew plentifully. Then he began following the *ayepe* just past the creek. We don't know why he travelled this way or where he was going. He

LEFT: *Keringke Rockhole*, 2003, acrylic on ceramic, 20 x 20 cm
RIGHT: Keringke Rockhole

32

was an *altyerre* being, and these ancestors often changed their form from one place to another, so we don't know what else he might have become, further on in his travels, or what he was before he came to us – we only know what he did in this *apmere*.

As the ancestor kangaroo hopped along, the *ayepe* started to stick to his legs. He hopped further but more *ayepe* got caught around his legs. He kept hopping for some time but more and more *ayepe* was sticking to him. The ancestor kangaroo went on hopping, hopping until he couldn't move anymore. His legs were completely tangled up in *ayepe*. He began to crawl, dragging himself along the ground, and, in this way, he got a bit further up into the gully.

Finally he had to stop. The *ayepe* had become too much for him. He had crawled a little bit more, but then he lay down right where this waterhole is today.

The ancestor kangaroo knew that the *ayepe* would weaken as it dried in the sun, setting him free to move again. While he was lying still, waiting, many flies landed on him. They tickled and irritated him until the ancestor kangaroo flicked sand up over his body. This sent the flies buzzing away from him for a few moments. Each time they settled back on him he flicked up more sand. Slowly, as he flicked sand up, he dug a great, deep hole. That is now the Keringke Rockhole: *Keringke* because that means kangaroo track. He was here for many days because the *ayepe* around his legs took a long time to dry. Eventually, when it had dried, he broke free and hopped away over the top of the hill.

If you look above the rockhole today you can see his footprints very clearly in the rocks. There are also deep scratches in the rocks, where his tail beat against the rock as he flicked sand at the flies. Some of those scratches are from smaller kangaroos that came to him while he was stuck here.

Keringke Rockhole, 2005, lino cut on paper, 39 x 28 cm

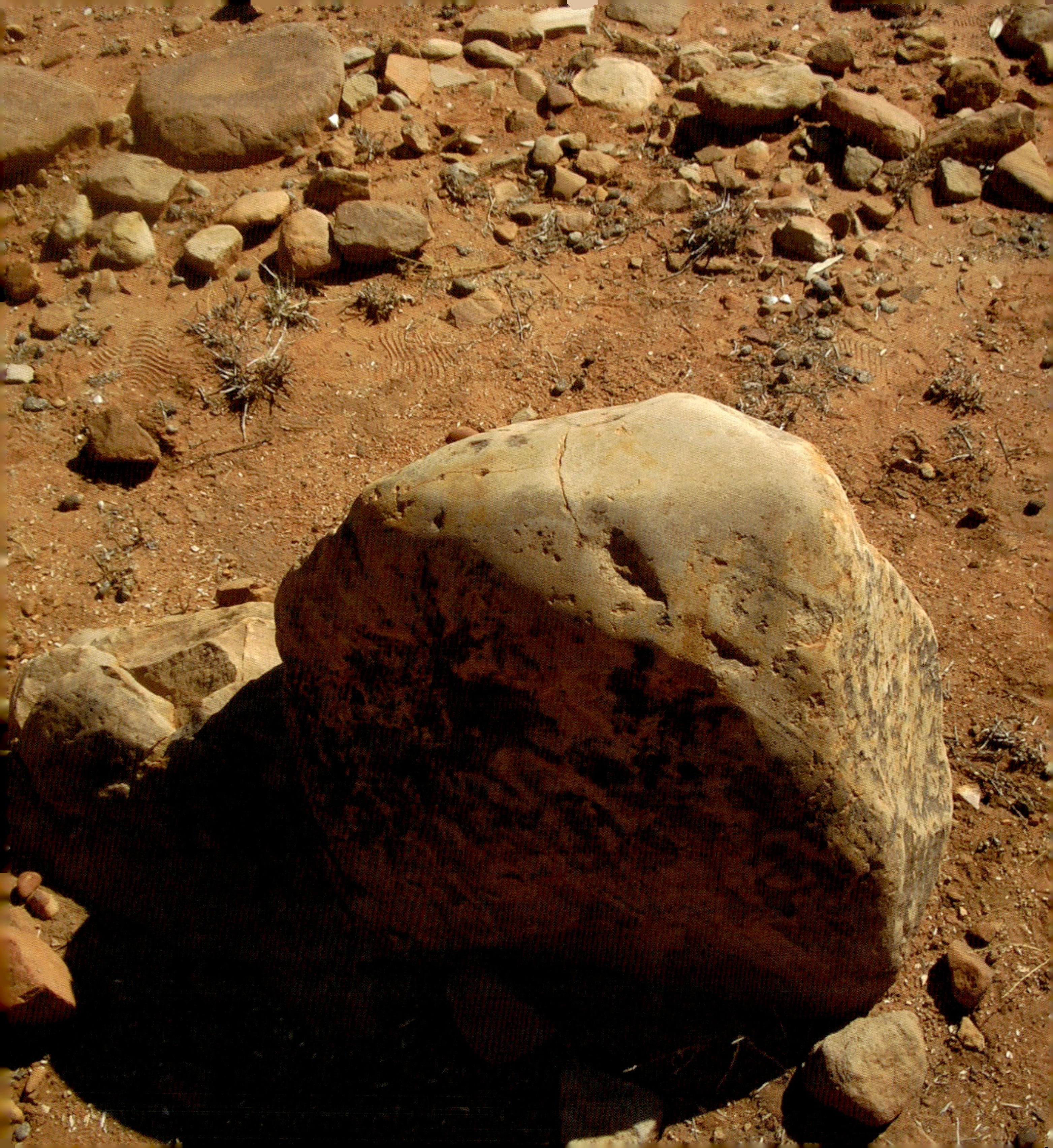

Tyenge Artweye akerte, My family, my country

My grandfathers, Atyelpe Therirrerte-arenye and Werirrte-arenye, were both important men. They were charged with many responsibilities for their families and their land. Their names, Atyelpe Therirrerte-arenye and Werirrte-arenye, indicate that they are incarnate totemic *altyerrenge* at these specific sites. Atyelpe's father held the same name, Atyelpe Therirrerte-arenye, as does my uncle today. Morris, my brother, is now Werirrte-arenye because he is the eldest left for all that homeland area, so he is Werirrte. Responsibility for the land we come from, and our ties to the sites we return to in spirit form, pass on to us through our father's side. In this way, the men took responsibility for all the aspects of ceremony and law which pertain to their land. This included undertaking the ceremonies in a certain place, at the right time, with the correct people there. Ceremonial law relationships were guided by skin relationships too and we used to take our skin name from our father's side. When a woman began married life or had her children, she used to move to the place where her husband came from. Her male children took responsibility for their father's land and all the children took their totem from their father's father.

My grandmothers were Louisa Riley, whose conception site is near Keringke Rockhole, and Molly Baldwin, who was conceived at Nturkunpa, near Arltengke. According to our old ways, your conception site is a place you

OPPOSITE: *Antekakarle*, lizard rock.

must look after, and you have responsibility for that place.

I relate to *apmere* from both of my grandfathers. I follow the paths they gave me. I have responsibility for my mother's and grandmother's conception sites, and my skin name is Kemarre so that is how I relate in law and business to Keringke. The combination of all those things guides how I relate to other places, other people, to culture and country. Some women take their *altyerrenge* responsibilities from their mother's side so that is how they relate in law and business. It is very complicated from outside our culture, but we understand this way of organising things because our ancestors have taught this knowledge for many generations.

I get my totem *alekapare*, the collared sparrowhawk, from Werirrte because he was the owner, he was of that place, Werirrte-arenye; he represents our totemic ancestor from the place called Werirrte – a place near Salt Bore. He was also sometimes called Jim Utjepa, and white people called him Jim Doolan, or Goggleye Jim. One of his other grandchildren is called Zita. She was taken away from her family in 1948 when they lived at the Little Flower mission at Arltengke. She was only little when they took her but she remembers our grandfather very well, and she and others have told me many things about him so I know that country and some of his stories. His conception site is Atnetarrkwe,

Werirrete, Jim Doolan, c. 1940s. Photographer Roy Dunstan, courtesy State Library of Victoria (detail).

near Uyetye, so that's where *irrernte-arenye* goes upon our deaths.

My other grandfather Atyelpe's totem was *atyelpe*, the native cat or quoll. He was a rain maker and he remains within Therirrerte, where he came from, representing that powerful native cat ancestor. I would have been part of the women's *urrwempele* ceremonies too, a very powerful women's

LEFT: Atyelpe, Bill Hayes, 1962. Photo courtesy Strehlow Research Centre (detail).

RIGHT: Kathleen shows grandchildren Bart Doolan, Luke Wallace and Jacob Doolan how to make themselves known to their ancestors at the Antekakarle rock.

ceremony and very dangerous to men, but they finished up before I was old enough to learn them. I think Atyelpe, who was also called Whiplash or Bill Hayes by white people, also had *altyerrenge* responsibilities to *atirrkwe*, the marsupial rat. It had a white tip on its tail but they aren't seen here anymore. I remember him having native frog ceremonial ties, and also bat ancestor ties. I think he was responsible for many *altyerrenge* objects. Atyelpe's father, my great grandfather, was called Therirrerte-arenye Atyelpe, or Fred Atyelpe to white people. His totems were *urlampe*, rain and *atyelpe*.

My aunties used to tell me about my grandfather's father, Therirrerte-arenye, Fred Atyelpe. He was a powerful *ngangkere* and law man who spoke quite a few Aboriginal

Arnerre, a shallow hole to store water in.

languages: Arrernte, Pintupi, Pitjantjatjara and Arabana were some of them. During his lifetime Fred Atyelpe still walked around everywhere on foot. He must have travelled around everywhere before he stopped on the stations. He was old by that time, a really grand, well-travelled old man. My old aunties told me that he began to learn to speak English at Ross River station. They remembered one story about how a priest and a nun came travelling along, and they asked him in English, "where is Arltunga?" Fred Atyelpe replied like this to them, "that road. Go straight and then come back, and then go and then come back and then go and then come back". He meant it was a curved road, but the priest and the nun couldn't understand him at all! He was talking to them in English. Everyone says it was really funny when he used to speak English.

One of my grandmothers was Molly Baldwin – she was my father Walter's mother. She was called coloured by us and half-caste by other people because her father was a white man. He was employed by the police for a while at Arltengke, or Arltunga. He was a white man, and I think he was from Ireland or Scotland. We can't find out anything about him. I don't know why she was called Baldwin either – I think it was because his name sounded like Baldwin when it is said in Arrernte – because his name was actually Jim Bolton.

We know this white man didn't want anything to do with his daughter, baby Molly, or her mother Ankora. I think he just used Ankora for sex. She was one of the first in my family who went to work for the white people on the stations. She was a good worker too, and it had turned out all right for her until the family went to have a look at Arltengke. Although Arltengke was not their homeland, but just next to it, my grandparents knew many Aboriginal people from Arltengke, and Molly came from Nturkunpa, a place near there. My family had all heard about the gold mining and the white men and I think they went to Arltengke to see what was going on. Arrernte weren't interested in gold, but they were interested in what was happening to their homelands and sites, and they were interested in rations.

Ankora must have been a young girl when that white man saw her at Arltengke and he used her. My great, great grandparents, Atjita and Mernulpa, took their family back to live out bush, so Ankora had that little coloured baby called Molly at Uyetye. That little baby girl was kept safe, no one took her away, because they never found her hidden at Uyetye. Ankora then had an Aboriginal husband and other children and Molly grew up safely and had a proud Aboriginal husband, my grandfather, Werirrte.

That's how my family first experienced Arltengke and the white people there. They knew there was a police station at Arltengke and that white people lived there. My family kept away after Ankora was pregnant because everyone was learning to be very careful about the whites. Aboriginal children who were coloured were sometimes just taken away from the family by the white patrol men and sometimes the church helped with that too. Molly was kept safe. Her son Walter, who was my father, was baptised at Arltengke when he was about seven years old, so it could have been the missionaries there who first reported his mixed descent background to the authorities.

Walter was taken away when he was about seven because of Molly's mixed descent – even though his father Werirrte was a full Aboriginal man. Walter looked exactly the same colour as I do, but he was taken away to the Bungalow, in Alice Springs. I think that Molly and Werirrte must have taken a journey to Alice Springs for rations, and Walter was taken away from them in the street in Alice Springs and taken to the Bungalow at the old Alice Springs Telegraph Station.

From the Bungalow, all the boys were sent to stations when they were old enough to work, which meant they were supposed to be at least fourteen years old. My father Walter Doolan was given to Ross River station as a worker when he was about twelve or fourteen. That station was on part of our family's traditional land, part of Walter's homelands, where there are still lots of stories and sacred sites. We call that place Inteye Arrkwe. My father already knew that country because he had lived there with his family, in the bush

Children from the Bungalow visit our horse race camp site close to the original Alice waterhole. The lad above with the checked shirt is Alec Kruger. At lower left, also in a checked shirt, is Walter Doolan, c. 1938. Photo courtesy Roy McFadyen

around Uyetye, until he was taken away to the Bungalow.

When he returned to Ross River station from the Bungalow, some of his family were still living in the area. Werirrte and Atyelpe worked around there although, as older men, I don't think they wanted to work on the stations. They used to walk around going about their business, but sometimes they used to help out. Atyelpe would do a bit of gardening for a day, watering the plants. His father, Fred Atyelpe, turned up over there too sometimes, and he kept a herd of goats to supplement the rations which were not enough to feed the families around the stations. But they all used to go away again. The manager at Todd River station, near Uyetye, didn't worry about them coming and going. He knew the men would always come back to their homelands, and he would give them work again. This is what my grandparents did, and what their parents did. They lived in the bush with family keeping away as much as possible from the mission and the white people on the stations, which was their homeland. After Ankora's experience, they had good reasons to stay in the bush!

There were lots of other boys who were sent to work at these stations too, including another of my uncles from Finke who was at the Bungalow. There were even boys who were sent from Borroloola, a long way away. When they were sent out to Ross River my grandfathers, great uncles and aunties looked after those boys as well. That is how they grew up speaking our language, Arrernte. One of them is Alec Kruger who is an old man now, and he has written a book about those days.

ABOVE: *Tyepetye-ileme*, Kathleen drawing in the sand.

RIGHT: *Tyepetye arrentye yaye*, sand drawing of the Evil Spirit Woman story.

Arelhe Arrentye

Ayeye nhenhe apele Altyerrenge-arle aneke akwele Arelhe Arrentye-akerte. Atyeyikwe aneke arelhe awenke. Rarle anewengkartne-arle aneke, anewe-akerte re aneke. Itne apurte unthilirretyarte, arelhe atherre artwe anyente. Apmere arrpanenhe rareye unthetyarte. Apmere arrpenhe interle-alherle. Akwetethe rarle itne unthilirretyarte, aname-irrerle apmere arrpanenhe ikwere.

Arelhe ikwere atherre apurte merneke arlkwetyarte-arlke. Unthetyeke alhemele kere atwerle, arelhe atherrele ntange utnherlenge. Artwe re akenhe kere inerlenge, apmere anyente re imernte intemele. Anewarte interle akenhe arelhe akenhe anyente intetyarte akwintye ikwerele-arrpe-arle. Ure-ante mpepele. Alakenhe re itne interrirretyarte.

Kele arelhe akngerre yanhe itirretyarte, "ilengare rame ampe atnyeneye?" Kwenhe. Re atnerte akenge-ame-akenge-arle-irretyarte. Re alhwe antywetyarte aneke arrwekerle. Ampe-kenhe alhwe re antywetyarte.

Wale, ikwere-atherrenge re anetyarte, atyeyikwe, anewayte. Re itirretyarte, "ilengare atyenge-atyeye ampe atnyenetyenhe?" Kele imerte arratye anteme areke marle renhe ingweleme antewe-irrerle-anerlenge. Kele re itelareke, "awe, ampe atnyenetyenhe apeke alakenhe irrerle-aneme". Kele re imernte marle renhe mwantye anteme arntarnte-aretyarte, "urreke the ineyamenge!!" Kere alewatyerreke apeke. Re papethe tnyetyarte.

Akenhe marle re akenhe merne arlatyeye apeke tnyerlenge, "arnterre tnyetyelaye! Angathe ware tnyaye!" kwenhe. Arelhe re papethe tnyetyarte, marle akngerre-ame-akngerre irretyarte.

"Iparrpe ulkere atnyenetyakenhe atnerte akngerre-ame-akngerre-irremenge," arelhe-arle itirreke. Rarle akarelhetyakenhe re aneme aneke.

Kele arratye aneme marle-arle ampe renhe atnyeneke. Ratherre-arrpe mpwarerreke. Arlwekere akweke-arle mpwareke. Akweke re inteke. Akenhe menhenge apmere ikwerele aneke urreke anyikwe-werne irreyeke. Kele akweke re akngerre-awerne aneme irreke. Irlkngaye akweke arle akwete aneke, werlatyenye, ratherre akngetyarte ampe akweke renhe urtnele kereke unthetyeke alhemele anewartele.

Mwerre renhe mpwaretyarte; urtne arrpenhe akapertele merne-akerte, urtne arrpenhe amultele ampe-akerte-arle. Akenhe arelhe re akenhe aretyarte kele re imernte arelhe arrpenhe atyeyikweke alakenhe angkemele, "ampe yanhe iwerle-aneme-alhaye! The arntarnte-areyemenge," kwenhe. Kele arelhe atyeyikwe alakenhe angkerlenge, "urreke-awerne awe! Ampe akngerre-awerne irrerlenge the ngenhe anthetyenhe arntarnte-aretyeke. Akweke akwete-arle re, werlatye-arenye," kwenhe.

Kele atnyentye urrpetye alhelenge ampe anentye-anteme-aneke. Antere akngerre anthurre anteme re aneke. Arratye anteme melikwe akweke renhe iwerle-alheke. Arlte urrpetye arelhe arrentye renhe mwerre atnyeneke. Mikwe-arle apetye-alpeme werlatye anthetye-alpeke mwerre urrke.

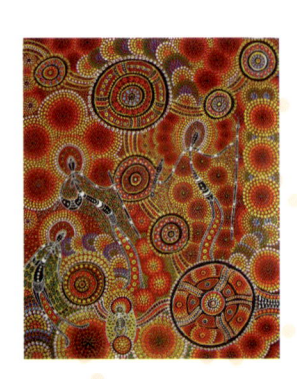

ABOVE AND OPPOSITE (detail):
Arrentye Sister, 2007, acrylic on canvas, 50 x 40 cm

Arlte arrpanenhe re imperle-alhetyarte. Akenhe arelhe arrentye akenhe ingkerne akweke rawerne arrerneke iperteke. (Re iperte arrwekele tnyeke-arle). Ipertele anetyeke atnyartne-tnyerle-ketyenge. Anetye-ame kele ikwere-werne-atheke anthepe irrerlenge arne-akerte. Akweke re akangkemele arerlenge mwerreke-athene atherremele-arlke. Akenhe arelhe arrentye re renhe alhe mpepe atwerlenge arne ikwerele, intartneke alhetyeke akweke rawerne, alhe alhwe untemele. Arelhe re renhe iparrpe anthurre akemelhe-ilemele, alhwe renhe awantyerlenge. Urlkernemele anthurre akunye-awerne. Atwekawe renhe-awerne alhe alhwe-akngerreke. Akenhe imernte irlpe pewe-ileme itethe ilirtnemele. Akenhe nhakwe akenhe mwerreke-athene kereke-arlke, merne-arlke untherle-anerreke.

Kele anyikwe imernte alhe ultatye-irreke, "akurne-apeke-irreke aye! Aretyeke alperratyekaye," akwenhe. Ratherre apetye-alperreke. Akweke yanhe-awerne areke akenge-akenge anerle-anerlenge. Melikwe inetye-alpeke, "ampe akweke nhenhe-ame iwenhe-iperre?" kwenhe. "Ankwe-iperre awe!" Arelhe arrentye-arle angkeke.

Arelhe iletyarte "ankwe-iperre" iknge. Akenhe melikwe angkwerre-iwemele anterele-arlke apernemele. Mwerre-awerne akweke re ankwe-irrerlenge.

Akenhe arelhe arrentyele akenhe alhwe renhe akwetethe awantyetyarte. Akwetethe re iwerle-alhetyarte mwerreke-athene.

Akenhe arelhe arrentyele awethe iperte tnyerlenge arrurle-arrurle mpwareke arteke. Ampe akweke lyete unthetyeke aneme. Inngerre wangketyarte, melikwe aretye-alpetyarte akenhe arelhe arrentyele ilerlenge, "arneke-arleke apeke atnyerne," akwenhe "aretyakenhenge." Alakenhe re re iletyarte.

Alakenhe re re mpwaretyarte akwetethe renhe. Akenhe ratherre arlenge-werne alheke ampe iwerle-alheke-iperre. Merne-arlke, kere-arlke akngerre rarle ratherre atweke, tnyeke-arle.

Ingkerne arelhe arrentyele akweke renhe tnyante anteme atweke. Alhwe awantyeke imernte irlpe uye pewe-ileke, uyarne renhe akemelhe-ilemele. Re imernte itirreke anteme ampe renhe arlkwetyeke. Re akenhe ure akngerre iteke. Akweke renhe itekawe! Arlkweke re. Ingke akweke anyente-arle re impeke alkngwirremele. Arelhe re kele unteke. Re itelareke, "atyenge ratherre nterteke-irretyenhe nhenhe aremele". Kele alheke.

Akenhe mikwe uthene anyikwe uthene akngerre-akerte apetye-alpeke apmere-werne. Apetye-alperreme ratherre, "aye! Angepe mape arawe-irreme!" Akwenhe. "Akenge apeke irreke akwenhe!" Ratherre itwe-irreke, "arelhe nhenhe-ame nthenhe?" Arrangkwe, ratherre untheke. Areke imernte ratherre ure akngerre-arle ampeke. Walye-arlke aneke. "Iwenhe renhe iterleke? Kere akngerre apeke re iteke," akwenhe. "Ampe apeke re akngeke." Akenhe melikwe areke anteme, "aye ingke akweke nhenhe interle-aneme!" Rawerne ake alhwe

42

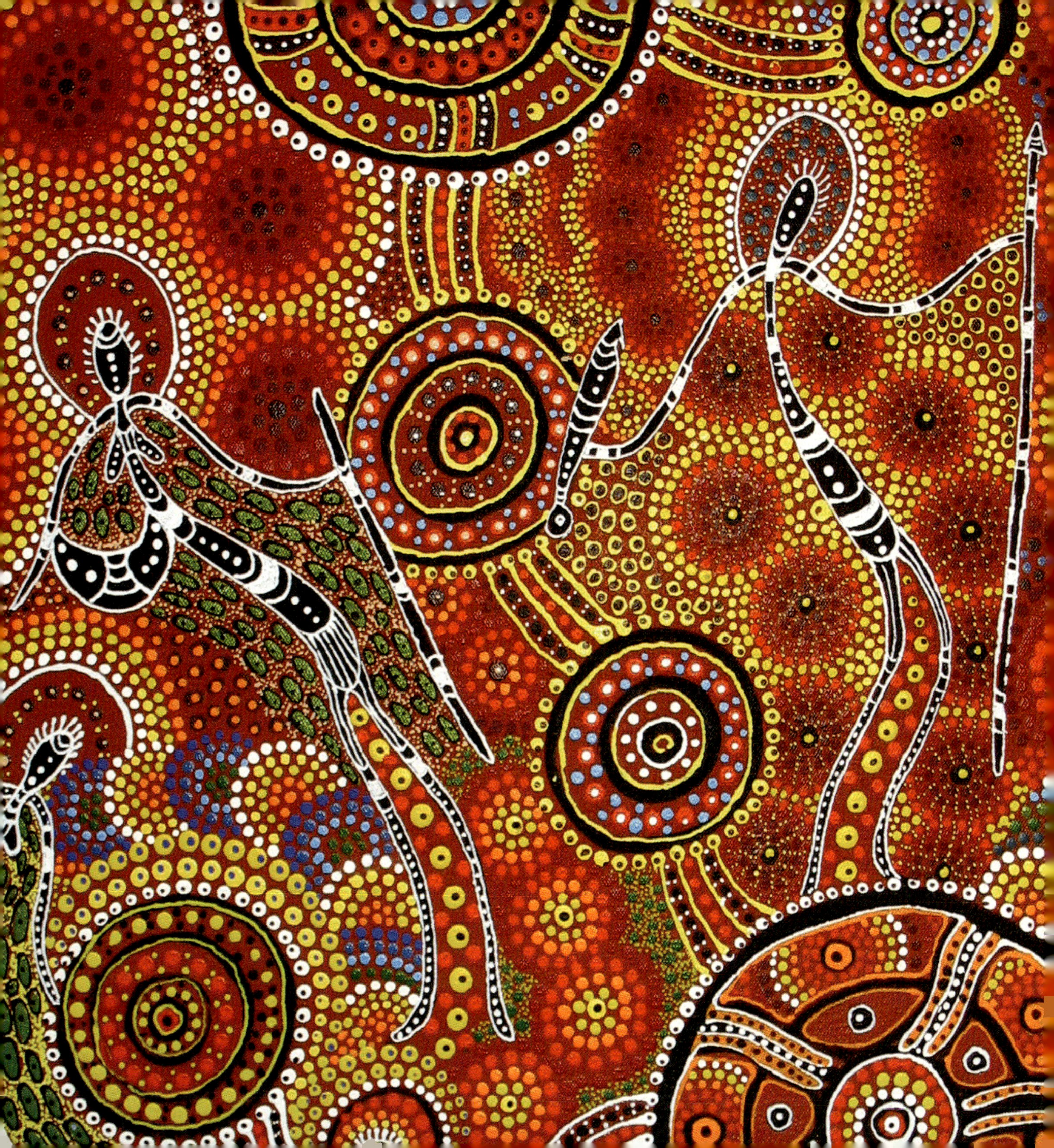

akngerre atwelheke, "nhenhe araye! Ampe ilernekenhe arlkwekeyaye!" re artneke.

　　Ratherre kere-arlke iwerle-alheke arelhe ikwereke nterteke-irremele. Kwetere, irrtyarte-arlke-akerte. Arelhe arrentye arlpele alheke. Ratherre apenteke impatye ikwerenhe anthepe-arle-irrerle-apetye-ame. Alhemele arlpele anthepe-irrerle-aperle. Alakenhe re itne irrerle-arle-apeke arlpe akertnele. Arlpe arrangweke anthepe-irretyerle-aperle awethe, alakenhe.

　　Kele renhe anteme arratye aretye-alheke anthepe-irrerle-aneme. Artwe re nterneke artepe anthurre renhe irrtyartele. Arrernelhartneke irrtyarte-arle mwerneke. Ratherre renhe atweke tnyante re, ilwetyeke-ante. Urele aneme iteke arelhe arrentye renhe. Alkngenthe akenhe atetheke-arle atherrke-atherrke rarlke arraterlenge re arrentye-arle anekenge.

Evil spirit woman

Arrentye is like a devil monster. This story is about an *arrentye* who was caught and punished by the people she stole from. It takes place during the time our ancestors still roamed in our world. Two sisters are living near Ulerarrlkwe. The older sister is unmarried but her little sister has a husband, and before long the older one begins to wish for her little sister to have a baby. Eventually the time comes, and the younger sister gets pregnant. Her big sister can hardly wait for the baby to be born.

　　When the younger sister gives birth, the older sister says, "give that baby to me. I'll look after him while you go out hunting". But the younger sister says, "no, he is too young to stay with you just yet". So she takes him hunting when she and her husband go out together. The older sister really wants to get hold of the little one, she wants to hurt him. Because the little sister looks after her baby he grows safely until one day he is just too heavy for the younger sister to carry while hunting and she asks her older sister to look after the little boy.

　　When the younger sister is out of sight, the older sister makes a little hole in the ground and sits the baby boy down in it. She begins dancing for the baby, who looks at her, laughing happily as she dances by waving a little stick. She dances up close to the baby and hits him hard on the nose with the stick. The little boy falls backwards and blood comes from his nose because she hit him so very hard. The older sister hurts him because she wants his blood, so she licks it off the baby's nose.

When the little boy's parents return they know straight away there is something wrong with their baby. The little sister asks what has happened to their little boy. The big sister lies. "oh…he just got sick," she says, but she doesn't tell the truth. This cruelty goes on for a long time because every time the younger sister goes out hunting, the older sister stays with the baby. The younger sister comes back from hunting and shares her food with everybody. She has no idea what the older sister is doing to their baby when she and her husband are away.

Yet every time they return they find the baby very sick. The older sister makes up many stories about the baby falling over, but in reality she is hurting the baby because she wants his blood. The younger sister goes hunting again but she feels something bad is going to happen.

By now the baby is a bit bigger and can walk around. The big sister makes the baby sit down as usual and she dances around him with her stick. He laughs with pleasure until she goes in close to him and hits really hard. It is too hard, so hard that the baby dies.

The big sister bends over him, blows in his ears and tries to bring him back to life. When she knows for sure he is dead, she makes a huge, big, hot fire. She throws the baby on the fire and when he is cooked she eats him. Having finished her feast she runs off because she has killed her sister's little baby boy.

The younger sister and her husband come back, but there are only crows flying around, and no one else is there. They search everywhere, crying out for both the little boy and the big sister. Of course, there is no answer. As they look around they find one of the baby's feet. They are very, very sad then. The younger sister begins hitting herself on the head with a stone and her husband makes cuts on himself in sorrow.

Then they follow the older sister's tracks over the *arlpe*, sandhills, past Ulerarrlkwe and all the way into the *urlere*, the dry, sandy country, they follow her. They can see her dancing footmarks in the sand. Eventually they walk over many sandhills and they catch up with her. The husband throws his spear and kills the evil woman. Then they make a huge, big, hot fire too, and throw her in. The flames of the fire are very green because the woman was so evil. When she is destroyed they go to another place and start a new life. The big sister was an *arrentye* – an evil, devilish spirit.

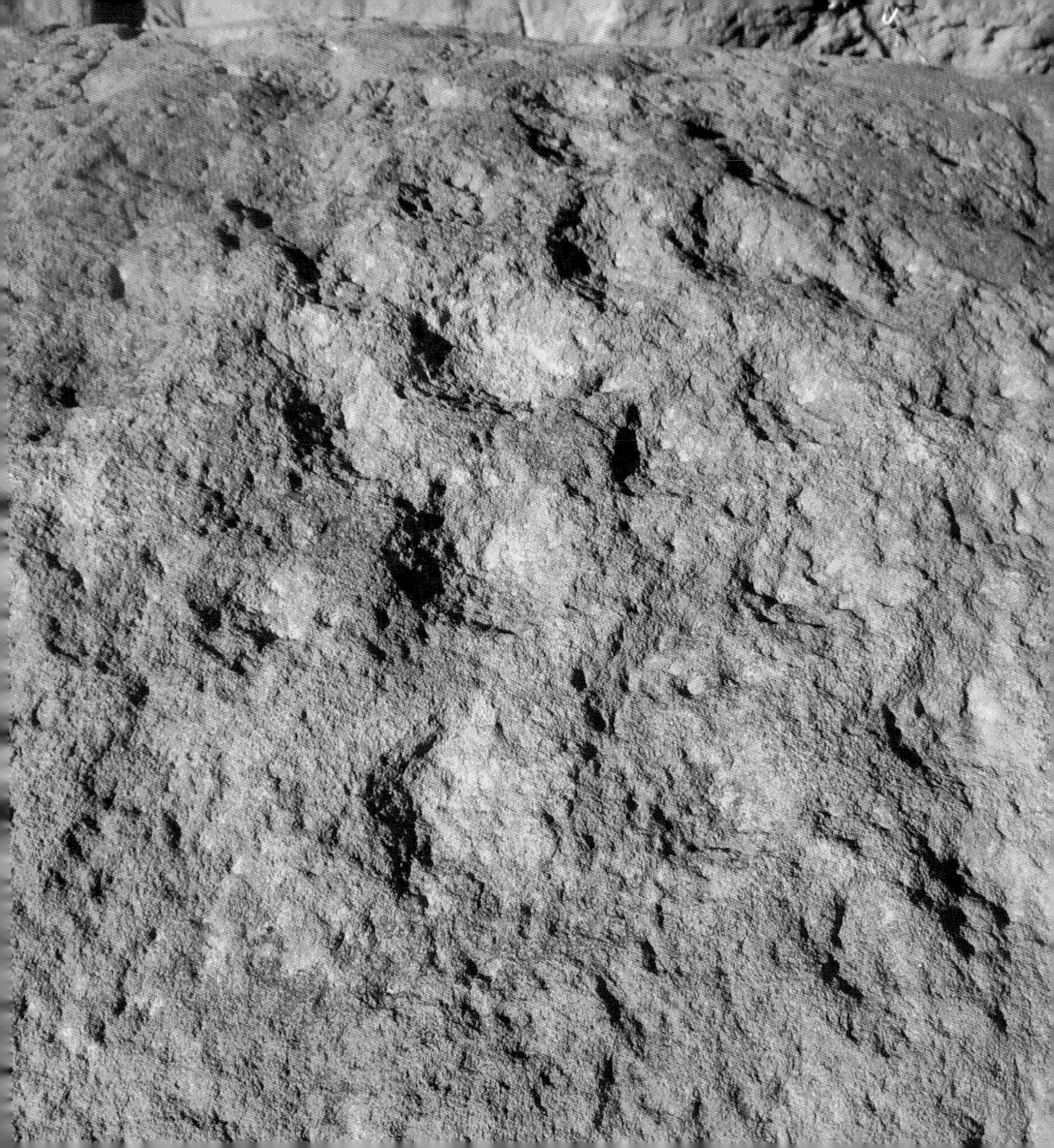

Apmeraltye, People of one land

When we still lived on our lands, everyone looked everywhere to get enough food to keep us all fed. We children ran around looking for lizards, birds' nests and everything else, and the old people used to walk along and look for bigger lizards, kangaroos and goanna. By the time I was nine, we used to go out hunting alone. We hunted in a group all by ourselves – this helped feed us, and having something to bring back to the camp to share with everyone made us proud. I started to earn story-telling from my grandparents by catching or collecting bush food to give them.

When I was growing up, our grandparents still knew how to make all kinds of useful things: knives, axes, boomerangs, shields, water bags, digging sticks, coolamons and dancing sticks. One sort of stone knife they made was called *thurle*. This knife was made with a particular stone which was sharper and stronger than any other stone. Sometimes the knife handle was made with spinifex resin, heated and mixed with ash. This dries into a really hard substance. To make their axes, my grandfathers used the sinews from kangaroo legs to bind the stone axe head to a wooden handle. Sinew from the leg of a kangaroo makes strong string. To make it soft enough to use, they chewed the sinew first. People still use kangaroo sinew if they are making a spear thrower or spears. These days, if the men make them, it is for selling and not for hunting!

Hunting with spears requires a lot of skill. The best way to catch an emu or a kangaroo

OPPOSITE: Rock carvings of eggs in a nest.

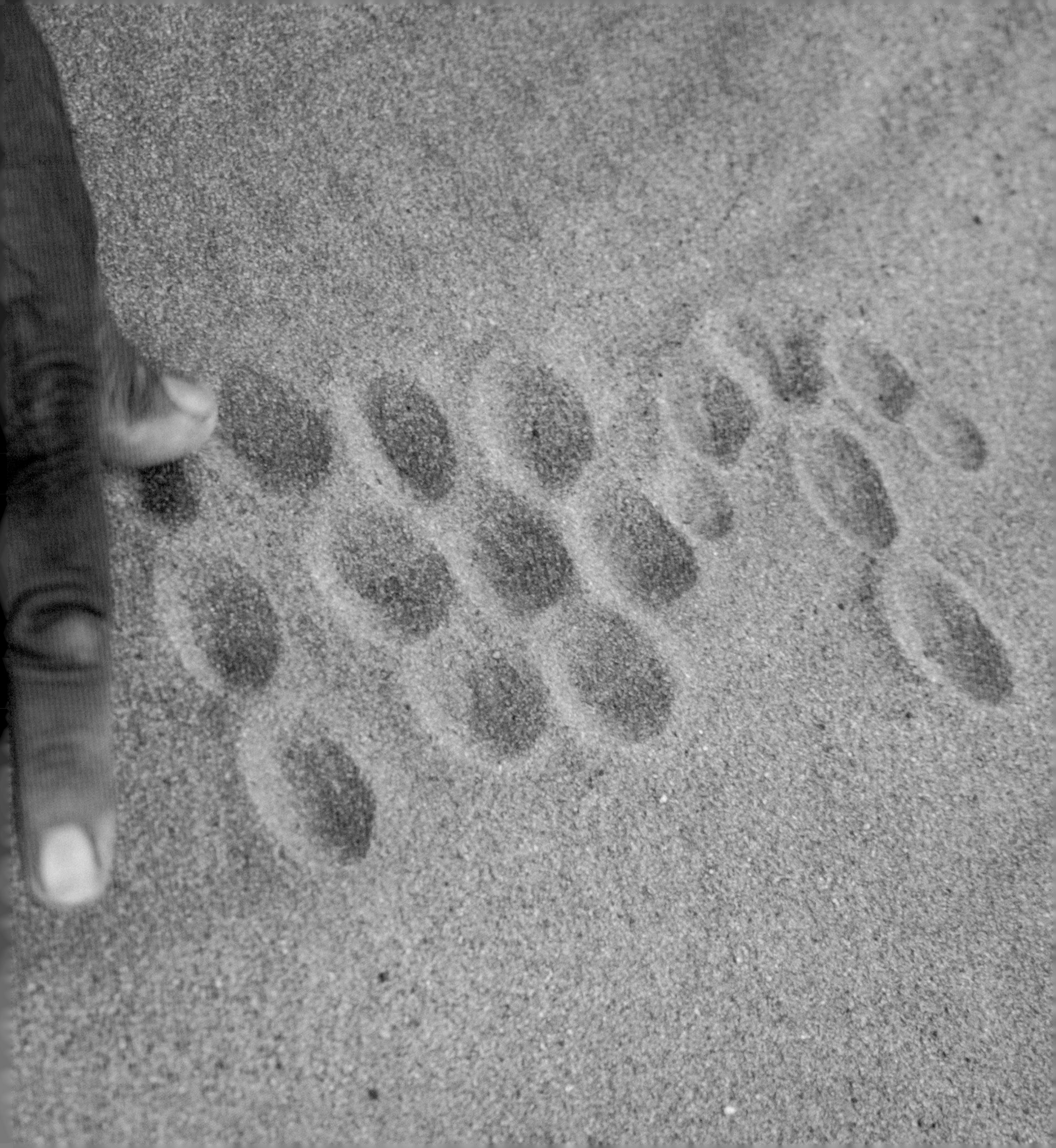

is to throw a spear right through the animal, trying to make it stick out both sides, so that it catches on the scrub and the animal can't run away. Hunting was very hard work and at times people had no luck with their spears, and growing up I remember being hungry sometimes. Because food could be scarce, we made the meat last for a long, long time by drying it and grinding it into powder. That was the only way to preserve food – put the meat near the fire, dry it out with smoke and heat, and after it's well dried, pound it and grind it until it is a fine powder, like flour, and this way we could keep and carry it around. People carried this dry meat powder in a bag made out of kangaroo skin, or in a coolamon.

We still use some of these old tools, like digging sticks made out of witchetty tree, which is a really strong wood. Digging sticks need to be nice and strong. Mulga is another very strong wood. It stays strong for a long time. To make a digging stick strong and sharp you must heat the wood over the fire, rotating it evenly. This dries and seals the wood. We had to grind the ends with a sharp rock to make them good points for digging with, but now you can use an axe or a knife to make the ends sharp. If we don't use a wooden digging stick, we use a crowbar to dig for witchetty!

When my grandfather Atyelpe died, others tried to let go of their culture and knowledge. But it was still part of them – everything they knew was still in their minds, in their memories. No one alive was left to replace Atyelpe properly. No one was left to inherit from him in the old way. It was a huge problem and in that grief for our old people, we almost lost everything we still know about ourselves. We have inherited pieces and some details but not all the knowledge of our elders. Our culture is not intact anymore but we have some strong pieces of it.

OPPOSITE: *Tyepetye-ileme*, sand drawings of tracks, nest and eggs.

CLOCKWISE FROM TOP LEFT:
Rock carvings of bird tracks

Following Emu Tracks, 2007, acrylic on canvas, 18 x 12 cm

Tyepetye, sand drawings of coolamon, fire, little budgies, birds' tracks and the women who collected the birds.

Arlewarrere Atherre-akerte

Akenhenge Arlewarrere atherre aneke. Artwe ratherre anetyarte urreke arlewarrere akngarte-iwelhetyenhe. Arrpenhe arnkentye-arenye aneke akenhe arrpenhe anewengkartne-arle aneke, ampe atningkeke artweye-arle aneke.

Ratherre kereke alhetyarte. Kikwe-arle ampe atningke akngetyarte ikwerenge akenhe atyeyikwe akenhe ahentye-aneke. Anyente alhelenge kere iparrpe atweme akenhe ampe atningke-akerte alhelenge ampe-arle arrkene-irrerlenge kere aterele-anthemele.

Akwetethe re itne alhetyarte. Kikwe-arle ampe atningke-akerte alherle kere aterele-anthemele akenhe atyeyikwe ahentye-anetyakenhe, "ampe atningke kngetyale. Kere aterele-anthemeketye," kake ikwerenhe re iletyarte.

"Akunye-areye. The akngeme-arle," kikwe-arle angkeke. "Alhetyeke-anteye ahentye-aneme. Kele, akngetyenhenge re." Kikwe-arle kereke arrangkwe apetye-alperle. Kere akweke, alewatyerre-ante, atyunpe-ante apeke itwe ware atwerle. Atyeyelikwe-ante kere kngetye-alperle. Kele imernte apmereke irretyerte-alpeme atyeyikwekenhe-ante kere amperlenge arerlenge. Atyeyelikwe kere anthetyenhenge kine, ampe mape-akerte. Renhe uyarne iletyarte, "ampe iwerle-alhe! Kere atningke ulkere atweyemenge. Ampe atningkeke artweye itelarelhemele," kwenhe. Irrtyarte-akerte tnerle-alherle akenhe ampe-arle arerlenge-arle, "aye, anwerne alheme kine!"

Kele ampe ingkerrenyeke anthurre alhelenge! Aywepe-arle-rlenge apeke akenhe ampe-arle ingkerne unterle-unterle-iwerlenge kele imernte arlenge-ante anyikweke irrenhemele. Apertetyeke alhemele imernte kere apeke aretye-alherle akenhe ampe itne arnterre arretyemele. Kere akenhe awerlenge-arle. Kele aywepemele kere akenhe unterlenge.

"Arrpenhe apeke arerlenge arrantherre nterte anthurre anetyenhenge!" Anyelikwe ileke.

Akenhe rawerne awethe apertetyeke alheke. Arlte arrpenhe anerlenge akenhe arratye atweme, arlte arrpenhe akenhe ampe-arle aterele-antherlenge. Alakenhe re anetyarte, akwetethe re. Akenhe nhakwe akenhe, atyeyikwe, anthetye rarle, kere-akerte akarelhelenge.

Arlte arrpenhe-arle atyeyikwe alheke akenhe kake ikwerenhe re imernte, "nthenhe-ame re?" Uyarne akwete arerletye-ame. Re imernte aremele apwerte akertneke arne mape alkereke-irrerlenge, "aye, nthakenhe-ame irreme?! Atyenge atyeye apeke."

Kele re rarle aneke. Rarle arlewarrere akngarte-iwelheke aneme. Re "Pwerte Irrpmernenhe" aneke. Re kwenhe akwetethe arrengkere anthurre alhetyarte. Kele re imernte arratye kere atwemele. Kelikwe re imernte areme (re artwe akwete-arle aneke), "ampe mape-ame nthenhele?" Pwapwe akweke mape re imernte aremele, "aye, arrentye apeke atyenge mpware-irremenge." Akwenhe.

Whirly winds

Alkngarelhemele areke ampe ikwerenhe akngarte-iwelhelenge akenhe re anteme akngarte-iwelheke arlewarrere anteme.

Lyete ulkere itne arlewarrere anteme aneme. Akwete re ratherre apenterrerlenge. Apwerte irrpmernenhe arrwekele arne alkereke iwemele alhelenge akenhe imernte arlewarrere akweke ikwerenhe-areye plain-le-arle.

This story is about two ancestors who travelled our country in human form before they became *arlewarrere*, or whirly winds. Many winds have a very specific meaning or journey, they tell us about things which happened here in the old days, or warn us about events that could happen now. Sometimes the wind is one which will bring news to us, will contain spirits, *ngangkere* or even harmful illnesses. When I was little we used to love to run into a big whirly wind and see if it could lift us off the ground. Sometimes they were really strong and they picked me up and threw me down way away. Some of the whirly winds are really dangerous – strong enough to break a house or split a rock.

Two of our ancestors of the *altyerrenge* became whirly winds. They were brothers. One brother had a big mob of family – he had plenty of children who loved to follow their father, running around everywhere, even when their father and his brother went hunting. I think I was just as bad when I was a little one and I would follow my grandfather. It was so hard to learn to keep quiet!

The brothers were really fast runners and clever hunters who often brought home plenty of meat for their big family. The brothers could run so fast that they made trees bend and rocks split open as they travelled through their country. One day they kicked up so much dust that they became the winds themselves, with dust flying from their feet and swirling in the air around

Whirly Brothers, 2003, acrylic on linen, 46 x 30 cm

Whirly Brothers, 2005, acrylic on linen, 30 x 30 cm

them. These days we see them racing here and there across the country as whirly winds, spirals of dust pluming up into the sky, still hunting elusive bush animals.

At the time of this story the brothers had tried to go out by themselves to look for kangaroos. It was difficult to get away alone and eventually the brother with many children gave in, letting the children come hunting so they could watch and learn. The children would always finish up making too much noise and scaring away most of the animals before their father could catch them.

The children's uncle never allowed the children to go with him, but he always returned with food for the family. The children shrank away from him though, because he didn't let them go with him when he hunted.

If they followed him, when they tried to creep up on the kangaroo and the kangaroo ran away he used to say, "you mob can stay at home when we go out hunting, or tell your mother to come behind with you". But those children always wanted to see what was happening in front, and to learn how to catch the kangaroos.

These ancestors changed one day when hunting. The brother who was the father of all the children went out quietly, trying to hunt alone. He didn't know that the children were following him. As he was hunting, creeping up on a really nice big kangaroo the children came running out from everywhere, but he still took off after the kangaroo with all the children running after him. They ran and ran so fast that they got caught up in the wind he created, and from then on they remained joined up together as a whirly wind, running all over the country, with all the little winds joined around the big one.

Meanwhile, the children's uncle looked everywhere for all the children. Where are all those children? he wondered. But when he couldn't find them, he guessed the children must have followed their father anyway. He went out to join them and as he ran toward the others, he saw them take off, running so fast they threw up big spirals of dust. He too became a whirly wind, but one that is a single, big, strong wind which is still hunting alone.

Whirly Brothers, 2006, lino cut, 39 x 28 cm

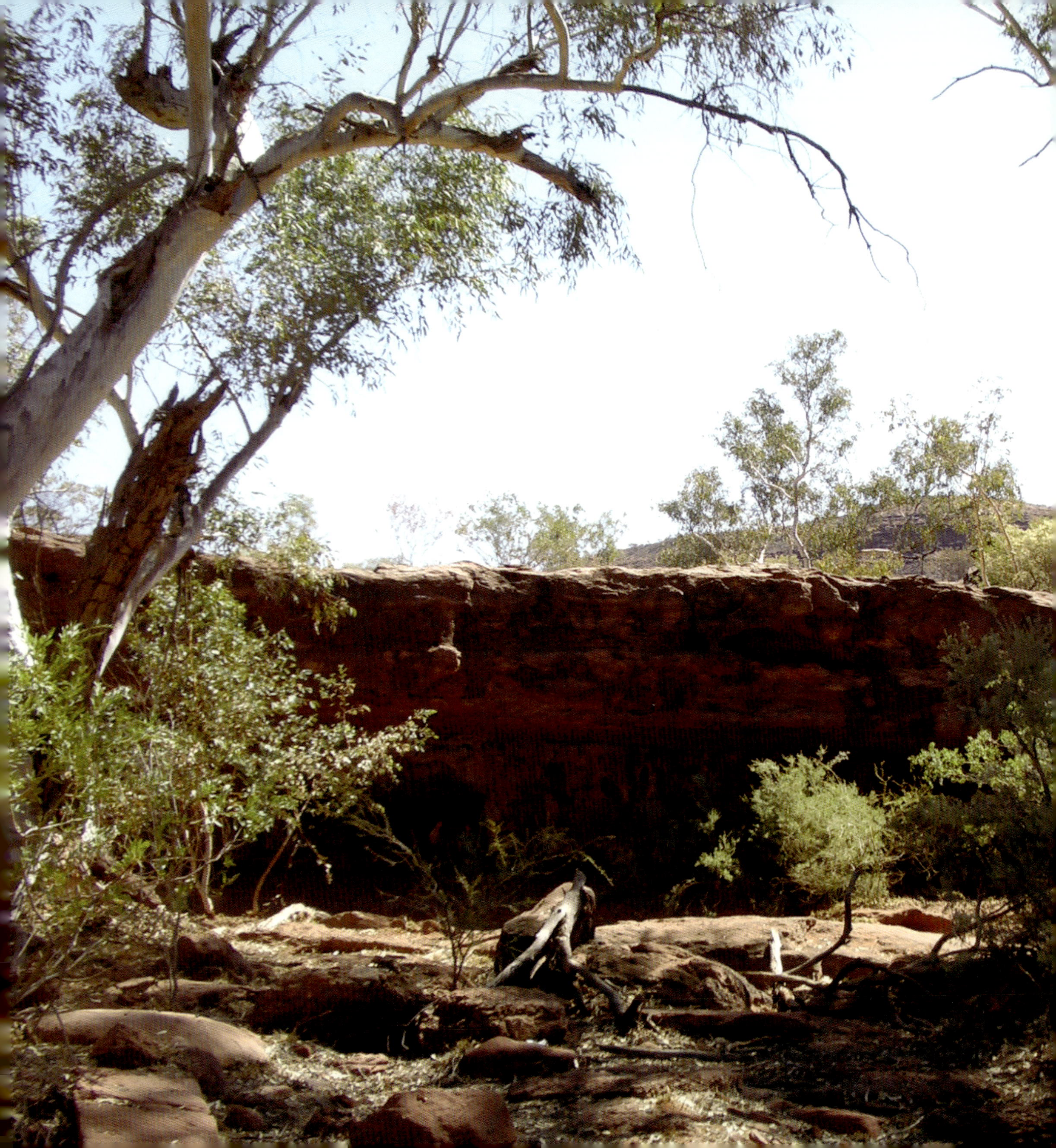

Uyetye

OPPOSITE: Looking at the cave at Uyetye.

My birth certificate says "Place of Birth: Unknown", but I know where I was born – I was born in front of the cave at Uyetye. We don't know exactly when I was born, but my mother and grandparents told me it was just before winter, when *Arralkwe*, the Seven Sisters, was just going down in the sky towards the horizon. When Arrernte first came into contact with white people we were given either July the first or January the first as a birth date. I was given July the first, 1948 by the station owners at Todd River station, because when they first saw me as a small baby they made a guess that I was born closer to July than to January.

I was given the name Kathleen Doolan at the station, too. Then, when I first came into the mission to stay, they baptised me as Catherine Doolan. I was never called Catherine though, only Kathleen. I was given my husband's name, Wallace, when I married, so I am Kathleen Kemarre Wallace now. I don't know if I had a bush name, maybe something, but I don't remember now. We didn't have names like in English. I was known by my skin name, Kemarre, and the responsibilities and relationships I have through *altyerrenge* and *apmere*. Everybody knew who you were by skin and country, not by English names like now days.

Uyetye was the main place where we used to live when I was a baby. Uyetye was considered a really safe place for us to camp. My family hunted in this country; they found

Ghost Gum Women at Uyetye, 2009, acrylic on canvas, 60 x 46 cm

This painting is about a woman whose totem is *awele-awele*. She used to go to women who were really fair skinned and ask them down to the waterhole. From there she took them to a cave, and put a rock in front of the cave so they couldn't get out. She got a few of these fair skinned women into the cave in this way. She picked *awele-awele*, wild tomatoes, to take to them, and she used to go hunting for goannas and *yalke* for them. I think she wanted to keep those women for herself. One day she went back and the rock was pushed out and there were white trees standing in front of the cave. The women who she had kept in the cave had become those white gum trees – ghost gums. Those trees are still at Uyetye.

plenty of kangaroo and euro and sometimes they went out to get goannas or red kangaroos on the flood plain – from the cave you follow straight along the creek bed and out onto the flats. There were no cattle at Uyetye when we lived there so everyone used to sit near the rock pool. That big mound of dirt we see today wasn't there then. It was a good rock pool; the water runs down into it from up on the hills behind, and it also comes up all the way from the other creek over on the flats. This still happens when there's a big rain and even in drought we can still get good water if we dig there.

When the rain was really heavy the water flooded the cave and we made a wurley to shelter in then. Most times we slept outside but sometimes people slept under the rock shelf in the cave when they needed to be cool. The cave roof is one giant big rock slab that is buried right back into the hill. The cave itself is not a sacred site – this was a place for everyone and lots of families would come here and sit down – but it is a place of great cultural significance, and there is a men's sacred site nearby.

Now, the cave at Uyetye is not fenced off from cattle. The soakage out the front is full of sand. The men's sacred site nearby has apparently had things taken from it. The cave roof has not been repainted in many years – the station owner doesn't welcome our occasional visits to this place. It is very sad that Uyetye has not been looked after properly. It was a place of great safety and significance for many people for many years, and now the cattle ruin it.

There are many stories our old people told us about Uyetye, some of them to teach us things we needed to learn. In one, a woman looking for *altye*, relations, was a young widow who grew tired of staying with her husband's family after he had passed away. She travelled across the desert side of the country towards Uyetye.

They saw her coming, the families at Uyetye, and she was uncertain about how they would receive her. They were cautious. They spilt into two groups and one group went up

Kathleen and Bart Doolan digging for and cleaning soak water at Uyetye.

along the hill to look around where she came from and see if there were more of her people there, hiding. The others went out along the creek towards her.

When they drew near her she sat still on a rock and they remained some distance away. The woman had to talk loudly in order for them to hear. Her language was different, maybe from Alyawarr, so they could understand her a little bit.

"I am a Perrurle woman. I am searching for *altye*". She was *ngangkere*, a healer, and they took her back to Uyetye and showed her the *alwekere*, the women's camp. There she stayed. She remained single and became *altye*, family. She grew into an elder, living with the other Arrernte families there at Uyetye…

And this is the story for the cave at Uyetye, where I was born. The spirits of those old people still live here. Lots of *irrernte-arenye* reside here, all the people from this place. For many years the men from here kept that roof painted with that *awele-awele* story, kept it looking fresh. We were all taught something from that story, a story to explain how important it is for people to share their food and take care of each other, not to be selfish.

OPPOSITE: View from track travelling in to Uyetye.

Awele-awele Uyetyele Aneme

Altyerrenge aneke Apmere Uyetyele. Awele-awele atningke-arle aneke yanhe re. Awele-awele-ante itne arlkwerrirretyarte, merne yalke-arlke Altyerrenge. Kere impe inetyarte. Apmere nhenhe itne anetyarte, atwentye akngerre mape-ketye, apmere Uyetyele. Yanhenge-ntyele ware itne arratetyarte kereke-arlke unthetyeke, merne yalkeke, arlatyeyeke kele imernte itne apmere ikwere-werne apetyerte-alperle.

Wale, itne yanhe ikwerele anerrirretyarte. Awele-awele-arle anerlenge itne awele-aweleke-ante ware atheke-irreke.

Arelhe ampwe anyente-arle aneke. Ahe akngerre re aneke. Mape-arle atere-irretyarte ikwere-ketye, re imernte awele-aweleke itnenhe ilkaretyarte. Kele nhake mape akarelhelenge rarle ilkareke-iperre, kele imernte itne anteme ilkaremenge. Ampe mape inemele akenhe arelhe re akenhe rakerlenge-ante. Akwetethe re alakenhe irretyarte. "Akngerre-apenhe mape atyinhe-arle impe!" Re angketyarte. "Akweke mape-ante arlkwe, akngerre-apenhe mape-arle atyinhe-ante!"

Akwetethe re re alakenhe mpwaretyarte. Kele itne angkerreke anteme, "arelhe ampwe nhenhe arrpenhe mapeke itirretyakenhe, ikwere-ante itirreme kwenhe. Anwerne awele-awele arlkwentye akngerre kine." Artwe ampwe mape-arlke anteme areke, "arratye kwenhe re. Ikwere-ante itirrepirreme." Kwenhe, "arrpenhe mape itirretyakenhe. Anwerne akenhe apmere anyente-arenye mape, antherretyeke kwenhe!" Kele akwetethe re mpwaretyarte.

58

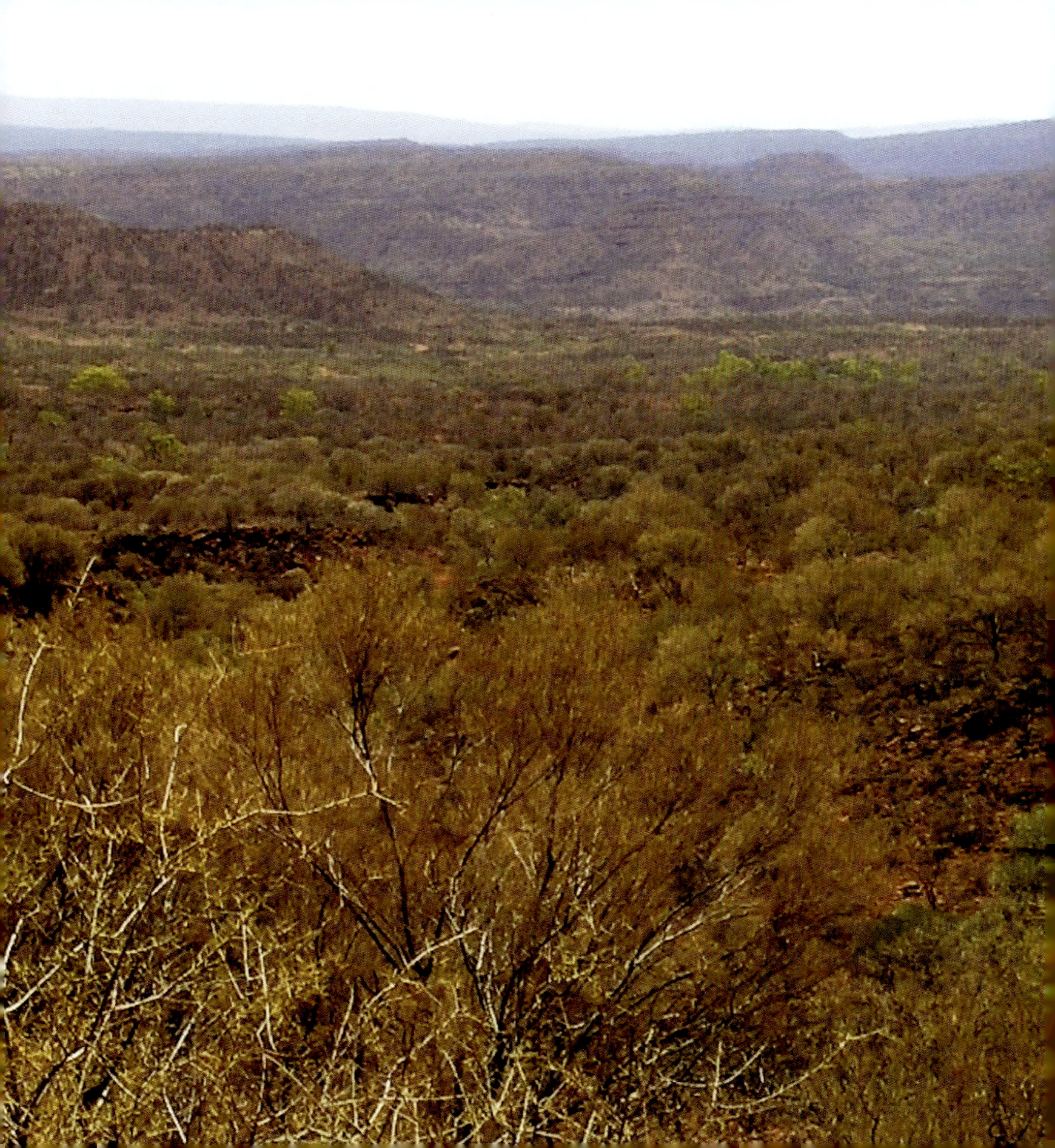

Kele arlte arrpenhe akwele artwe ampwe, apmere akwete-arenye kine, ikwere apele ahentye-anetyakenhe, "akenge kwenhe arelhe yanhe irrepirreme. Arrpenhe mape nthetyakenhe. Tharle renhe artimperre-arle-iwetyenhenge!"

Artwe ampwele merne awele-awele renhe alyeke. Arelhe re imernte ilkaretyeke alhemele akenhe nhenge imernte alknge atwerlenge. Arne arrirlpe-arle alknge-arle atantheke, pwenge ilemele renhe.

"Wertaye? Nthakenhe-irrekaye?!" Artwe artimperre-arle-iweke, apetyemele angkeme.

"Alknge akurne-irrekaye!" Arelhe re angkeke, "merne awele-aweleke ilkarekenge alknge atweke," kwenhe. Artwe ampwe-arle ngangkere-arle aneke, re renhe alknge mpwareke uyarne akwete. Arelhe rawerne artepe anetyarte, Arrurtele, inteyele, apmere Uyetyele.

"Arrurte"-arle inteye arritnye. Arrurte kwenele re artepe anetyarte, alknge pwenge re, angayweke re. Akenhe artwe re "aye akurne-awerne, arrpenhele apeke arlkwetyeke ntherlenge arrangkwe." Rarle ikwere alhwarrpe-irreke. Re anteme renhe kere nthetyarte, awele-awele-arlke, arelhe ahentye-aneke renhe, merne alangkwe, yalke-arlke renhe. Artwe ampwe re aneme artimperre-arle-iwekiperre, re arntarnte-aretyarte.

Akenhe tyerrtye itnarrpe aneme merneke ilkarerlenge. Yanhe ikwere-anteye re ilweke, inteye kweneke.

Arelhe re urreke ilwetyenhenge artwe ampwe re inteye akertnele kweneke intelhe-iletyarte, merne awele-awele aknganentye. Kele arelhe ampwe rarle awetyarte, "iwenhe-ame mpware-mpwaremaye?" "Awele-awele kwenhe the mpware-mpwareme urlpele" kwenhe, "ingkernenye mape apele arelte-anetyenhenge" kwenhe. Arratye re.

Yanhe aneme akwete. Irrernte-arenye anteme ratherre. Arelhe tyerrtye arrwekelenye yanhe aneme, irrernte-arenye, apmere akwetethe mape. Unte awetyeke apeke angkerrerlenge-arlke, alyelhewerreme-arlke, apmere yanhe-werne alhelenge. I yete anteme apmere inteye re, Uyetyele, Arrurte kwenele, awele-awele Altyerre lyete aneme. Lyete arelhe ampwe yanhe aneme, irrernte-arenye.

Awele-awele, 2003, acrylic on canvas, 30 x 30 cm

Bush tomatoes

There used to be plenty of *awele-awele*, bush tomato, growing around Uyetye and they were a good source of food for us. In the old days, a really greedy woman had lived at Uyetye. She lived there with other people, in a family group, much as we all did. But this woman, she was always the first one to check the *awele-awele* plants to see how the fruit was growing. The others living there knew she checked the plants early in the morning, and they knew she was greedy too, but they always let her go first. Later in the day, they would go and look themselves to see if the tomatoes were ready to pick. The woman would pick all the ripe fruits in the morning before others went out looking, and she ate them all straight away, without sharing anything with the others. That greedy woman didn't think about the other people's need for the fruits. Gradually everyone else began to miss out on any *awele-awele* fruit except her.

After some time, an old man who lived at Uyetye got really angry with her because of her greed. He knew very well that she was cheating the rest of the people out of the ripe fruits. He was *ngangkere*. We know he didn't like what she had been doing, stealing food from the whole group, not thinking about other people getting fed too. He decided to use magic to punish her, to stop her stealing from everyone, so he used his *ngangkere* powers to sing one of the *awele-awele* plants.

Awele-awele plants have long sharp spikes on the branches. The *ngangkere* sang the plant with ripe fruit, so that when the woman took the fruit from it in the morning it sprang back at her and hit her in the face. Two of those sharp spikes pierced her eye balls and she was left completely blind. The woman could no longer go out and collect food; she couldn't see at all and had to sit in the cave all the time unless some other person guided her about. The other people still shared all the food but the woman had to take what she was given.

The *ngangkere* man started painting the *awele-awele* on the cave roof, talking all the while to her. "I am doing this painting of the *awele-awele*," he said. We don't understand why he did the *awele-awele* painting there when she couldn't see it. Perhaps he wanted her to use her memory or look inwardly since she could no longer look out around her. He was the man who sung the plant which made her blind. He was very kind to her when she was blind. He brought her good meat, *awele-awele*, other food and medicine – he looked after her then. Other people looked after her too and the cave was painted with many *awele-awele*. Perhaps he wanted her to understand that she must go without something in order for everyone to share and survive.

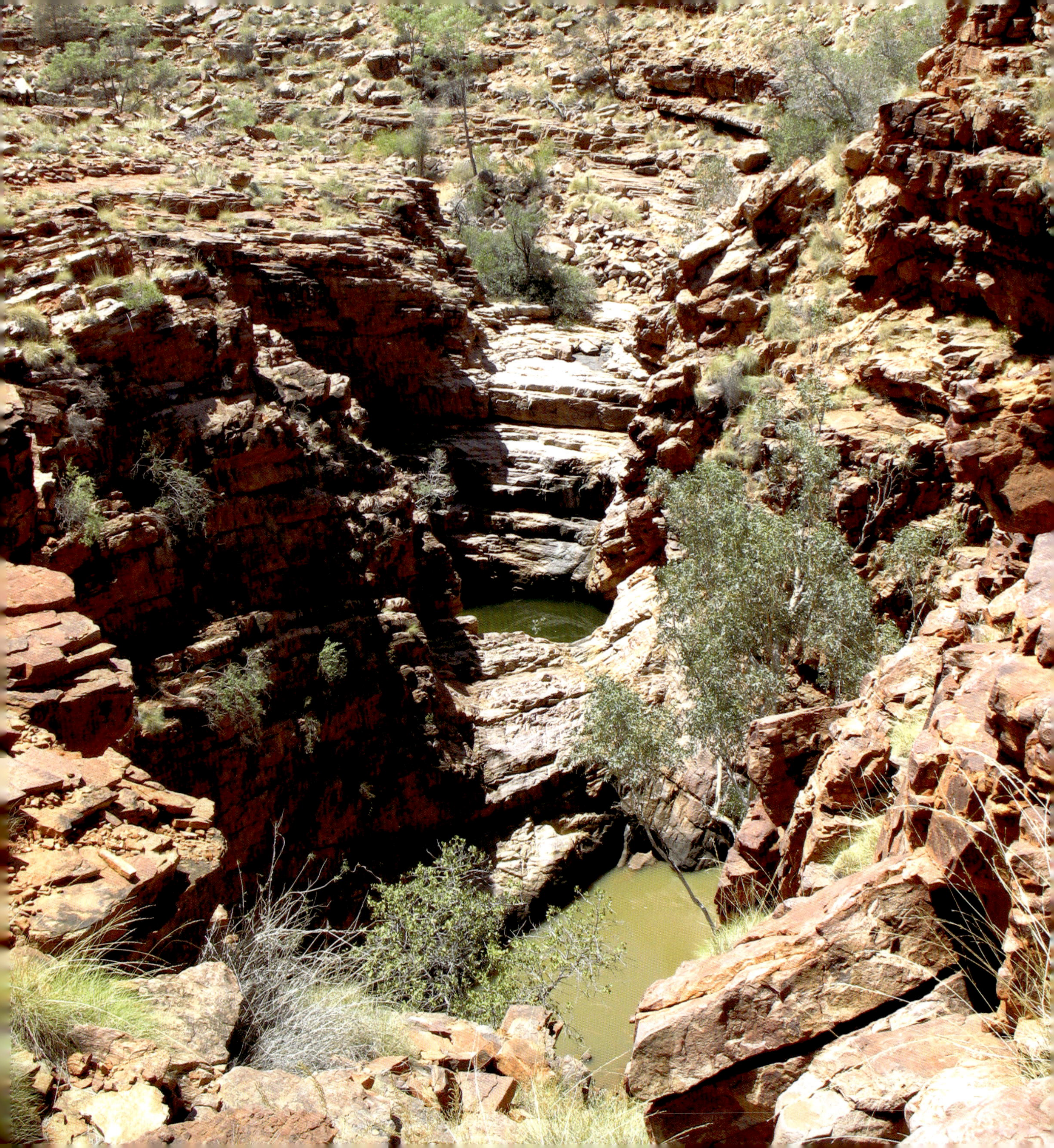

Kwatye, Water

Before, everyone knew where the water was – the springs, the rockholes, the creeks and the soaks. We used to visit all the springs through the homelands a lot. We kept right away from the stations then, travelling at night or in the day walking along the ranges where it was steep and rough. We knew all the short tracks to get around quickly from one place to another. In those earlier days, everyone had walked from place to place hunting their food as they went. Later we had camels to ride too. When it was getting dark, we camped at a spring where we were well hidden. At each spring we had somewhere to stop and camp. Sometimes we used to get water from the spring, but the next day move to another place. Atyelpe showed me many rockholes where water was to be found. One small rockhole was up the side of a little hill not far from the place where all the *utyerrke*, fig trees, grow. Sometimes when the men hunted they based themselves around that hill. They got *kwatye* to drink from the little rockhole there which they kept clean and covered over with a large rock.

That rockhole was just a small hollow in a big rock on the side of this hill. The old men kept a large stone over the opening so the water would last longer and stay cleaner. Sometimes they would pick lemon grass or medicinal plants and soak those in the waterhole to keep it tasting good. I can't find that rockhole anymore. It's dry up here now and full of sand. No one has looked after this

OPPOSITE: Two of the three rockholes called Atneperrke.

ABOVE: Alherrulyeme: At the bottom of this big rock the sand is falling away, and one day the rock will fall down and there won't be any water in there. I want traditional owners to work together to put the rocks and sand back so the rock won't fall down and it will be here for people to use again.

RIGHT: Kathleen in the creek bed at the base of Alherrulyeme Rockhole.

place that way since those old men finished. For a while there used to be an old tin hanging on a tree near the rockhole. My grandfather and his friend, or someone else working cattle at the mission, must have put it here. I thought I might find it again today, but it's gone. The rockhole was only about as wide across the top as a big man's foot but went quite deep inside the rock. The water stayed cool for a long time after the rain had finished.

Many springs have healing properties, and are also where *irrernte-arenye* and other spirits live. Alherrulyeme is another small rockhole which my grandfather showed me. We used to visit here often and find water in it. Atyelpe showed me this big rock with a deep hole going into it. That's why it held water for such a long time after the rain. There were plenty of bush figs not far from here. Some of the rockholes we talk about are very small. Alherrulyeme is small and it's right up on top of the river banks, in that big rock up there. My grandfather used to look after all of them – even the little tiny ones. Those old men kept on doing that long after the mission and the stations settled onto our homelands. Atyelpe and the other old men and women still taught us where all the rockholes and springs were so we could walk around and always find water when we were ready to camp or needed a drink, even after the bores and windmills were put in. The water at the springs and rockholes tasted better than the bore water.

There is another rockhole, a really big one not far from Therirrerte, called Mernathenge. It has water all year round, but to get water there you have to climb a really steep range. People didn't live up there because hot sand and wind blew straight in from the Simpson Desert so it's not a nice place to camp, but old people knew there was always water there. They only went there to get water or to hunt when it was needed. Men and women used kangaroo skin bags to carry water down from Mernathenge to the rest of the group. It was good, fresh rain water from that big rockhole up in the range.

This place, Atneperrke, is named because *atneperrke* means intestine from kangaroo and the rockholes here connect to one another in

Arterrke, 2008, acrylic on ceramic vase, 28 x 30 cm
Arterrke has fresh water. Special mulga with red trunks grow there. The spring and the mulga are on top of a tall hill. The spirits of that spring are a man and woman.

ABOVE: *Atneperrke*, 2005, acrylic on canvas, 25 x 25 cm
Two spirit women are holding their coolamons and digging sticks. They were hunting emu when they came to Atneperrke. There are three rockholes going up into the rocks. There's a big one at the bottom, then next one, then little one up higher in the rocks. That's where the emu have been drinking and where the spirits are standing. The old people used to hunt here just like these spirit women still do today.

OPPOSITE: Jacob Doolan, Bart Doolan and Noah Tyley at the fresh water rockpools of Mparnwenge where native lemon grass grows.

a long string, which looks like the intestine when you clean it out after hunting kangaroo. This rockhole is also known as John Hayes Rockhole, it's over near Inteye Arrkwe, Ross River Homestead.

At Mparnwenge there is a fresh water spring with water running through little rock pools under a canopy of trees. It's fresh mineral water where *aherre-aherre*, native lemon grass, grows in big clumps around some of the pools.

There is another plant that grows at Mparnwenge, *arrwatnurlke*, striped mint bush. In Atyelpe's lifetime the hunters would grind some leaves into powder, make a separate pool of water and mix the powder into the pool. They used to make a dam to keep the water back, so only a trickle could run through. They diverted water from the trickle to a little hole, making sure the water from the hole could not go back into the main pools from which everyone drank. *Arrwatnurlke* has a little white flower and a nice smell but it works like an anaesthetic when you swallow it, so when euro or emu drink that water, they become sleepy – they fall over, then lie down to sleep. That is when the hunters would kill them, while they were fast asleep. The animals didn't feel anything. That was how the men sometimes used *arrwatnurlke* to catch emu or euro without trying to chase them with a spear. Instead, at Mparnwenge the hunters would sit up on top of the hill very quietly watching the euro coming down from the rocks. Everyone kept hidden, watching while that euro or emu drank the water in the little pool. Then they quietly followed the animal until they saw it go to sleep.

We use *arrwatnurlke* as bush medicine too, but only on the skin – it's really strong medicine, so we don't ever drink it. These are some of the things that my grandparents knew about and which they showed me, even after we began living at the mission. I liked to learn from those old people, because they were very clever and very good at survival. They gave me my country.

Mparnwenge is not far from another spring called Irlkerteye. Irlkerteye is a spring which is well known to us for its water. My great, great

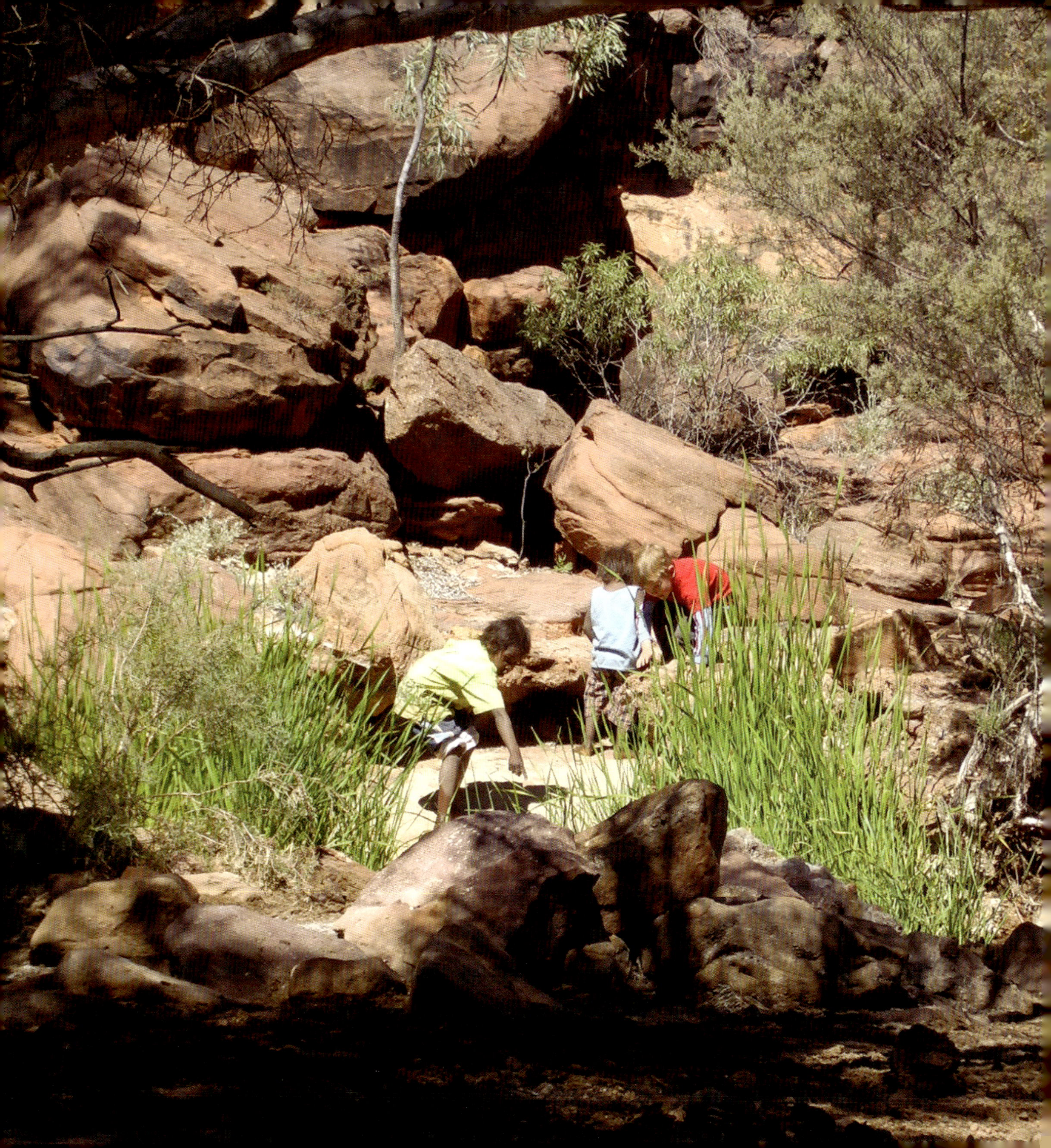

Fresh water at Irlkerteye.

uncle was taken away by white people from Irlkerteye when he was about ten years old. His name was Urlamp-arenye, but he was given the European name Jim Hayes by the station owners called Hayes. I wasn't born at the time this happened but I have been told about this event by my aunties from when I was a small child. My great, great uncle was taken away by station owners from Allambi. They used to ride horses around looking for their cattle. They came to this spring one day and found some of our people. They didn't know that anyone was still living out bush around here. The station owner's daughter saw this young boy at the springs and she took him on her horse all the way back to the station. His father was away hunting and the boy and his mother were too scared to stop the girl taking him. His parents and all the rest of his family were very anxious and so they followed the next day. They followed all the way back to the station on foot. There were a lot of them and in those days they wouldn't have had clothes. It was quite a big walk, too. That was my great, great uncle Kwementyaye, who became Urlampe-arenye. *Urlampe* means white cloud, and he was chosen to be Urlampe-arenye by the men, when it was the right time. As a child, he decided to stay with the station people and learn from them as well. Later he became an important man for our people, and a rain man, and he worked with the white station owners. He has passed away now.

That family and its descendants visited and stayed at that station for a long time, and my old uncle grew up as a stockman there. The station owners gave him both his names – a first name and their surname. Even then they didn't know there were more of us living on the other side of the range at Uyetye. We were all connected as family and in those days everyone was still walking around the country.

At Irlkerteye the unusual thing is that some of the spring water is salty, you can taste it and tell that there is too much salt in it to drink. But over there behind the rocks, the water is good, fresh water. In the days when the white people first brought there cattle here, they found this water was only salty, no good! None of us showed them where the fresh water was!

Ant lion sisters

There is an ancestor story at Irlkerteye about two women, who were sisters. They used to walk around this country, but they kept to the hills because that was safest for them. The sisters used to go out looking for goannas, and when they caught one they would come back to Irlkerteye to do their cooking in the hills, safe from danger. The older sister kept a watchful eye on her younger sister who would sometimes wander away when she went to look for big *tyape*, witchetty grubs. *Tyape* are a main food found easily here, near the springs. The sisters would look for yams and dig them up here too. The yams don't grow here anymore since the cattle got in and those other grasses strangled the yams out.

The sisters often hunted all day, coming back in the evening to their hilltop camp to cook up their food. Sometimes the big sister got tired, feeling she was the one doing most of the work, so she would send her little sister back down the hill on her own to get the water they needed from the spring.

Each time little sister climbed down from the hill alone to get to the spring she frightened off the rock pigeons drinking from the spring. When the birds heard her coming, they would fly away, making a noise with their wings. This noise always frightened the little sister. Some days she ran straight back to her big sister telling her, "there is someone waiting down there, he is going to kill me". She would say, "I am frightened! I can't go down there alone". So the

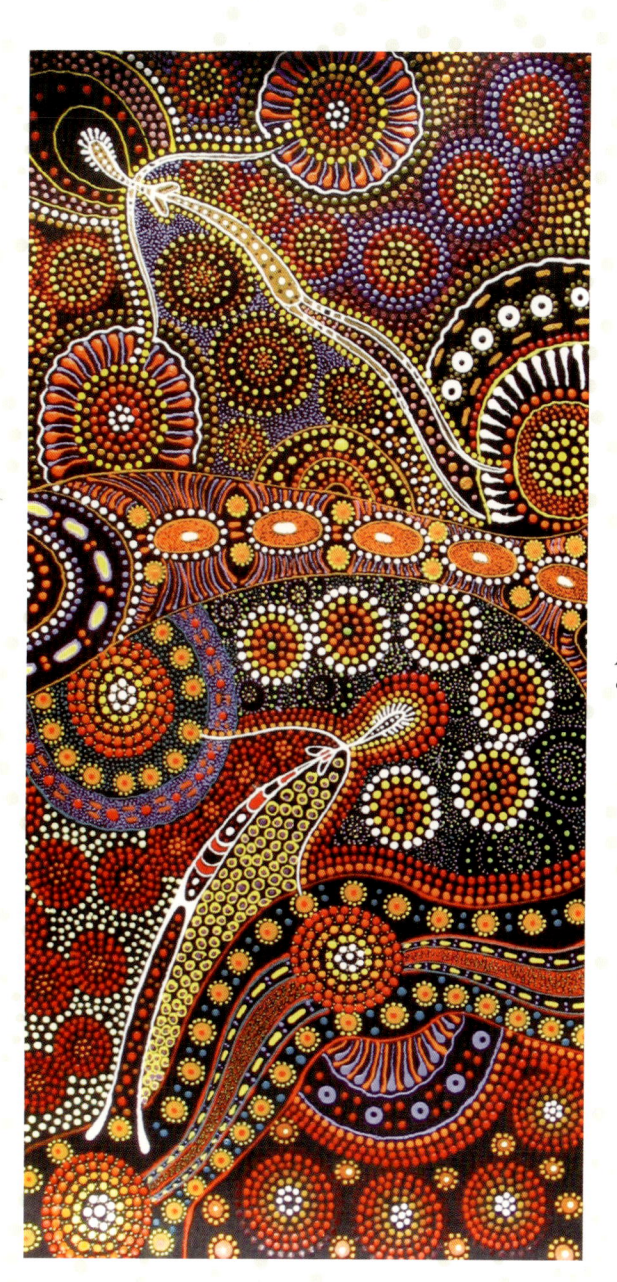

Ant Lion Sisters, 2005, acrylic on canvas, 50 x 20 cm

ABOVE: Ant lion beetle burying itself, and ant lion beetle trap with tracks, at Irlkerteye.

RIGHT: Salty pools at Irlkerteye.

big sister would have to stop preparing their food and climb down to the spring with her little sister. This made the big sister even more impatient with the younger sister, and once again she felt that she was doing more of the work. The little sister always thought that someone else had frightened the pigeons away – she didn't think it was her noise that made them fly off.

The sisters would bring a little bowl down with them. They had made it to carry the water back up to the fire. It was made of bark cut from a gum tree where the lump on the branch was. They carefully peeled the bark from the lump on the tree and made it smooth inside, rubbing it with stone until it was quite shiny and smooth. A good bark bowl like that would hold their water for months and months.

One day the little sister decided she would catch the man out who she thought was waiting for her at the spring. She climbed down by a different path, intending to get around behind him. Instead it was the man who caught her and drowned her. We don't know why this happened to her and we don't know who he was. It is possible that because she had always been so scared, always expecting something bad to happen to her, it did happen. After her death, the little sister's spirit fell out of her body onto the ground. She became *angkweye-angkweye*, an ant lion beetle.

The big sister was still preparing their meal up on the hill. She sat waiting there for her little sister and the water they needed for their meal. When it had grown completely dark she thought, what can have happened to her? Something must have happened. I better climb down and find her. The big sister did climb down to the spring in the dark and there she found her little sister's body floating in a big pool of salty water.

The big sister climbed back up the hill. She felt terrible. She was really sad and shocked. She cried all night and didn't eat anything. In the morning, she climbed back down to the pool to take care of her sister's body, but the body was gone. That is when the big sister became aware that her little sister's spirit was still there, calling to her. Her little sister had become *angkweye-angkweye*, so the big sister then turned into a spirit as well and they are both here today as *angkweye-angkweye*.

When I was a child many of us still used to visit the spring at Itnewerrenge and camp here. The families who camped here used to clear the scrub and sand back to keep the fresh water running so we could have a good camp. When they built the mission they put in the stone well and a windmill here to bring water up for the cattle. It's now an old ruin, the sand and trees have choked up the spring; there is no water in the well and the windmill is broken.

That old spring is all overgrown now, but this place was also a site where the men used to do their ochre rock painting associated with the *alangkwe*, bush banana plants. It is not something that I can talk about – it is the men's story. There are often many *alangkwe* growing in this area. When we have a lot of rain, we come here to swim sometimes in the rock pools along the river.

Near the spring at Itnewerrenge there is a small deep cave in the rocks by the ochre paintings. A long time ago, when people used to live freely, they often walked passed here and camped near the spring. It was a good spring to get water from, but there was a terribly bad *arrentye*, or man-eating spirit, at Itnewerrenge. The *arrentye* there was so strong, it drowned little children if they were too curious and wanted to find out if they could see it. That is how several children were caught and killed at Itnewerrenge. Being too brave is a bad thing when your curiosity puts you in danger. Everyone could see it was *arrentye* that killed them because it left long fingernail scratches on the children's faces. No one could ever hunt out or destroy that bad spirit. As far as we know there has always been a very evil *arrentye* at Itnewerrenge.

People only visited the spring in groups and children were always told they were not allowed to go close to the spring by themselves. Mothers and other family members said, "children, do not ever go to the spring alone or the *arrentye* might grab you and finish you up". But some children, as you know, choose to ignore their parents. They would be very curious and occasionally a child would come down to the spring alone just to see if anything was going to happen. We don't

LEFT: Left to right, Tara Palmer, Germaine Williams, Luke Wallace, Maureen Ellis, Bart Doolan and Jacob Doolan swim at Itnwerrenge after summer rains.

ABOVE: Kathleen swimming at Itnewerrenge after summer rains.

Bad Spirit at Itnewerrenge: Arrentye, 2007, acrylic on linen, 90 x 150 cm

know if it was a man or woman *arrentye*, but it killed those children who were too curious, who wanted to see it, or find it, who did not listen to the people warning them to stay together for their safety.

There are *irrernte-arenye* at Itnewerrenge, too. *Irrernte-arenye* often tried to help in this sort of circumstance, but they couldn't do anything to stop the child who was alone. The *arrentye* spirit at Itnewerrenge is really powerful so *irrernte-arenye* couldn't stop those curious children being drawn to it. The *irrernte-arenye* tried to keep the children away, but nothing worked. When a child was killed by *arrentye* everyone used to grieve for them and then bury them. They knew exactly what was responsible for the death because *arrentye* left marks on the body with its long sharp fingernails. *Ngangkere* came here many times looking for it, hunting *arrentye* to destroy it forever from Itnewerrenge. Even *ngangkere* could never find it, because this *arrentye* could hide away from them. It is a tricky, strong, bad one. *Ngangkere* have never killed it or removed it. That *arrentye* still lives here, even today, so we have to look after our children very carefully when we are here, make sure they are not left to explore alone.

When we were children we were told never to go by ourselves to the springs. We never did. There were always groups of us; I never went to the springs by myself. Every one of us would be safe if we kept together. We were all frightened by the stories we listened to and the sights we saw that were about *arrentye*.

There were many reasons for children to be cautious and to listen to their parents' words carefully. Another spirit woman who is capable of being quite evil is called *aleperentye*. She takes our children and sends her own magical children to their home to replace them. The magical children become very ashamed when others look at them, so it is clear to people what has happened when such a change-over has been performed. If anyone harms the magical children, then the *aleperentye* woman will come and seek vengeance, protecting her young ones. After some time the *aleperentye* will swap the children back over, replacing her magical children with the original ones. No one really knows why the *aleperentye* does this, but it happens. You might hear her at night time, making a humming noise as she creeps around your house. When we hear her we have to grab all the children and cuddle them tight, so she can't take them from us. We also use big fires to keep her away.

Aleperentye, 2008, acrylic on linen, 34 x 25 cm
In the painting, the *aleperentye* is following children who have gone to collect bush foods. When they have travelled far from home, she comes towards them wearing the disguise of a woman painted up for dancing. When she gets close enough the children recognise her as *aleperentye*. They become really scared; they are shaking, not knowing what to do.

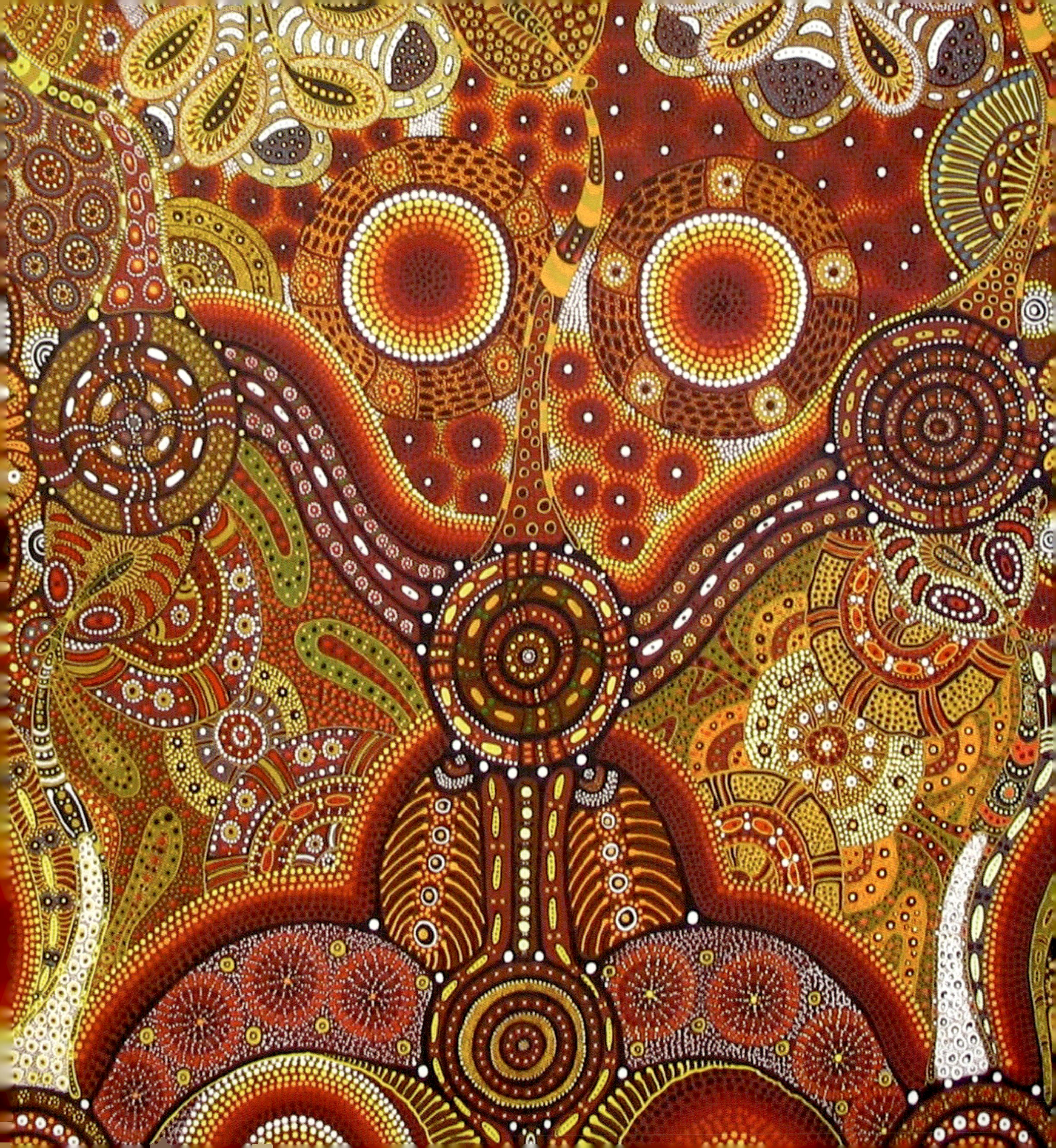

Ngangkere, Traditional healer

Ngangkere describes our traditional healers, but the word also means the healing itself. In English we sometimes call the people who have *ngangkere* a witch doctor or magician, but that's only because there aren't any better English words to describe *ngangkere*. *Ngangkere* are taught to know and use special energies to heal people and to keep order in both our world and the spirit world around us. They can heal many things, or bring illness, and they can travel through their spirits in many ways we do not understand. *Ngangkere* are aware of spirits, energies and other things that the rest of us do not know exist.

No family ever travelled without a *ngangkere*, and often the *ngangkere* was a member of the family. Families needed *ngangkere* healing power because they looked out for bad spirits, and other things which don't concern us and which are only understood or known by *ngangkere*. When we lived at Uyetye there was one old lady I remember who was *ngangkere*; she used to spot *arrentye* going along the river. From what she would show us afterwards, it had a really sharp shape like a pointy stick with a red skin. She used to sing out to all the people to sit quiet, so we did. Then, she used to go down to the creek and get that thing and come back with blood in her hand, and that sharp thing. As children we used to watch her. Things like that used to happen at Uyetye when I was small.

OPPOSITE: *Five Ngangkere Search*, 2005, acrylic on linen, 90 x 90 cm (detail)

OPPOSITE: *Ngangkere Journey, Spirit Guides*, 2005, acrylic on linen, 90 x 120 cm

It was just like that; sometimes things happened – still happen, only *ngangkere* know what it's all about. The *ngangkere* said that thing was *arrentye*. *Arrentye* are in every place. *Ngangkere* watches out for them, kills them in the *ngangkere* way, keeping us all safe. All we saw at Uyetye was a sharp pointy thing with blood on it which she then covered in ochre, red ochre. She used to come back and show that to us.

When I grew up we always had *ngangkere* with us when we travelled and camped. They still have a very important job to keep us all healthy and safe these days, too. Some of my grandparents were *ngangkere* and they told me about the *ngangkere* journey people take in training in order to be able to use their powers. I have painted this story because it is important to understand that these powers are still held safe, still reside strongly in our country. With this painting I can tell you about part of the journey that the chosen person takes in their training before they receive their powers. *Ngangkere* can make people ill or well, through considering the need of the person and administering the energy of the *ngangkere* for which they are a conduit.

There are several ways in which a person can become *ngangkere*. One way involves a person becoming a kind of student with *ngangkere* who are appointed to supervise the learning journey. Not everyone is suitable to learn to administer *ngangkere* and it is a long learning journey to become a good healer.

Some *ngangkere* are very good and may end up with several different *ngangkere* energies to use for specific sorts of illness like maybe for healing sick children, for looking for lost spirits, for healing sickness in the chest or for mental wellbeing. Those are a few. But, this painting is telling you about the long journey that a learner can take in order to have the ability to conduct the healing energies conferred on them.

In this first part of that journey, the spirits of the people who are learning to be *ngangkere* leave their bodies, and, in a dream state, their spirits start to travel underground. The knowledge they need to learn and remember starts to come to their spirit as it travels. They have to complete a whole journey, remembering everything they have been shown along the way, to be able to manage the healing energy of the *ngangkere*.

In the painting opposite the learners are just starting the journey underground and it will take them a long time to finish it. At certain places their spirit comes back up into the country – the spirit guides shown in the painting will always help them to come up. Each time they come up they must be able to recognise the place they come to, learn its healing properties, and remember everything. They see the place with their spirit, then they go back underground and on to another place. Every place must be recognised, learnt and remembered in this way.

At the finish, while they are going along the final tunnel, they see everything they learnt over again. As they go towards the end of the tunnel they start to be overwhelmed and distracted by many nice things. Sometimes it might be really nice places, smells, sounds or other things that try to distract them from their learning. If they forget anything about the significant places and the healing properties associated, their spirit will be taken back to the start again, going back underground to begin the journey again.

In the painting, little spirits hold the energy the learners need for the journey, and they guide them into the significant places. They are always present where the spirit of the dreamer comes up, in order to guide that spirit. Each sacred place has its own healing

Iwepe, the nest of the itchy grub.

songs and stories and when the dreamer is awake they must be able to recognise the energy for healing held in each place, and know how to sing those places and tell their stories. When they are awake, they must be able to describe perfectly each of the places to the *ngangkere* who is teaching them. When they know everything they need to know about each of those places, *ngangkere* enters them. For some people, they feel this as though through a hole in their hands, which means that the spirits put that energy into them through their hands. The *ngangkere* is then able to use their knowledge and these energies for healing people. *Ngangkere* have many ways to work with spirits and with healing. Many of them we don't know or understand unless we are *ngangkere*. The special healing sites in my country are Therirrerte, Keringke, Uyetye, Irlkerteye, Mparnwenge, Itnewerrenge and Antewerle, so each *ngangkere* on our homelands needs to know and recognise those places in order to conduct *ngangkere* healing.

I remember about 35 years ago, I got really sick. I was still quite young, maybe 25 years old, and my husband and I were married and living in an area called "over the fence" in one of our old houses in Ltyentye Apurte. While I was ill, an old spirit man came to me. He was a really short person with a very long beard, right down, dragging along the ground. He was a horrible little man, like an *iwepe*, an itchy grub. They have hairs which go into your skin and make awful itchy lumps swell up. The hairs are called *ikngethe*. He appeared and talked to me while I was ill. I got all swollen up: I was in agony! I was really sick and when I went to sleep I used to get all swollen on the side facing the little caterpillar man, and then if I turned the other way I would swell on the other side. He was there because he wanted to give that *ngangkere* to me, but I said *No!* This is another way people can become *ngangkere* – spirits can approach them and try to give them *ngangkere*.

In the end I had to go to an old lady who was *ngangkere*, living at Ltyentye Apurte. She had the power to take him away, to get him to go to her. That old woman told me the little caterpillar man was trying to give me a really strong *ngangkere* and if I had taken it I would have been very powerful, but that sort of power means I could also make people really sick. I didn't want to! They might feel really bad like I felt! He stopped coming to me after that, since the old woman had put him back in a safe place. It was a horrible little thing that caterpillar brought, it made me really sick!

My grandfather, a well respected *ngangkere*, taught me many things about *ngangkere* and healings. He taught me that *ngangkere* can come from anything: perhaps from a little caterpillar or even a snake that comes to you. It could be any live thing, even a bird. It depends on many things as to what power comes to you to make you a healing person.

Kathleen listens to her niece, Mia Mulladad.

Five Ngangkere Search, 2005, acrylic on linen, 90 x 90 cm

If you are not the type who is given the healing journey through your dreams, it might start off with you getting sick, and in my situation the sickness was like the stings of the *iwepe*. Although a real caterpillar did not sting me, the caterpillar *ngangkere* made me very sick.

Sometimes *ngangkere* will try you out for your potential to use healing power. The caterpillar tried to give me healing power by making me sick with the illness it wanted me to hold the healing power of. But if the person who is being tested says it's too hard for them, as happened to me, then the power and sickness can be taken away, and you are left alone after that.

Mia, my niece, lives at Ltyentye Apurte now and she received new *ngangkere* from my old ancestors when she was out bush near here. Mia already had three other *ngangkere* before she got this one. This is what she told me about how she got the new one.

First of all she felt her head was spinning, that was *irrernte-arenye* there making her feel like that. She was out past Deep Well station there, that's *irrernte-arenye* country, all around there. And she was sitting down by the fire when her head went dizzy, so she put salt in her tea instead of sugar! She was telling me all this, and she felt, oh, what's happening to me? Something going wrong. And then: I'll go and dig. And she went and dug witchetty, got a big one, really big. That was *irrernte-arenye* giving her the big one. All her family was saying, "where you get all the big ones?" It was *irrernte-arenye* giving her those big ones, and one was really big. But she couldn't understand: why they giving to me? It must be *irrernte-arenye* giving me. All that other family came – "where you get all the big ones? Tell us!" But she was feeling sick in her tummy, that was *irrernte-arenye* making her sick too, to give her more power. Then they gave her *ngangkere* again, a different one – little kangaroo one. That's only for little kids, she told me. And then when she was coming back she turned around and she saw *irrernte-arenye* – there was a mother and father and kid ones.

They were watching her come back. Father had a spear, mother had a stick, little one was standing watching. And she kept thinking, who are those people? But then she was tired and fell asleep, and that's when they came to her and they were speaking real Arrernte, true Arrernte. "Yeah, they spoke to me in real Arrernte, in real old Arrernte. Where are they from?" I told her, "they are my grandparents, they were them".

They gave her this power from kangaroo mob and she was real happy to tell me all this, and now she got new one, new *ngangkere*, couple of weeks ago. She felt, oh, I got stomach ache. But that's because they took her spirit away. Before, she couldn't recognise this place, because she came from a place not far from us, she's Alyawarr, other side from Todd River station, more north, and we're there too. Not far, it's family too. Now she is here. Now she can recognise this place. She goes, "Oh, I've seen those spirits!"

As you can imagine, I was really pleased to hear Mia's story.

Ngangkere have many important jobs to undertake and one of those is to look after *utnenge*. Everybody has *utnenge*, a living spirit, but *utnenge* might leave a body that is sick – it will go somewhere else. We understand that when the body is very sick the spirit leaves, and it may go underground to hide. It will stay there until the body starts to get better, or until *ngangkere* can guide it back to the body. Only once their spirit has returned will the person be well again.

Sometimes the *utnenge* can be found and returned through *ngangkere*, but sometimes the spirit hides inside the earth where nobody can find it. In this situation, three or four *ngangkere* might all look for the spirit in its hiding place, but even then they might still not find it. Sometimes, when the *ngangkere* sleeps, the *irrernte-arenye* might come and guide the *ngangkere* spirit, following the path the sick person's spirit took, hoping to find the *utnenge* and bring it back, returning it to the body of the sick person and making them well again.

If the *ngangkere* can't locate *utnenge* alone or with *irrernte-arenye*, a *wirlpirlpe*, curlew, might lead them to *utnenge's* hiding place, so *ngangkere* watch where *wirlpirlpe* goes. *Wirlpirlpe* has got really big eyes for seeing well at night – it can also see spirits going about their business. The bird may watch the spirit come out of the sick body, because at night the *wirlpirlpe* goes from camp to camp watching and looking. Sometimes *ngangkere* can then follow the *wirlpirlpe* tracks to *utnenge's* hiding place, only to look into the hiding place and find nothing! But there will be marks indicating the spirit was hiding there before. Sometimes they find *utnenge* is still in the hiding place. *Utnenge* goes everywhere trying to hide and sometimes it can't be found by *ngangkere*.

Utnenge will dig holes for themselves or go in to a lizard's nest trying to get underground to escape and hide. They don't go near *irrernte-arenye* though, they stay quite separate. Sometimes *utnenge* stays hidden, blocking itself into a corner in a little underground hole. *Utnenge* might make a door with dirt or sand to keep everyone away. They shut themselves in. *Utnenge* could be hiding anywhere in the whole country, anywhere at all!

If *ngangkere* can find *utnenge* in time, the weak spirit will be very cold. *Ngangkere* will put it in their chest, holding onto it really tightly so it can't get away again. They make *utnenge* warm again before putting it back into the sick body. Then the sickness goes away and the person gets well.

If the spirit is not found quickly enough the person dies and the *utnenge* will become *irrernte-arenye*.

Some *ngangkere* are especially good at helping little babies. Even though there were important actions we undertook to keep babies healthy and safe after birth, it is not uncommon for a little baby's spirit to leave the body if it gets very sick, so it's important to take good care of them from the beginning. First, when babies were born, we used to hold the baby in cleansing smoke. You dig a big hole, put in a special kind of wood, and burn grasses underneath. The smoke that comes up heals and cleanses the baby. It's to help keep away bad spirits. The little one would have black marks painted right across their forehead and tummy, and was also given a headband made from their umbilical cord. That was to keep bad spirits away, too, so that when they grow up, they will grow up strong. The headband was kept for a long time, until it grew old. It protects the person. Some people still like to do that – they wrap the cord in cotton and put it around the baby's hand or pin it on their jumper. People don't make a headband from the cord for the baby anymore, some just hold onto it.

You can put red ochre on children to protect them from some of the winds which can upset their stomachs, too. The red ochre is painted on their foreheads and pressed into their bellybuttons so they won't get sick. In the old days, when we were children, people applied ochre on us in that way. But regardless of all these things to keep them safe, babies' spirits sometimes leave their bodies – even a loud noise can frighten the little one's spirit out of their body. If a baby does get sick *ngangkere* may be able to retrieve the little spirit and guide it back to the body to live. Otherwise *irrernte-arenye* goes to their grandfather's country.

This knowledge of the body and the spirit is given to us so that we understand that without the spirit the body is just a shell. Without the living spirit the body dies and without the living body the spirit returns to the spirit world as *irrernte-arenye*. This is how it is for Arrernte.

We don't know what happens to the spirits of other people.

  We still have *ngangkere*, who can help us with all sorts of sickness and who understand and communicate with our spirit worlds, but even they can't take away the grog or the boredom. That is something for each person to do themselves. *Ngangkere* can, however, still conduct healing energies and teach those willing to learn.

Utnenge Spirit, 2003, acrylic on canvas, 30 x 46 cm
This painting shows a journey taken by *utnenge*, the spirit of a sick person.

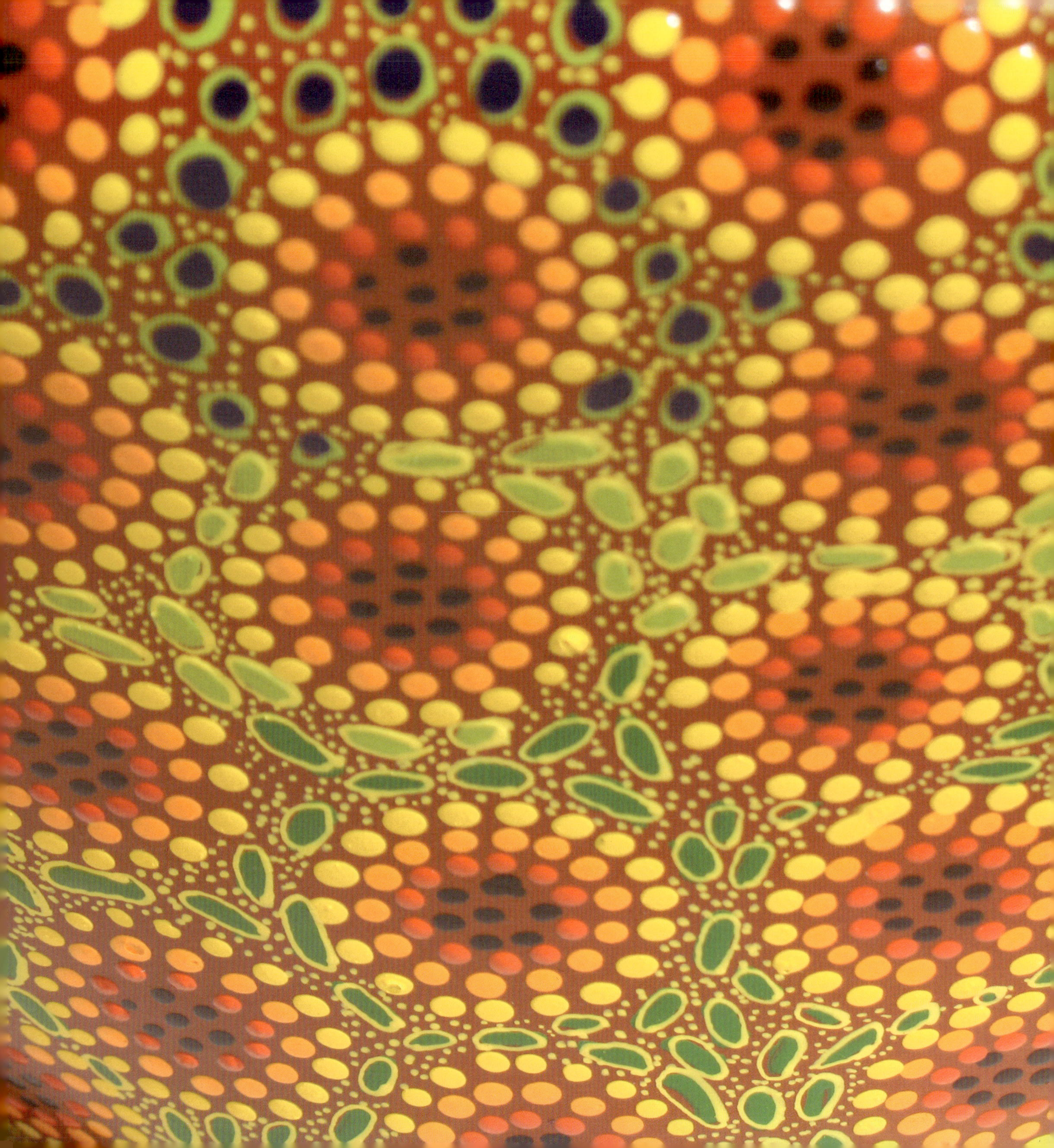

Ahurratye, Drought

When the drought hit in 1959, our safe and independent lifestyle at Uyetye ended. Until the late fifties, there were maybe twenty or thirty people living in family groups at Uyetye and we still had quite a few very old people living with us, real old ones, but we don't get that anymore. No one is living that long these days.

At that time, in the late 50s, my grandparents were still keeping us out of the way, moving around the hills and springs, but keeping us all out of sight from the stations and from Arltengke. When we were out and about, all of us children used to run back to the cave if we saw a truck coming towards the station – Uyetye was the safest place to hide. Other people used to bring their children there too – they heard that children were still being taken away from families, as they had been taken from Little Flower mission at Arltengke.

Some of the station people helped us out by being quiet about where we were. I remember hearing about one man at Todd River station who looked after our people. He knew people were at Uyetye but he never used to report them or get them sent to the mission at Arltengke. Children were still running around everywhere, bush way. Another good man at Todd River station was there when I was a child. He used to look out for us, sometimes bringing rations to my grandparents, leaving them for us near Uyetye. He never told the authorities about us either. Although I was born at Uyetye, it was wrong

ABOVE AND OPPOSITE (detail):
Dancing Wind, 2007, acrylic on ceramic, 24 x 42 cm

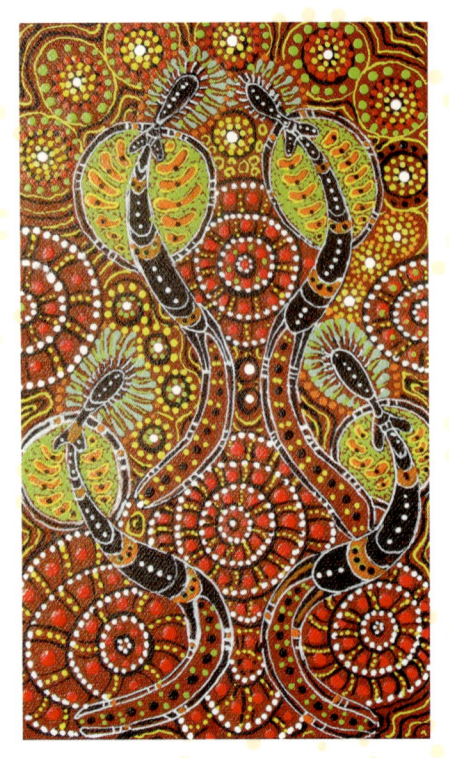

Seeds, 2007, acrylic on canvas, 18 x 12 cm

in white man's law – I was supposed to be born and registered at Arltengke so then, if I was coloured, they knew about it right away. The government was always trying to keep count of us in those days.

In 1953 the Catholic Diocese built the new mission at Ltyentye Apurte because the Little Flower mission at Arltengke was no good. The water was bad after the gold mining and the country was too hard, too poor to keep the people going. They called this new mission Santa Teresa because that was another name for Little Flower. They were the names of a Catholic woman who was made a saint, and given the names Little Flower and Saint Theresa.

At Ltyentye Apurte, they built the mission on a particularly important sacred site. They should have talked to the old people from here about that first. My great grandfather was alive that time when they built, and they built on that sacred site which was part of the men's business – it was a big rain making site. Now the spring at the site is all covered up with sand and it's built around. I don't know what my grandparents were thinking or saying when it happened. At first we didn't know that the mission had moved from Arltengke. Even my grandfather didn't know because he was keeping us out of the way, keeping around the hills and springs. I imagine he might have felt shocked or sad when he saw the mission at first at Santa Teresa because it was on one of those old men's sacred sites. That was wrong, I think, *akurne*, sad, no good.

Then the drought came. In the normal seasons, we all knew where to get the *tyape* and witchetties. And kangaroo was sometimes quite easy to get, but even then seeds were much harder to find. All around us there were many different bushes and trees, but it was especially difficult to find seeds unless the rain, sun and wind had all come at the appropriate times. When it is dry or too hot, the plants die back and there is no seed. No seed meant no flour at all for us to eat. Seed was an important part of our diet. The flour was good for us, we missed it really badly when we had none.

Hunting for Seeds, 2006, acrylic on linen, 64 x 46 cm
This painting is about hunting around for seeds. Looking! We are still always looking, especially looking for seeds. That's the waterhole and that is the spring – both springs. Those are the tracks where the people go. Sometimes there is no track, but people still know where to get the water. They know the country. The figures at the top and at the bottom are family, looking and looking.

Seed Spirits, 1999, acrylic on canvas, 50.8 x 40.5 cm

There is a story about three young women from the *altyerrenge*. They used to go around collecting seeds for older people, ones who never used to go out or couldn't go around collecting seeds. They used to collect a lot of seeds and make little damper cake which they gave to the old ones. They also fed damper to the smaller kids while the mothers were out hunting. The three women used to go to a place where they knew there were plenty of seeds. They would work all day to look after the old people and the young ones left behind in the camp.

OPPOSITE: *Alangkwe* seed

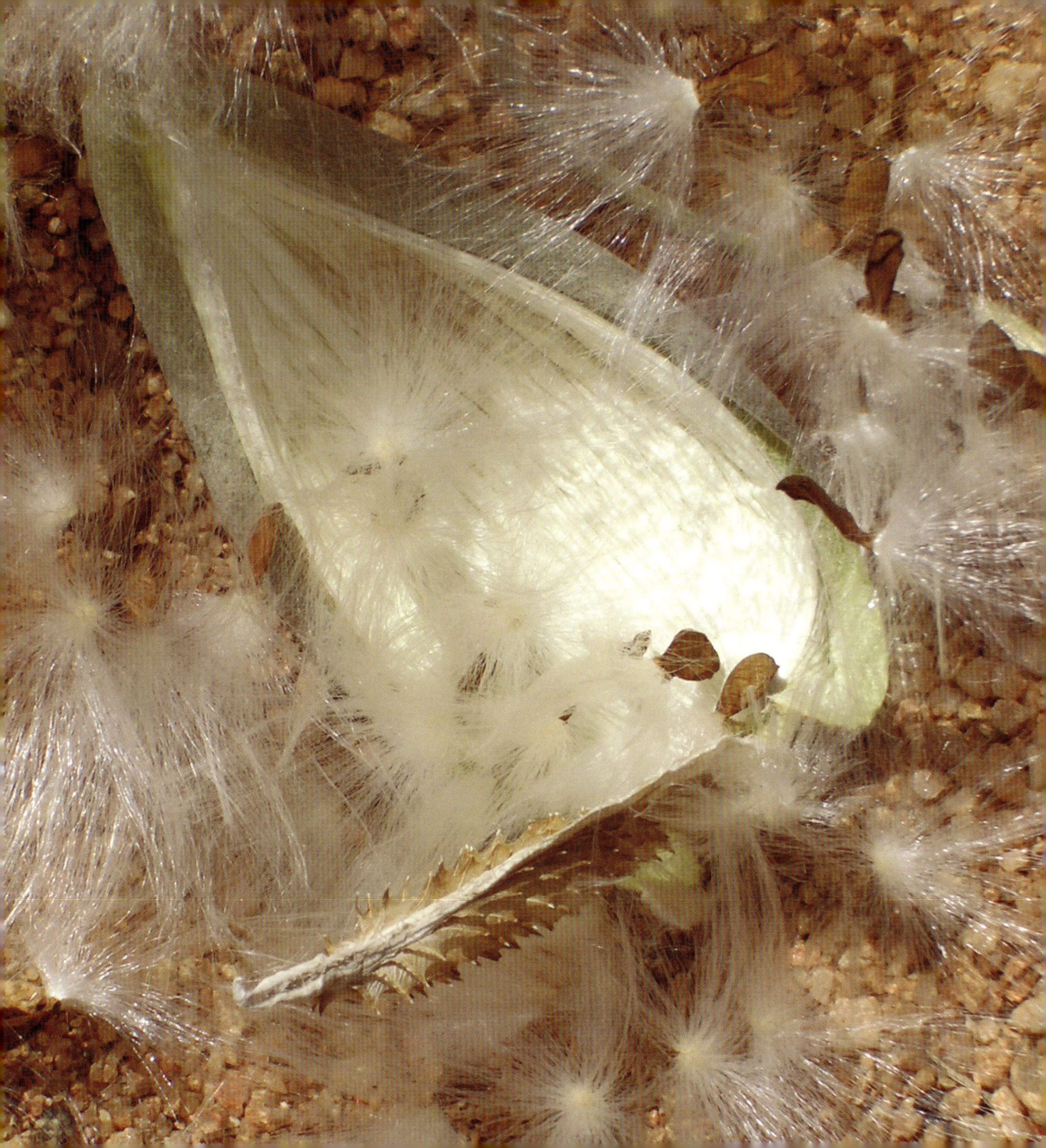

ABOVE: *Dancing Wind*, 2007, acrylic on ceramic, 24 x 42 cm
Growing the seeds – five women are dancing to make grasses grow seeds. They dance all night long and in the morning they rush around in a whirling, dancing circle. Rushing around, their feet make a big, swirling dust cloud. We still see them in springtime or after rains when the seeds start to grow into different plants. These whirly winds dance across the landscape, scattering more seeds, and drawing the plants up from under the ground.

RIGHT: *Hat Box with Landscape*, 1994, acrylic on cardboard, 35.5 x 25.7 cm

There always were *tyape*, and still are. You can still get some grubs from the tree bark and some from the root, but the seeds are harder to find. Now, it's become even harder for seeds to grow too. The different grasses and weeds that came in with the cattle have killed many of the grasses and plants which produced all the seeds. At the moment we are not getting enough rain, even the bush tomatoes have all gone from this area. Every year we had a big mob of bush tomatoes. We still find bush tomatoes in some places but not in others. When they dug gravel out of here for the road, the bush mushrooms stopped coming up. They don't grow here anymore. Mushrooms were rarer. They're all gone now. Same with that bush cucumber. That drought in the 1950s was so bad, and things had changed so much, that even at Uyetye there was nothing else to eat out in the bush. We had no choice anymore – we had to start going to Santa Teresa mission to get rations, because we couldn't gather and hunt enough food anymore.

It was extremely long that drought, lasting for seven years. Some people stayed out bush as long as possible but eventually all the kangaroos became too skinny to eat. They were nothing but bone. Lizards and goannas were the same too. We couldn't hunt them, and bush foods weren't growing anymore. The

2006 drought was not as bad as that one which went from 1959 until 1966. In those days when I was out there, it was really dry. We were all forced off the country and onto the mission, but the mission didn't have enough either. Santa Teresa mission was not set up to provide for everyone. The Santa Teresa mission was set up to have thirty or so people living there, to look after the babies, their mothers and elderly people while everyone else worked on the stations. When the drought forced everyone off the country there were about four hundred people at the mission.

They couldn't feed everyone at Santa Teresa, so some people had to go into Alice Springs. Even people who were good hunters, and who had lived all their life out bush on our homelands, had to try and live in town. Some got given jobs like looking after pigs or goats to earn their food. This was a bad drought. Gradually all of us went to Santa Teresa mission or into Alice Springs to get rations and to camp because of the drought. It was the last straw that broke us from our lands.

ABOVE: *Merne Arliwerme - Edible Plants Come Up (grow)*, 2006, acrylic on ceramic, 37 x 15 cm
This wind pulls up the seeds, makes them come up to grow. Four women danced after rain. They danced all night and when the morning came they whirled around so fast they became that wind. A good wind, that helps pull the growth up from the seeds.

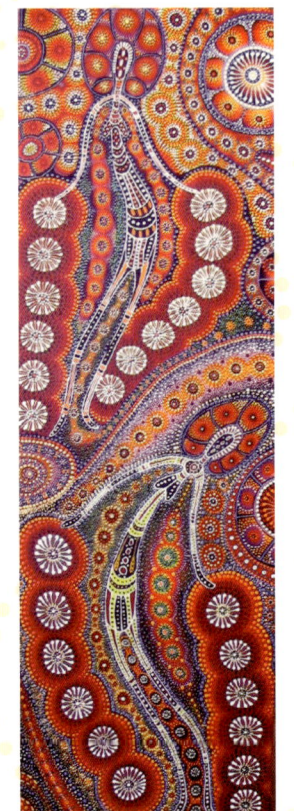

LEFT: *Collecting Seeds*, 2007, acrylic on canvas, 18 x 12 cm

RIGHT: *Women with Seeds*, 2005, acrylic on canvas, 90 x 30 cm

Artwe Anyente Mpwernikwe Akweke-akerte Uyetyele

Urreye akweke aneke Uyetyele, yaye ikwerenhe anewarte-arle aneke. Mpwernikwe ikwereke ahentye-anetyakenhe, "ayenge kwenhe ahentye-anetyakenhe akweke yanhe anwernenge anetyeke," kwenhe. Akenhe akweke re awelhetyarte, "kele, ayenge-arrpe alpeme intetyenhe artepeke ulkere interle-anetyeke." Akenhe yaye ikwerenhe angketyakenhe ikwere re, "ampe akweke kwenhe re," arrangkwe.

Kele alakenhe rarle aneke, akweke re artepeke ulkere anetyarte, akenhe ratherre apmerele anerlenge. Anewarte intetyarte akenhe akweke rawerne iknge intetyarte, anyente-arenye. Ure akwekeke ware interle.

Artwe nhenhe kereke alhetyarte, arratye akenhe inerlenge akenhe yaye ikwerenhe merneke alhelenge, ntangeke-arlke, awele-aweleke-arlke. Akenhe akweke nhawerne akangkemele inketyentyele mpwernelikwe kere-arlke iterlenge. Nterte ware arlengeke-arle anerle mpwernikwe-arle angkeketyenge. Akwekeke alhwarrpe-irretyakenhe-arle aneke. Kele kere-arlke mpenge-irrerlenge itwe-irrerlenge akweke re akangkemele, "mpwerneke atyinhe kere akweke-awe," kwenhe akenhe re akenhe renhe ilterlenge, "ngkwenge akngetyakenhe kere nhe-arle nhenhe!"

"Unte ampe yanhe merne yanhe-areye ntherle!" kwenhe re anewıkwe renhe ileke.

"Kele, atyenge-arrpe arlkwerle-anetyeke ayenge alpemenge," kwenhe, urreye akweke angkeke, "atnyetye arlkwerle-anetyeke". Atnyetye arlkwerlenge re atnerte akurne-irrerle-anetyarte.

Ingwele-ante apeke yaye ikwerenhe merne nthetyarte artwe anewikwe ankwe-interlenge. Ingwele-ante kere akweke ntherle, merne akweke ntange, rarle arltele utnheke mape. Akweke rawerne atnerte akurne-irremele atne-ulhetyeke alheleke. Akwetethe rarle artwe ampwe ikwere ahentye-anetyakenhe.

Kele akweke re itirreke, "tharle iperte tnyetyeke alheme," kwenhe, "ayenge iperteke atne-ulherle-anerle," kwenhe, "tharle yanhe renhe atwetyenhenge, iperteke atnyetyeke mpwarlerle atne ikwereke atnyetyeke!" Re iperte akngerre tnyetyarte akwetethe renhe. Ikwerenhe itirrentye-arle aneke artwe re renhe alwerneme re iperteke atnyetyeke.

Kele re ampe akngerre-anteme-irreke. Artwe re renhe alwernemele atwetyarte re. Akenhe re akenhe iperte ikwere-werne iknge arrewemele unterlenge. Artwe untemele apertemele utepe-iknge-irretyarte alpeme, akwetethe rarle.

Urreye re kere-arlke ineke rarrpe; kelyawe, alewatyerre-arlke. Atnyetye-arle-ante atnerte akurne-iletyarte.

Kele re ampe akngerre aneme aneke, artwe kele arratye aneme renhe alwerneke. Iperte ikwere-werne atheke ampe re unteke akenhe artwe-arle tyelpelh-ilelheke apwertele. Apwerteke aka atwetyenhe atnyetye-alperlenge. Artwe re ilweke, urreke iperteke atnyetyenhe re ilwerlenge.

Yaye ikwerenhe arlkeke, "nthakenhe-irrekaye?!" "Apwerteke atnyetye-alpeke," kwenhe, "rarle ayenge alwernerne," kwenhe.

Ratherre apmere arrpenhe-werne alperreke, artwe renhe iperteke artemele.

Boy and Man, 2006, acrylic on linen, 152 x 120 cm

Brothers-in-law

Looking after your family members is a very strong part of our culture. Sharing the food, shelter, hunting and child rearing were considered most important tasks for the family group, and everyone's needs were considered. In this story our elders warn us about the damage that can be done when someone is selfish, mean and disrespectful to their family. This can cause great distress to others. This story is about a little boy who had to live with his sister and her husband, his brother-in-law, because his parents had passed away. She was the only family he had left. The boy was just a young child. The man, his brother-in-law, should have been responsible for hunting meat for all of them. In our culture they were now his family to take care of.

The brother-in-law was a good enough hunter and he often caught good meat but he would not share what he caught out in the bush, the kangaroos and things, with the boy. The little boy used to say, "Brother-in-law, you have got a big mob of meat there". But the man used to say, "go away! You won't get any meat from me!" He never did share good meat with the boy, so the little boy had no alternative. "All right," he said, "I will go away. I will go and look for my own food. I'll get lizards, I'll find something for myself to eat." This is why he had to dig up roots, grubs and other poor-quality foods.

Because of this poor diet that little boy used to get sick. After eating too much of the poor food, never being given any of the good meat he needed, his stomach would hurt and he would have to do a lot of poo. When the boy had a bad stomach ache, he used to dig holes for himself to poo into. Secretly, he would hope the man would fall in them. As the boy grew up, all the while he dug lots of these little holes and he thought: one day I am going to trap that man in one of my poo holes.

Sometimes during the night when the brother-in-law was asleep, the sister would wake the little boy up and give him some good kangaroo meat. She would only do this when the man did not know because she was frightened of her husband. She was a good wife and a good hunter too. She often dug yams and caught goannas. She always shared these with her little brother when her husband was asleep.

As the boy grew the man became meaner towards him, making him go and sleep on his own, sending him off to find his own shelter, never allowing his little brother-in-law to sleep near the fire on cold nights. He told the boy to go away and make his own fire. The boy's sister taught him how to make fire and so he learnt to make his own. Things went on that way for a long, long time as the boy grew up. At no time would the man share anything of importance with the boy.

The boy learned how to survive on his own, very young. He would go out hunting and get goannas for himself and even little kangaroos. His brother-in-law still caught the really big kangaroos while the boy could still only catch the weak or skinny ones. Still that man wouldn't share with his young brother-in-law.

Reflecting on this over time had made the boy feel deeply angry towards this selfish man. The man grew a fat stomach, so the boy started to dig bigger holes still thinking: I might do something to trap him one day! He made bigger, deeper holes. Sometimes the boy would purposely tease the man, and then run away towards those holes, hoping the man might fall into one when chasing him. But the lazy man only ran a little way, never falling into any holes. When the boy was about fourteen years old he started digging very big holes. He was really angry and cross about how his brother-in-law had treated him since he was a little boy. The man lived with the boy's sister, so naturally the boy thought: Why isn't he kind to me? He has got my sister, he should be kind to me. We are a family.

He would ask his sister about it, but she was very afraid of her husband who wouldn't listen to her either. She was frightened of him because sometimes he got rough and angry with her. Whenever she asked for food for her brother, the man would say, "just give him the bones". Then the man ate all the good flesh and gave only the bones to the growing boy. The boy said, "I am not going to eat those bones, I'm not a dog!"

When he became a man, the young boy teased his brother-in-law again and again until finally he made the man chase him. But instead of falling into a hole, as the boy had planned, the man tripped over himself, knocked his head on a rock and died. The woman was a bit sad for her husband but the boy was not sad or sorry. Brother and sister moved away from there, to a place near Uyetye, where they lived safely with the other families. Then they were happy.

The boy didn't finish up killing his brother-in-law as he had thought he one day might, because the brother-in-law had enough bad luck to finish himself off. He probably deserved the accident and it was better that the boy didn't have to take that responsibility.

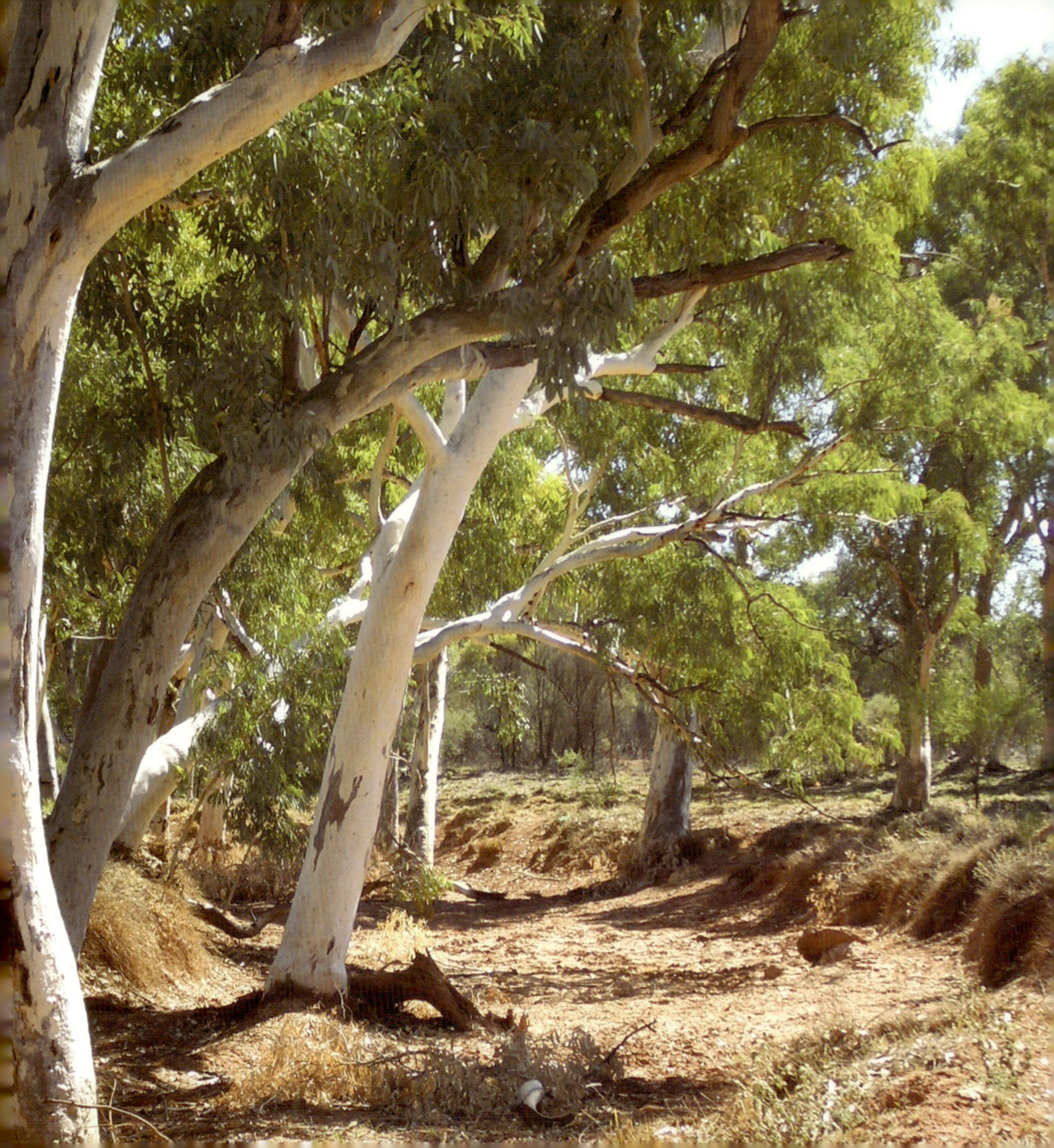

Ltyentye Apurte community, Santa Teresa mission

I was eleven years old in 1959, when I came into Santa Teresa mission to live. For some time after this, members of my family kept their business and culture active, taking trips back out to the sites and camping and hunting for periods of time. Our homelands were rich with springs, stories and sites of significance to us but there were many, many changes to our culture, country, family and way of life. The way we had lived was finished. The drought was the final barrier to our old ways of survival.

I was taught many new things at the mission but it was really very hard. At first the nuns told us to stop speaking our own languages and speak only in English. I didn't know any English at all so I used to sit quietly, only speaking to the other girls when the nuns couldn't hear. The only words that I understood in English were "yes" and "no". When we tried to speak in our own language we were forced to stop. I struggled in the mission. We were ordered to learn very different things, in the European way, and punished if we didn't obey, and I struggled to learn everything in another culture and language. Slowly I learnt English, sewing, domestic work, cooking, cleaning, religion, and some art and craft. Along the way I forgot some things, too.

A lot of families from Uyetye had moved into the mission at Santa Teresa or earlier to Little Flower mission at Arltengke. Some of these families are now known by names they

OPPOSITE: Tyelkempwe creek *altyerre* men's site.

Tyepetye-ileme, sand drawing showing family camp site.

got on the stations – Ryder, Williams, Oliver – but originally they had all come from around Uyetye. Our grandparents, our ancestors, all came from around there. White people had given us all different surnames, so those surnames don't always make sense to our family connections, but we still know our own family relationships, through our skin names and our *apmere*.

When I was taken to the mission by my parents, I was just left behind there. I didn't know beforehand that they were going to leave me. My parents put me there so the nuns could look after me. The nuns gave me dolls to play with, I was about eleven. I waited with the dolls, not sure what to do with them, expecting my parents to come and get me when they finished talking to the nuns. After some time I realised that my parents were not coming back for me. They were not around anywhere so I started going after them, I took off back towards to Uyetye. I didn't know my parents had gone to live in Alice Springs. The nuns stopped me at Tyelkempwe, a creek on the way; they caught up with me there and took me back to the mission. After that I stayed put at the dormitory. Then I had to go to school and start learning a different culture, learning in a very different way. I couldn't understand why I was left there until much later; now I understand that we could no longer survive in the drought in the bush and my parents had to go to Alice Springs for work or rations.

My family, my mother and father particularly, wanted me to learn about other things. They knew how much the outside world was changing because they had both worked on stations, and my father was raised in the Bungalow in Alice Springs. So they took me to the mission because my grandparents couldn't keep us all alive out bush in the drought. My parents couldn't get station work after the drought hit so they couldn't get rations out to us at Uyetye.

I didn't like living at the mission when they brought me there at first because everything stayed in one place, we never moved around the country at all! The nuns told us, "you have to do this!", "Do it this way!" But my mind was full of wondering about my homelands: What's happening out there? Have my family gone to this spring or rockhole? Is the rockhole full or empty out there? But at the mission they kept saying, "you must do this, you must stay here, and you must learn this". So I learnt. I had to learn to do things the European way until I was old enough to leave the dormitory and get work on the community, when I was about seventeen.

In the mission there were Aboriginal people from all over the place, with a lot of different dialects, not all from our place, not all from our homelands. We had our own strong ideas of wrong and right behaviour, and sometimes this was not the same as what the nuns made us do. For me, to look at another person's eyes was wrong. We were taught by our elders to look away from another person's face because you could see their spirit in their eyes. It was dangerous and especially disrespectful to look at the eyes of your elders. But then the nuns told us, "you look at me when I speak to you! You look at me when you answer me!" They really yelled at us. It felt so hard to have to do it the wrong way, so the nuns would leave me alone. I felt really, really shy about looking at people's eyes.

Seven Sisters, 2006, acrylic on linen, 54 x 40 cm

Seven Sisters

One day, when the seven sisters were still young girls and before they had their noses pierced, they went for a walk with their grandmother. As they prepared to go walking they saw their grandmother putting a piece of stick through her nose and they asked her, "why did you have your nose pierced? And how?"

The old lady said, "this is our custom and when you grow older you can have your nose pierced too, just like mine".

And then the seven sisters asked, "do we have someone to pierce our nose?"

"Yes," the grandmother replied, "but we have to look hard for him, he is really hard to find, he is an old man now. He travels everywhere and when he travels around he does the nose piercing for people".

"We want ours done too!" the seven sisters said, but their grandmother reminded them that they were still just small, young girls.

Later, when the sisters had grown into young women, an old man came by their camp. As it turns out, it wasn't the right old man for nose piercing; it was someone else. That true old man was still away, but their grandmother was a very old woman now, and she couldn't see much anymore, everything was just blurry, so she said, "that's him!" The man was a trickster and he pretended he was the nose piercing old man. So all the sisters lined up for him, and he went and pierced one girl's nose and told her to sit down. "You wait there till the blood stops," he said, and he pierced the next sister's nose. He had to first pierce the nose, then leave the stick through the skin to keep the hole open. The trickster went from one sister to the next, telling each one to wait. "Don't go away when the blood stops. You wait," he said. All the time he was looking at them carefully, and he was doing their nose piercing really slowly and so all the women were in pain! But he just didn't want to do it quickly; he wanted those women to be around him. Then he got to the last one, the youngest, and he pierced her nose.

He sat down and he called the sisters over to him, "you come here," he said, "and I'll smoke you mob". So they let him do the smoking, thinking it was the correct thing to do, although he was just making reasons for them to stay with him. By this time their old grandmother was

Seven Sisters, 2005, lino cut on paper, 39 x 28 cm

asking: "what's he doing now?" She couldn't see, but she supposed he was just piercing their noses and then letting them go!

All the next day the sisters waited. "Oh, it's not healed up yet," said the trickster and he kept looking at their faces. "It's much too swollen up. You must wait another day." By then the women got tired of listening to him and tired of waiting. They felt all right, so one by one they started moving away until the eldest was the only one left behind, waiting to run away from the trickster.

The trickster came back to where he left the sisters waiting, just as the oldest sister's head disappeared down into the ground. The sisters knew that the trickster was trying to make them stay with him by this time, but they were magic and so they travelled under the ground to get away from him. The trickster was a powerful magician too, so he chased them anyway. He looked around and looked around and when he saw their tracks all stop in one place he too made himself go into the ground, and chased after them.

The sisters came out from under the ground, but they kept running because now they knew he was a powerful magician and they would have to keep going if they were to escape from him. In this way they travelled around our country and you can see all the tracks left behind by them. They went here and there, trying to make tracks everywhere that would confuse him, so they could get away for good.

LEFT TO RIGHT:
Seven Sisters, 2003, ceramic vase, 48 x 24 cm

Seven Sisters, 2005, acrylic on linen, 90 x 30 cm
They are dancing with dancing sticks, in the place where they come to dance – see, the big circle. They go around dancing in different places, and there are little tracks leading from one place to another.

Seven Sisters in the Stars, 2005, acrylic on linen, 90 x 46 cm
Dancing Women, 2004, acrylic on canvas, 35 x 25 cm

Seven Sisters, 2004, acrylic on wooden table, 83 x 46 x 46 cm

Although they made tracks to trick him, the sisters never really got away; somehow he was always there, somewhere nearby, watching them, coming after them. They could change their shape when they travelled too, so they changed into different creatures like perenties or birds. Most people could not see them at all and, although the trickster couldn't see them clearly as they travelled underground, or in disguise, he could see enough to follow them. Since other people couldn't see anything at all, the sisters could go underground or anywhere else they liked without anybody's interference.

Still, they were being followed by the trickster. He wanted to catch the sisters and make the youngest his wife. The sisters had many adventures, changing many times as they ran from him, while he continued to change shape too, even spying on them from the sky at times to see where they had gone.

When the sisters came out from travelling in the desert they found a little, sick man, covered in rough warty skin, who was too weak to care for himself. They felt so sorry for him then that they invited him to travel with them. Off they went, taking him with them, but soon they found that they had to carry him, and once he was in their arms he would not get down again because he felt so sore. The little man became a very heavy burden. Each day they stopped for a rest, they would sit under a shade tree and make the little sick man comfortable under another nice shade tree. He would doze off in the sleepy afternoon heat.

By now, the sisters secretly knew who the sick little man really was! They wanted to leave him behind because they were really tired of carrying him and of him complaining all along the way. So, one day, they tried to slip away after he fell asleep in the shade. But he was the trickster, and he knew what the sisters wanted to do! As soon as he woke up, he cursed them to their deaths for leaving him behind. The sisters thought they must have truly escaped him this time, and in a place near here where I grew up, a place called Arlirntarlpe they danced and danced in celebration thinking they had really gotten away from the trickster for all time. As they danced they made beautiful ridges and patterns in the rocks, which are near the river bed.

The sisters didn't know then, but the trickster merely changed himself from the warty, sick little man into a large, powerful carpet snake

RIGHT: *Seven Sisters*, 2006, acrylic on linen, 90 x 30 cm

OPPOSITE: *Seven Sisters in the Stars*, 2005, acrylic on canvas, 30 x 56 cm

and he raced after them again, carving the large bed of the river as he slithered – a giant snake in the sand country. The sisters understood that the trickster had found their tracks again, that he was coming after them and that now he wanted to marry all of them and have seven wives! They ran to the rocky hills nearby at Inteye Arrkwe where they hid in seven little caves. As he approached, they leapt out of the caves and flew into the night sky, where they turned into the stars we call Arralkwe, Seven Sisters – that is where they are today.

They went up and up, above the Milky Way, because they didn't want to be seen by its light. The Milky Way was too bright for them at first, since they were still hiding away from the trickster who was even still pursuing them. When they went into the darkness of the night sky they carried fire sticks. At first they didn't realise that their fire sticks had begun to shine, that they had become stars. One of the sisters up there has two fire sticks, the others took meat and other food for their journey.

Even though they are completely in the spirit world now, they still go hunting up in the sky. They always go back to the same place to form a little group which appears to us like little sparks in the night sky. They are Arralkwe, the Seven Sisters.

Since the sisters flew up into the sky and became stars to our eyes, they have seen many new places and things. We understand that they now have a really good hunting ground and never have to run away anymore from the trickster who was chasing them on earth. It is a better place up there for the sisters. The trickster is now an old man, and he is there too, but he has forgotten about chasing them and leaves them alone. He stays in one place, peaceful and looking after himself. He is hunting for himself now, happy in the night sky. The sisters are no longer afraid of him, they can talk to him when they meet up during their journeys across the sky, as they go freely on their own way, hunting for themselves.

The Milky Way is like a big creek bed, where the sisters go to sit and look for yams to dig, and to dance their dances. You can see they're still dancing because the stars are twinkling. To this day my people look to the Seven Sisters and watch them dance, and that way we know when winter is coming, because the Milky Way turns downwards in the sky. Looking for summer the people ask, "where are the Seven Sisters, where are they dancing tonight?" They are a really good sign for our people.

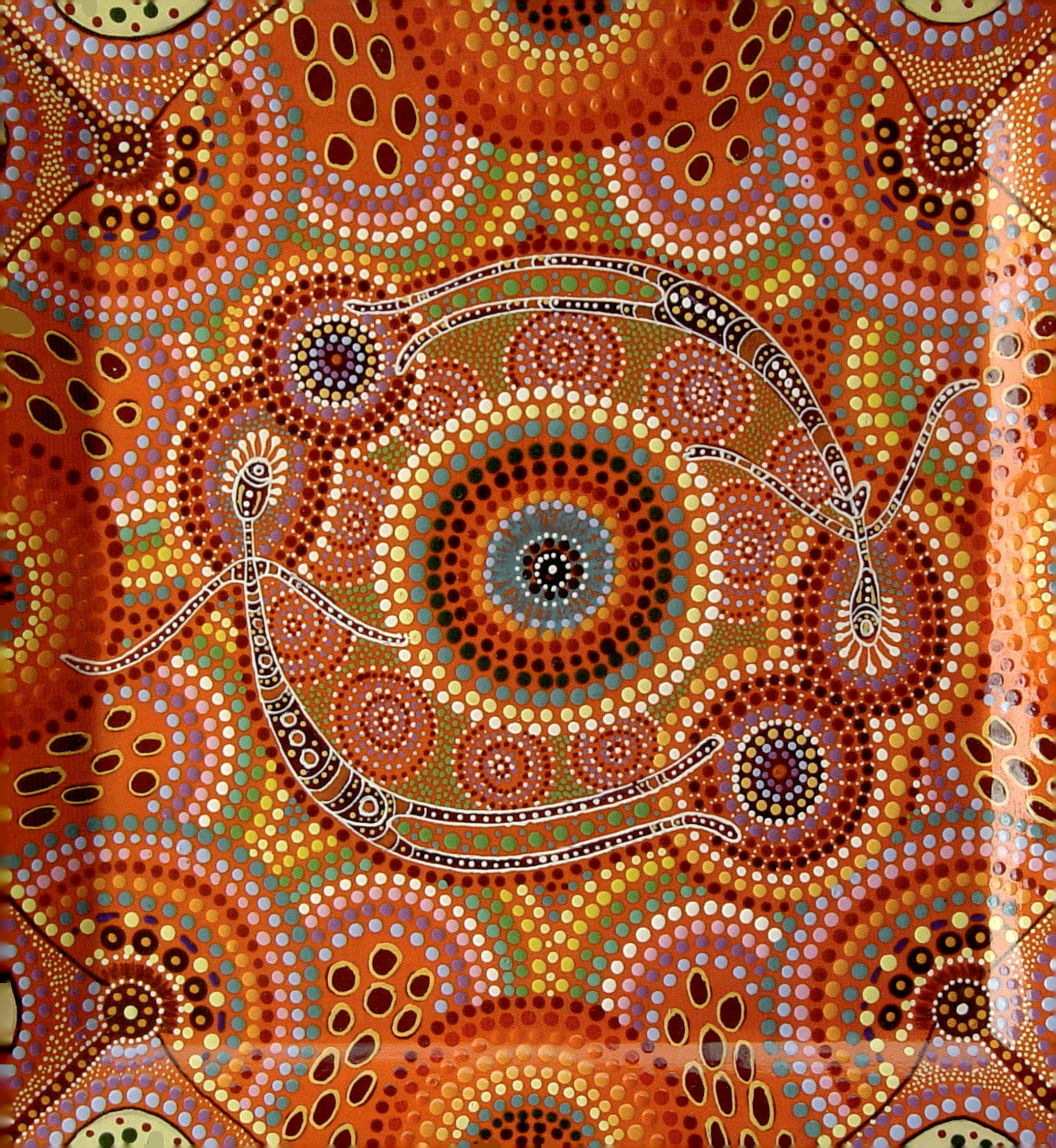

Awenke arle aneme, Growing into a young woman

We have ceremonies for young girls, teaching them to understand about growing up and becoming a woman. It's part of the women's ceremony. Over time, girls get told about women's business, Aboriginal law, children and husbands – everything should be taught to them at the right time as they grow. Before, girls were not given to their husbands until they were over seventeen or eighteen. When my father Walter and my mother Kitty got together she was about nineteen or twenty. *Awenke* means a girl of marrying age and women weren't allowed to leave the *alwekere*, single women's camp, to go with men until they were *awenke*. That was our way in the old days.

I had lived in the bush until I was 11 and then the dormitory until I was 17, then I moved out to live in the houses on community, with family members, while I worked as a domestic for the mission and until I married when I was 19. My marriage was arranged in our customary Aboriginal way, with my father and my husband making the agreement during men's business out bush, but he wasn't ready for a wife at first – he had to spend time out bush, do his men's business. He was my promised husband and he was the right skin to be my husband – that was very important to us.

Each baby born has a skin name; this was originally set out for us in the *altyerrenge*, like I said before. Our skin names guide our relationships and signify our obligations to each other. Everyone has obligations – to our

ABOVE AND OPPOSITE (detail): *Man and Woman*, 2004, acrylic on ceramic, 30 x 30 cm

OPPOSITE: *Young Woman Learning*, 2005, acrylic on ceramic, 42 cm diameter
The young girl is between the two women who teach her to look after herself. She is beginning to grow into a woman. They tell her everything that a girl should know.

country and our relatives. Our skin names help us understand these obligations and other things in society like who we can marry, where to join in ceremony and what part we will come to play in law and business. This is not as strong anymore, although our children still have skin names. Our ancestors understood their laws and they lived by those laws, as we still tried to do when I was young. The spirits of the ancestors are still in our homelands – they can still guide and watch us.

When I was old enough to be married my father made the agreement to give me to my right-skin husband, Douglas Wallace. He passed away in 1999 and so now I don't say his name at all. We loved each other from the start. Yes, we were happy right from the start to the finish, although like all couples we had to work hard together, and sometimes when we were younger we used to fight.

Before getting married in the mission church in 1967 – when I was old enough, and he was ready – we started to live with each other. Then my husband had to go away for a few months. He went interstate with all the men to pick fruit and earn money. Santa Teresa mission was really broke; there was no money and nothing to live on so the men were sent to work in Griffith in NSW for wages. They used to pick fruit there. The pays were sent to the mission and the married women were given a little allowance from their husband's wages. We weren't married in the church at that time, so I didn't get anything. I went back to my parent's house at Santa Teresa for those months he was away. I think the priest at Santa Teresa organised that trip for them to earn some money for the mission and they were gone about six or seven months.

I remember my husband told me that while they were away the men painted up and sang and danced, *urnterrirreke*, for the people in Griffith to see. They were proud of our culture and they wanted to show other people what kind of ceremonies we had in our country. *Urnterrirreke* was a dance that everyone could watch, it was nothing secret.

After my husband returned from Griffith we lived together again, and then married in the mission church in May 1967. I was nineteen years old and he was twenty-seven. I had lived at the dormitory until I was seventeen or eighteen. It was a different kind of *alwekere* that dormitory! I had lived there for about six or seven years with the nuns in charge, then they gave me a white dress to get married in the church.

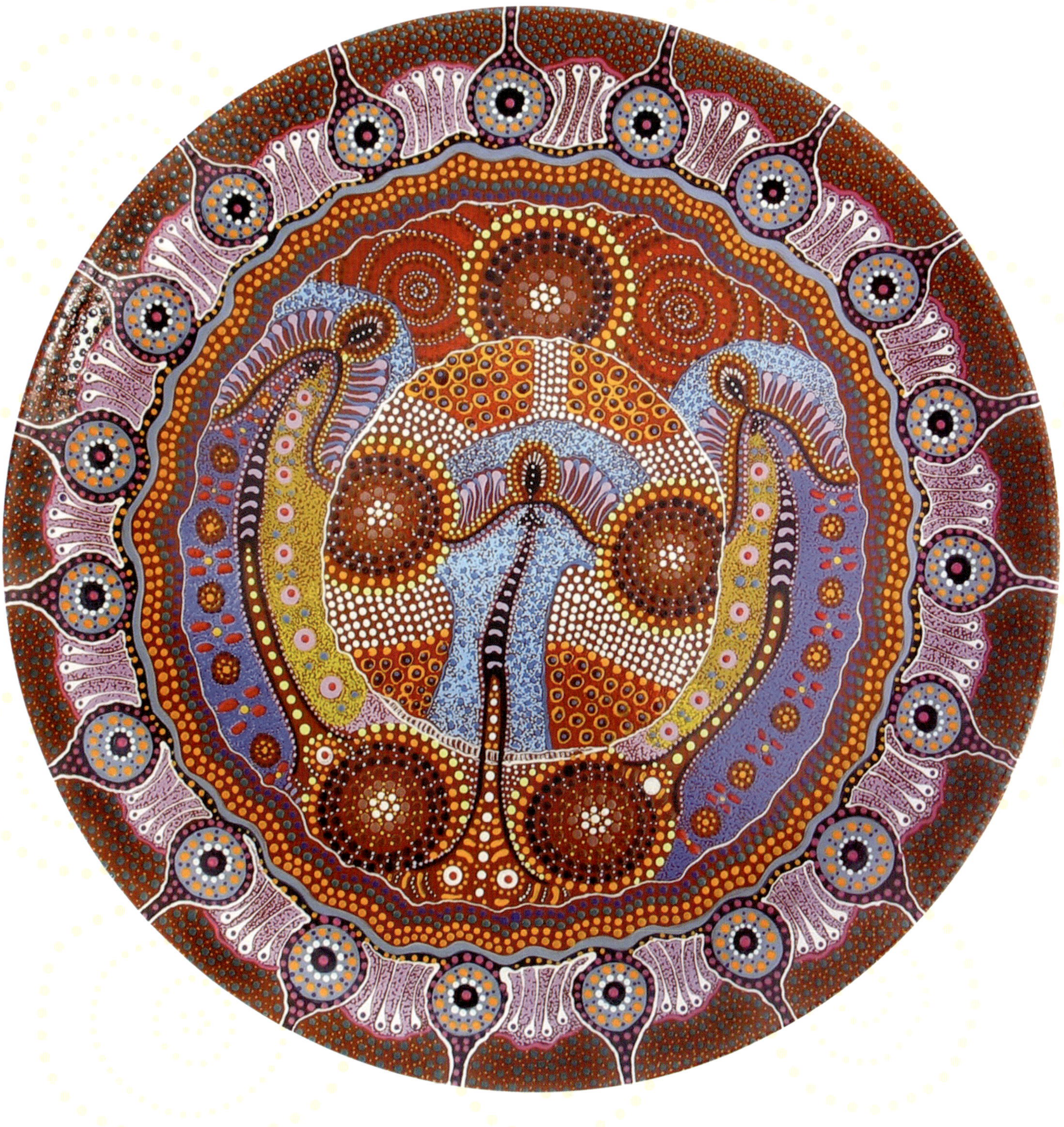

Arelhe Anyente Therirrertele

Arelhe Apitye-apitye-arle apetyeke. Re awenke mwerre akngerre aneke. Wale, re akngerre-apenhe aneke. Artwe atningke-arle ikwere ahentye-aneke, alhirreke ikwere. Wale, re areke, "artwe atningkenge ulkere atyenge alhirreme". Kele re aneme unteke itneketyenge.

Re alheke anteme akenhe itne renhe apenteke. Re imernte aremele, "ayenge-awerne anyente apetyerne akenhe atningke apetyemele atyenge ntertele". Rawerne unteke anteme, atnerte akngerre re. Re itelaretyakenhe kwenele amangkeme. Arelhe awenke-arle aneke mikwele apeke iletyakenhenge aneke.

Artwe itne ikwere nterteke-irreke. Arlpe akertne rarle untetyeke Apmere Atyatyekwenhenge-ntyele. Yanhe ikwerenge itne utepe-irreke akenhe rante aneme akwete untetyerlenge. Akenhe re atnerte akurne-irrerlenge awelheke. Mwantye re anteme apetye-ame. Artwe itne-arle utepe-irreke aneme.

Apwerte atwatyele re apetyeke. Arrwengwekenge-ntyele re irrpintyeke Therirrertele apwerte atwatyeke, alhwe akenhe thele-thele-arle-aneme.

Re arrernelhetye-alpeke kwatye arnerre anthurreke, akurne akngerre aneme, alhwe unteke akngerre. Re ampe akweke renhe atnyelhe-ileke. Kele re kwatyele alhewelheke imernte yanhe ikwere-anteye ilweke.

Yanhe-iperre aneme itne apmere yanhe ameke-ameke akeme ampe yanhe ikwere atnyelhe-ilekenge. Artwe mape-ante apmere yanhe-werne alhentye akngerre anteme. Arelhe-areye atere-irreme itne anteme ampe atnyelhe-ileketyenge. Alakenhe akwete re aneme lyete.

Lyete aneme kwatyele urnteme-iperre atetheke ware athertneme-arle. Arelhe ikwere intelhentye aneme, re apwerte akertne tnerle-aneme, arrwekelenye mapele renhe mpwareke.

LEFT TO RIGHT: *Desert Peas*, 2007, acrylic on ceramic plates, 20 x 20 cm

Desert flower spirits

Long ago, in the *altyerrenge*, there were two women who used to move from place to place in the country from Therirrerte across to Camel Flats. They were the spirits of the plant whose flower petals are bright, shiny and red with a big black centre where the petals meet. That plant grows up here and there and everywhere across that country when there has been enough rain. Those women move around, coming up and flowering here and there.

They would sometimes change from their spirit form to look like two very beautiful young Arrernte women. One day, while they were in this human form, a young Arrernte man came along that way and he caught sight of them. Well, he looked at them, not realising they were spirits. He thought they were very beautiful, but sadly they disappeared from sight as soon as they were aware of him watching.

So from then on every time the rain clouds came across that country he came back to the same place, just as the flowers began to grow, in the hope that he could catch the women. The spirits always hid their human form from him, remaining as spirits that he couldn't see. This happened every time he came looking for them, every time those rain clouds came bringing the rain to the plants. The flower spirits could always see the man but they continued not showing themselves as women.

One day the man went home and told his family about his bad luck, "I found two beautiful women out there near Therirrerte but now they always hide from me". He had really wanted to catch them so they would be his wives, but no men ever caught those women spirits. Now the only time anyone might see them is as flowers when the rains come.

Kwerralye Purle

Kwerralye Arrpwantye apele artwe aneke, Kwerralye Ilkngerre akenhe arelhe anewikwe-arle aneke Altyerrenge. Artwe nhenhe, arrweketye uthene, Apmere Irlkerteye-arle anetyarte. Yanhe-arenye ratherre aneke. Kere apwerte-arenye ware ratherre arlkwetyarte. Arelhe plain-werne alhetyarte kere alewatyerreke-arlke atwetyeke, merne arlatyeyeke-arlke tnyetyeke, merne atnetye inetyeke, awele-aweleke-arlke. Merne awele-awele, yalke-arlke akngerre aneke yanhe re uthnetyarte, marlele. Artwe rawerne utyewe anthurre-arle aneke, arlpennge akngerre rarle aneke.

Ingwele-ingwele rarle re alhetyarte. Ingwelheme akeme-irreme kereke unthetyeke. Ingweleme ware atwerle-aperle kere antere akngerre. Arelhe re akenhe merne yalke-arlke iterlenge, atherlenge-arlke ntange.

Akenhe artwe rawerne intetye-alpeyemenge apurrke apwerteke antyentye-iperre, kere atherrame apeke akngetye-alperle. Interle akwele anerle, ngkwerne arlpennge akngerre re. Kele anewikwe, "akunye-awerne ngkwerne prape arrpwantye akngerre. Kele antere inetyenhenge artwe ampwe althekalthe-iletyeke ngkwerne-arlke," kwenhe. Antere apernemele althekaltheke-ileme ngkwerne renhe. Kele re akenhe irrkerlenge-ame-irrkerlenge irrerlenge.

Arelhe arrpenhe-arle aneke. Rarle arrentye-arle aneke. Re artwe renhe nterte-ntertele aminetyarte utyewe-ilemele. Rarle ikwere alhirretyarte. Arelhe ikwere anewe itelaretyakenhe arelhe arrpenhe-arle aneke.

Arrurle arrpenhele, ingwe anyente-arle intetyame artwe re aneme aweke renhe ilterle-anerlenge, "angwenhele-ame ayenge iltepilteme?" Re imernte itirreke anewelikwe renhe ilteke-athene akenhe arelhe arrpenhe itwenge arteke ilterlenge apmere arlenge anthurrenge-ntyele, apwerte arrangweke arrpenhenge.

Kele imernte ingweleme-ingweleme re akeme-irreme arelhe anewikwe akemelhileke, "arelhe aye! Akeme-irraye! Unte-ame ayenge ingwartentyele ilteke?" kwenhe. "Yweke. The ngenhe iltetyakenhe," kwenhe. "Ingwartentyele kwenhe unte ayenge ilteke," artwele ileke. "Eee! Tharle ngenhe iltetyakenhe artwe ampwe," arelhe angkeke.

"Wale, ayenge kereke alhemenge," artwe ampwe angkeke. Arltele anteme re awelheke aminerlenge, "pwetyekaye!" kwenhe. "Eee! Angwenhele-ame ayenge aminepineme?" Re alkngarelhemele areke, "arrangkwe." Re kengentye ware kereke untherle-untherle-iweke.

Arratye atweke kere anyente, apwerte akertneke. Akngetye-alpeke kere renhe. Artwe ampwe atnarnpintye-alperlenge kere-akerte. Anewelikwe iterle-anerlenge merne-arlke, kere alewatyerre, arlatyeye-arlke, akangkemele arnarintyeke. Artwe re ware atnyetye-alpeke. "Artwe nhenhe-ame arrpwantye-ame-arrpwantye-irremele!" Arelhe anewikwe itirreke renhe atnyetye-alperlenge areme, "wertaye!?"

"Arelhe kwenhe aminepineme ayenge. Ikwere-iperre ayenge arlpennge-ame-arlpennge-irreme," kwenhe, "aminemenge-arle".

Kwerralye Purle, 2008, acrylic on canvas, 40 x 68 cm

Arelhe re akenhe antere akngerre akweke-arle aneke, urteke akngerre-apenhe nhe-ulkere. Arelhe rarle kere itetyarte artwe ampwe ikwere mirte akenge akngerre anerlenge. Kere re akwete itetyarte. Artwe re uyarne kere itetyarte ngkwerne arlpenngenge.

"Kele aneye the ngenhe althekalthe-iletyenhe," arelhe anewelikwe ileke. Akwetethe renhe ratherre alakenhe apernerretyarte. Akenhe artwe re akenhe arlpennge irrirtnepirtneme. "Iwenhe-iperte alakenhe irrepirremaye?" Kele ingwe ikwerele inteke ankwekenheke-anthurre-anteme-irreke, ure alepele re wetye-ame nthenhe-arle renhe iltetye-ame. Ankweke-kwenye ware akeme-irremele, "ingwartentyele ayenge ilteke," kwenhe. Akenhe arelhe ikwere anewe-arle awetyakenhe-arle aneke. Artwele rante awetyarte.

Akwetethe re aneme alakenhe anetyarte ingwe-arle arrpanenhele, angkentye awemele ure alepele iwerle. Nthenhenge-arle angkeme-werne-atheke iwerle, apale ware. Akenhe arelhe anewikwe-arle angkeke, "ankweke-kwenye unte intepinteme?" kwenhe. Akenhe re ilelheke, "ayenge kwenhe ingwartentyele ilteme," kwenhe.

"Arrentyele apeke ngenhe ingwarte-ntyele ilteme," arelhe re angkeke, "kereke unthemele are arrentye ikwereke!"

Arratye anteme re untheke, kereke unthetyakenhe, arelhe arrentye ikwereke untheke. Ngkwerne prape arlpennge akngerre re re untherle-aneke. Apwerteke-arrpele re untheke, "nthenhe-ame ayenge iltepilteme?" Arrentyele akwete re renhe iltepilteme. Artwe re arratye inteye renhe areke. Re anteme areke arelhe renhe arriwele artepele interle-anerlenge. Angeme ware, irrperrerlte-anerlenge ikwere. Re anteme ntyerneke unpe irntirte ntyerlenge.

Artwe re akurne akngerre awelheke aremele, "nhenhe re athewe!" Imernte nterneke irrtyartele, ware, lyeke-arle-arteke. Anyente-ngare renhe nterneke irrtyartele.

Arrentye-arle akweke ware akngelheke, "awe iwenhe-ame yanhe?" atyerre-lhileke imernte aremele irrtyarte-arle. Re akem-anteme-irrreke arrape-arle-anekenge, Akngelpe-akngarte-iwelhemele areke "awe, Ngkwerne-ngkwerne-ame ayenge arratye anteme aretye-alhene?" re apele angkeke.

Arrentye re artwe renhe ngkwerne atweke artnartneke-iletyeke. Re apele apwerte-arrpele alheke, apwerte arrpenhe-arrpele nhenhe akenhe re aretye-alheke. Nhenhe ikwerele re apele artnerre-akeke akenhe arrweketye arrentye re akenhe ikwere ntertele-arle. Arnpetye-ante-arnpetye-ante re akenhe artnerre-akerlenge. Apwerte-arrpele ikwerele re artnerre-akeke apmere-werne-atheke. Re akenhe renhe alwernemele aneme renhe atwerlenge, ngkwerne arrpwantye anthurre tyarre-akngerlenge. Apmere itweke-irremele rawerne, anewelikwe areke arne-arlke alkereke-irrerlenge. Ulpmernte-arlke arraterlenge re areke. Arrentye re kwenhe atwerle-aperlenge, arne-arlke ntewemele atwerlenge tnyante ultakethe. Artwe rawerne ilpelhelenge, ngkwerne anyente ultakekenge, akunye-awerne. Ampere arlenge nhakwele aneke akenhe ingke arlenge arlentye akine aneke. Atnerte arlenge arlentye akine.

Anewelikwe arnareke. Re ture ikwerenhe inerle-alheke, "aye, nhakwe akenge-irreme

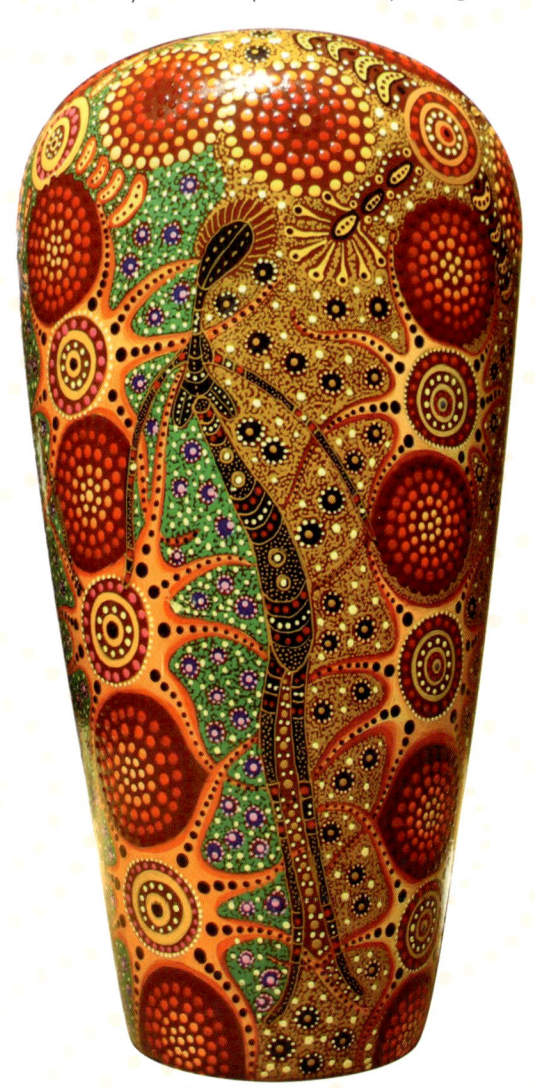

RIGHT: *Kwerralye Purle*, 2003, acrylic on ceramic, 48 x 24 cm

OPPOSITE: *Falling Star*, 2002, acrylic on canvas, 90 x 90 cm

114

atyenge aneweke," kwenhe. Re apele unteke. Re anteme areke arrentye renhe urrperle akngerre-apenhe, "eee! Akunye-awerne, prape alwernemele atweme!" Arelhe ratherre anewe akwele arerreke. Ratherre atwerreke. Artwe rawerne akenge akngerre intertnenge, inngerre-awerne ware atnyetye-alpeke. Rarle arelhe ikwere anewe artengele-aretyakenhe. Rarle akenge akngerre awelhekenge artnerre-akentye akngerre-iperre apwerte akertnenge. Ampere-arlke utyene anthurre aneme arnele-arle atantheke, iltye-arlke. Arelhe ratherre aneme tnyante ultakethe atwerreke. Arrentye uthene anewikwe uthene, atwerreke-atwerreke apmere akwintye itweke. Anthweke-anthweke re ratherre atwerreke.

Kele arelhe apmere-arenyele aneme arrentye renhe tnyante ultakethe atweke. Artwe re apele aneme akeme-akeme-irremele atnerte mwerre anteme awelheke. Tyerrtye-arle ante arlpennge akngerre akwete-arle aneke. Akenhe arrentye renhe urele iteke ratherre. Ratherre aneme alperreke. Ingweleme alhentye akngerre re Kwerralye Purle. Arlpennge akngerre, akertne-ame-akertne irrentye akngerre-arle Kwerralye Purle-arle irreke anteme. Akenhe arelhe-arle urteke akwete-arle aneke. Re Kwerralye Irlkngerre-arle irreke, angwerrele arratentye akngerre, iparrpe irrpentye-akngerre. Alakenhe re ratherre lyete aneme Kwerralye Purle uthene Irlkngerre uthene.

Morning Star and Evening Star

This story takes place in the country near Mparnwenge. It is a story about two ancestors from here, before they went up into the sky and became *Kwerralye Purle*, the morning star and the evening star, and we can use them to tell us the time as they make their way across the night sky, guiding us through the night and into the morning.

In the old days, this ancestor was a fine hunter. One day after he had brought fresh kangaroo home to his wife, he became a little sick. While he was out hunting, a jealous, bad, woman spirit had put a spell on him, even though there was no reason that he or his wife could think of for the evil spirit to do so.

Soon the malevolent spell made him sicker. Every night he began to hear her voice swearing and calling him names. His wife could hear the voices of the evil spirit too. The man couldn't sleep at all because of the awful voice keeping him awake! As this went on and on, night after night, a strange thing happened to him; his body became longer and longer and longer, especially his legs.

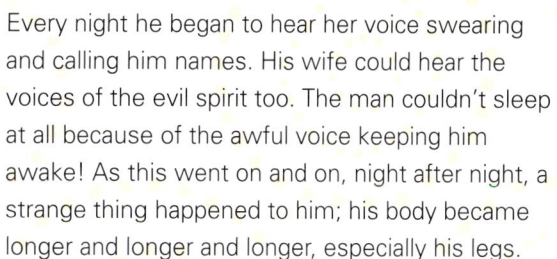

Sometimes the man tried throwing a fire stick at where he thought the voice was coming from because it seemed so close to him. He did not understand why this evil woman was so angry with him. The evil spirit seemed to be watching him all the time and she always knew everything about him. He tried to run off in different directions but the voice was always there following and taunting him. He decided that instead of trying to run away from her anymore he would find her and stop the evil voices.

Every day he looked, searching the caves in his country, but he couldn't find her anywhere. Eventually, one day, he found the cave in which she lay. She was huge, stinking and covered in flies that buzzed around her. He threw his spear at her as fast and as hard as he could, but it was just like a little pinprick to her. Then she turned around and took his spear out of her body, saying, "what is this? So, someone is trying to fight me!"

The man started running away, up and down over the hills he ran, as fast as he could, to get back to his wife. The evil spirit woman flew after him, screaming. His wife heard the noise and looked up; she saw trees flying as if a great whirly wind was coming, but she knew it was her husband, pursued by the evil spirit woman who was carrying a giant stick. By this time, the man's legs had grown so long that he tripped and stumbled as he ran. He became tangled up by them – struggling to run at all – but his wife, also growing taller all the time, came racing towards him to help him fight the evil spirit woman.

She managed to kill that evil spirit and save her husband.

Even though they beat that evil spirit, the man and his wife both kept growing taller and taller until they reached into the sky. He became the morning star and she became the evening star. *Kwerralye Purle* we call them now – big, bright stars.

Arrernte have many stories about the *altyerre* beings who are in the sky – many of them travelled up into the sky after having moved around the *apmere*. Some are known for their protection of us.

Stars and starlight are really important for Arrernte, allowing us to see at night and guiding the way as we walk over our country – our people see a certain star in its place and from that we know which direction to go. The first stars were burning sticks placed high in the sky. We know that when a stick burns very low a piece will break off and fall – these burning embers became falling stars, as they are known to us today. The ancestors told our people that a falling star might warn of a death in the family or group. This is what we were told, so when we see a falling star we spit on the ground to avert the death from our own family. Everyone does that to protect their own people. We also understand that sometimes the spirit people may catch a falling star to prevent the death.

OPPOSITE: *Star*, 2003, acrylic on ceramic, 20 x 20 cm
The four little figures are the morning star spirits. That's the big one there, that star spirit that comes up in the morning. The blue comes in around there like the morning sky, it's the light that shines with the morning star.

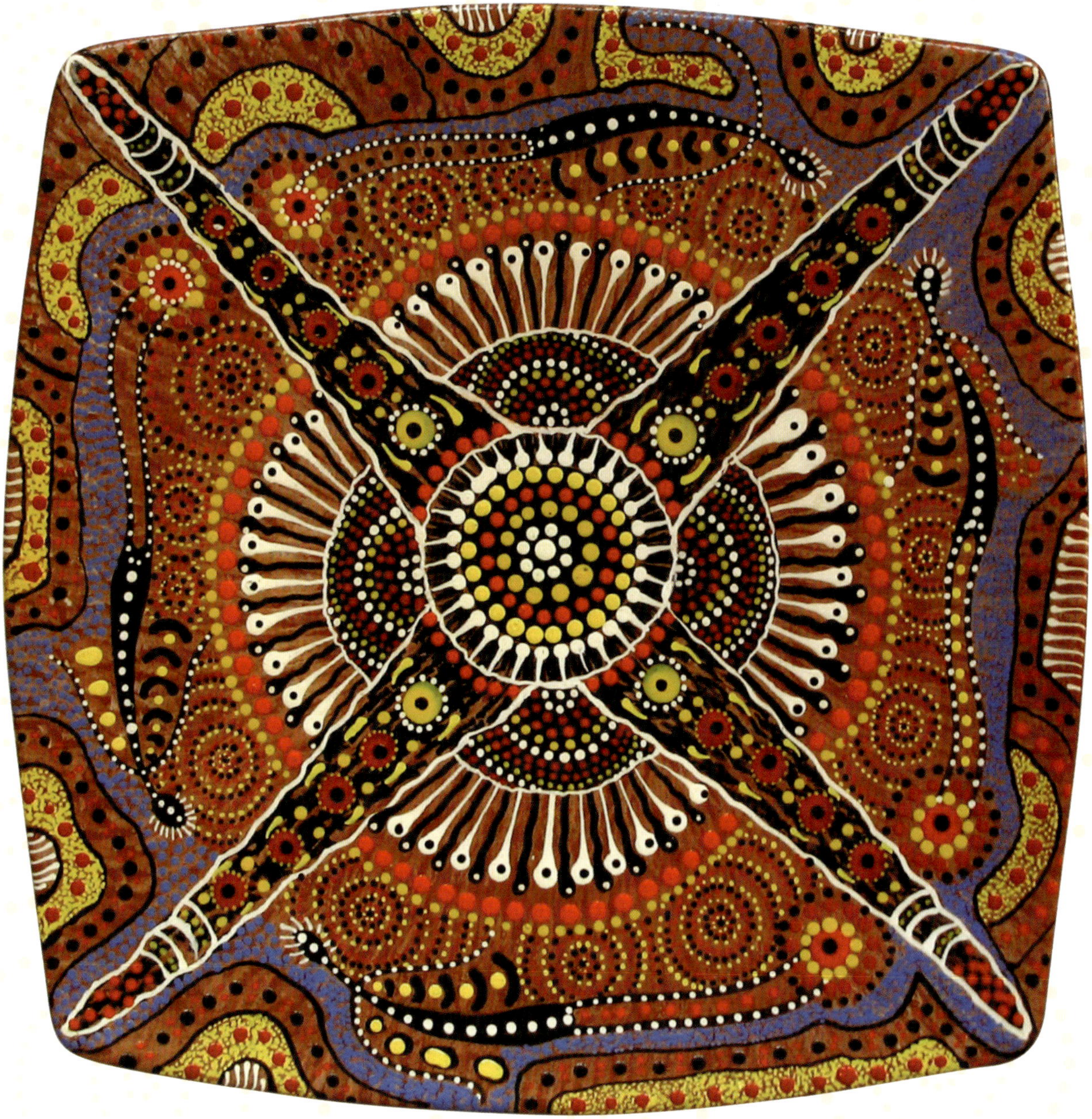

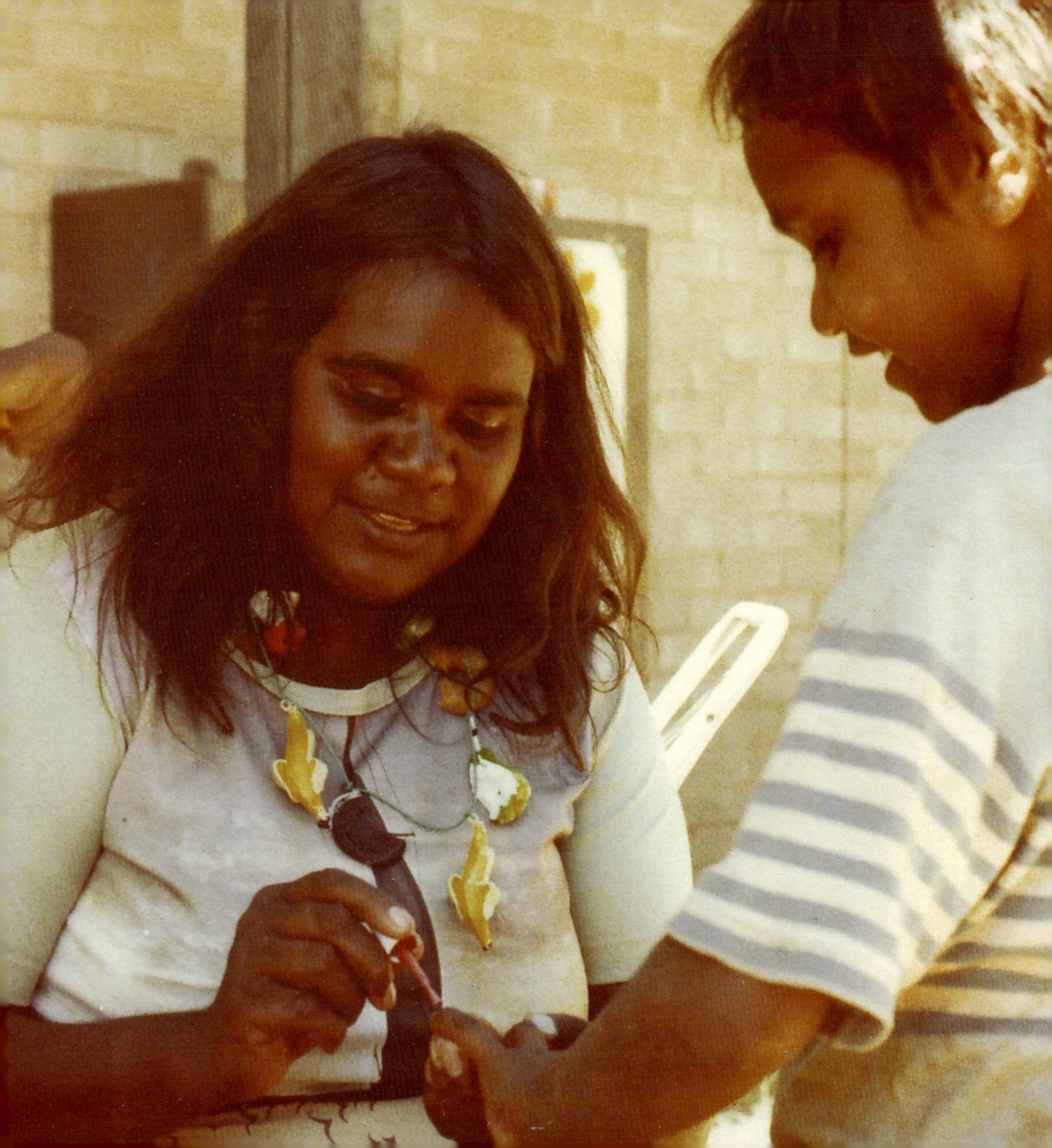

Amangkelhe-ileme, Growing up a big family

After we married in the church my husband and I stayed at the mission in the old village. Our first house was down in the part we then called Bottom End. My husband made a little tin house for us with a great big, shady veranda around the outside of it. Our house was down the slope from some stone houses; it was on the side of the little hill where the men used to make rain.

His family, the Wallace's, had a camp that was further down at the bottom of the road. They had a small stone house there too. We wanted to live by ourselves, we didn't want to live in that little camp with his family all the time, so my husband made us our first little house. We started looking after other people's children while we lived at that house.

Not our own children, because we never had any. We didn't think too much about it. We had certainly wanted to have a family, but I had a miscarriage. I was helping to dig a hole for a support to hold up the shady. It was hard work. At the time I didn't know I was pregnant, until I had that miscarriage. It never happened again.

Between the two of us, my husband and I raised thirty children. The youngest two are still with me, and they didn't know my husband, they came after him. We did not receive any support or rations for the extra children in the early days at the mission, not until much later, I think it was in the 80s sometime, when we started to get a bit of welfare to top up for their food and clothes.

OPPOSITE: Kathleen painting Lucille Young's nails at Santa Teresa school fete, 1978.

But in the early days we just made it all work out for the children who lived with us. Everyone needed food and shelter and clothes. We just worked, hunted and made do with what we could provide ourselves. Our houses were really small too, so we all lived in one room and outside under that big veranda.

There were so many children at the mission in those days, but by then some adults had started drinking alcohol. They visited town buying grog, or getting someone to buy it for them. When other people started to drink in town, we ended up with their children to look after at the mission. At first my husband didn't drink at all. At some point he started going into town with his brothers, and then he began to have a drink too. At one time he got to be hard on me, but I stuck up for myself, even though I am only short, and he must of realised it was the wrong thing to do, because after that he was never, ever hard on me again. He never treated me badly again and he always insisted that the children respected me and all their elders too. He taught the young men to be respectful of their wives and their culture, their Aboriginality.

Romance, 2003, acrylic on ceramic platter, 32 x 24 cm

So, a big mob of children started to come to our place for food, company and somewhere to stay. The drought was finished by then and there was not much of anything to help us and the bore water we used to drink at the mission was awful – really salty, bad water. We had to make ends meet and always made do so everyone could eat a meal. By this time, the children who had come to stay with us were all calling us Mum and Dad, because they were no longer seeing much of their real parents. There was no court case, no paper work, no government involved in this. Later, we did adopt some of the children in a European legal way, but mostly we dealt with it all within our systems of relationships. So much had changed and our cultural ways were breaking down, so those of us who retained – or tried to retain – the values and rules of our culture found ourselves being responsible for other family members, much more than we ever would have had to do living out bush. Many people were not coping with the changes and the loss of their old lives and old people, and so they went drinking and things went wrong. Now that has become the fashion.

Tyangkertangkerte

Urreke re ampe urreye anetyenhenge irrernte-arenye atherre utnenge ikwere-akerte akngernerle-apeke. Atnyeneke re Apmere Arnkarreke. Ratherre imernte, "utnenge nhenge nthakenhe ilerne irreye?" kwenhe, "ilerne arelhe awenkeke untheye?"

Apmere Arnkarre ikwerengentyele ratherre untheke apmere arrpenheke ilkaretyeke? Arelhe awenkeke akwele. Arrangkwe, ampe marle akweke-ante ingkerreke anemeke. "Angwenhe-ame anteme ilerne ntheye?" kwenhe, "marle-arle akweke ingkerreke nhenhe," kwenhe.

Wale, ratherre alherreke Irtnwerrenge-werne anteme. Arrangkwe kine, marle ingkerreke-arle akweke aneke. Ratherre apmere arrpanenhe untherle-apeke utnenge ikwere akngernerle-apeme. Apmere Irlkerteye anteme aneke. Irlkerteye arrangkwe kine areke awenkeke. Apmere mape atningke-arle aneke-werne akngeke. Arrangkwe kine areke, "ampe akweke marle ingkerrenyeke!"

Keringke-werne anteme alheke. Arrangkwe kine areke. Kele apmere arrpenhe-werne anteme alheke utnenge ikwere arntirrkwerle-aneme Therirrerte-werne. Untheke re, apmere arrpanenhe arerle-apeke, arrangkwe. Tyerrtyele akenhe irrernte-arenye renhetherre aretyakenhe. Apale ware itne aneke.

Akenhe ratherre Alerarrlkwe irretye-alheke. Arrangkwe. Akenhe ratherre apetye-alpeke Uyetye-werne anteme. Arrangkwe kine areke marleke, "marle akweke ingkerreke".

Alyathenge-werne anteme alheke, arrangkwe. "Apmere kwenhe itwe aneme, ilerne kele apetye-alpeke," kwenhe. Kele akngirtnerreke utnenge akweke renhe apmere ikwere-werne. Apurrke akngerre akwele ratherre aneke, arlenge arlentye-iperre.

Ratherre aretye-alperreke arne akngerre-apenhe renhe, Arrkernke-arle aneke, altywere-akerte. Ikwere ware arrerneke utnenge renhe. Arne renhe ngangkere ntheke, ilemele imernte, "ampe akweke nhenhe unte amangkelhe-ilaye, arelheke arrangkwenge," kwenhe. Arne re akenhe urlpmirreke ikwere-akerte. Akenhe ampe akweke re aknganerlenge kweneke. Ampe anteme aneke. Atnerte ikwerenhe rarle aneke Arrkernke ulpere re.

Ikwerengentyele ratherre ileke, "unte arritnye nhenhe ntherle, 'Tyangkertangkerte'," kwenhe.

Kele akngwelye artnwere akenhe apetyerlenge arne ulpere ikwere-werne. Atnerte-atnerte kine re aneke. Re artekerre kweneke mpwareke akngwelye akwerrke-areye.

Kele itne apurte amangkeke. Akweke re artnerrentye-irreke. Akenhe akngwelye akwerrke-areye unthentye-akngerre aneke. Arne Arrkernke re altywere-ilelhelenge ampe akethe-werne artnerre-aketyeke. Akweke re akethele anerle-anetyeke akenhe akngwelye akwerrke-areye renhe utnherlenge-arle akenhe akweke re irrpirtnerlenge-arle. Arne re akenhe martelhelenge akweke-akerte akngwelye akwerrke-areye irrpeme-ketyenge, altywere akweke aneme rlke irrpetyeke, akweke ware urlpme-irretyarte. Akenhe arratelhetyarte akngerre-irrerlenge. Alakenhe re unthetyeke-arlke irretyarte.

Wale, Tyangkertangkerte re akngerre-awerne-irreke, urreye akweke anteme. Arne re angkeke, "ayenge ingkeke arrangkwe," kwenhe, "anyente ikwerele tnerle-anerlenge," kwenhe, "unte-arrpe arntarnte-arelherle."

"Merneke araye, merne inmartwe kwatye-iperre arratentye akngerre. Yanhe ulkere arlkwerle-anaye. Merne alangkwe-arlke, kere kelyawe-arlke arlkwe."

Akenhe akweke re alakenhe angkerlenge ikwere, "nthakenhe-arle athewe mpenge-ileye?" kwenhe. "Ware arlkwaye," arne re angkeke. Tyangkertangkerte re aneme alhemele aretyarte tyerrtye-areye. Apmere akngerre Arnkarre aneke. Mape akenhe aname-irreke kwatyeke arrangkwenge kele anyente-arle arne re aneke. Anyentengare ware apeke re areke kere-arlke iterlenge. Akweke re wantelhetyarte rarrpe; kelyawe, arlatyeye, atnyetye-arlke tnyemele.

Akenhe akngwelye akine akngerre-anteme-irrerlenge. Akweke re arrkene-irreke itnekenge. Anhelhemele imerte untetye-alperlenge arne ikwere-werne. Akweke re akngerre-awerne-akngerre-awerne-irremele re aneme anhelheke akngwelye itneke. Arlke-arlke-arle-iwerle, akngwelye itne ampe urreye renhe apentetyarte. Itne renhe alwernetyarte. Akenhe re akenhe altyepeke kelyawe mape arrerneke, irrtyarte akweke-akerte, untetye-alperlenge arne mameye

ikwere-werne. Akenhe akwetethe re alakenhe irretyarte akngerre-ame-akngerre-irremele. Arlenge-ame-arlenge rlkele alhetyarte.

Akngwelye itne akngerre anthurre anteme aneke akenhe Tyangkertangkerte itneke akwete re anhelhemele arlkeme. Kele itne renhe alwerneke akwete.

Wale, re artwe akngerre anteme aneke re arlenge-werne alheke kere atwetyeke, arratye irrtyartele nterneke. Akngwelye itwe kine. Re nterte apeke apetye-alpetyakenhe. Re akwete re anhelhele-apeke akngwelye itneke. Akenhe itne anteme alwerneke renhe. Kere apele ulthentye anthurre-arle aneke. Re kere iwemele untetyeke kele itwe aneme, "awe, apmere kwenhe arlenge arlentye anthurre!" kwenhe, "ayenge-ame iwenheke arlke-arlke-arle-iweke?!" Itetheke rarle re unteke apmere Arnkarre-werne. Arne mikweke-athene re tnetye-alheke. Arne re akenhe altywere-akerte kine aneke. Alhwenge arrpenheke re irrpetyeke ikwere uye. Akngwelye itne renhe ingkeke tyarre-ineke arlkwerrirreke renhe. Kele.

Arne mikwe, Arrkernke re antyerrke-irremele ilweke Tyangkertangkerte ilwekenge.

OPPOSITE: *Tree and Puppies*, 2006, acrylic on canvas, 60 x 46 cm (detail)

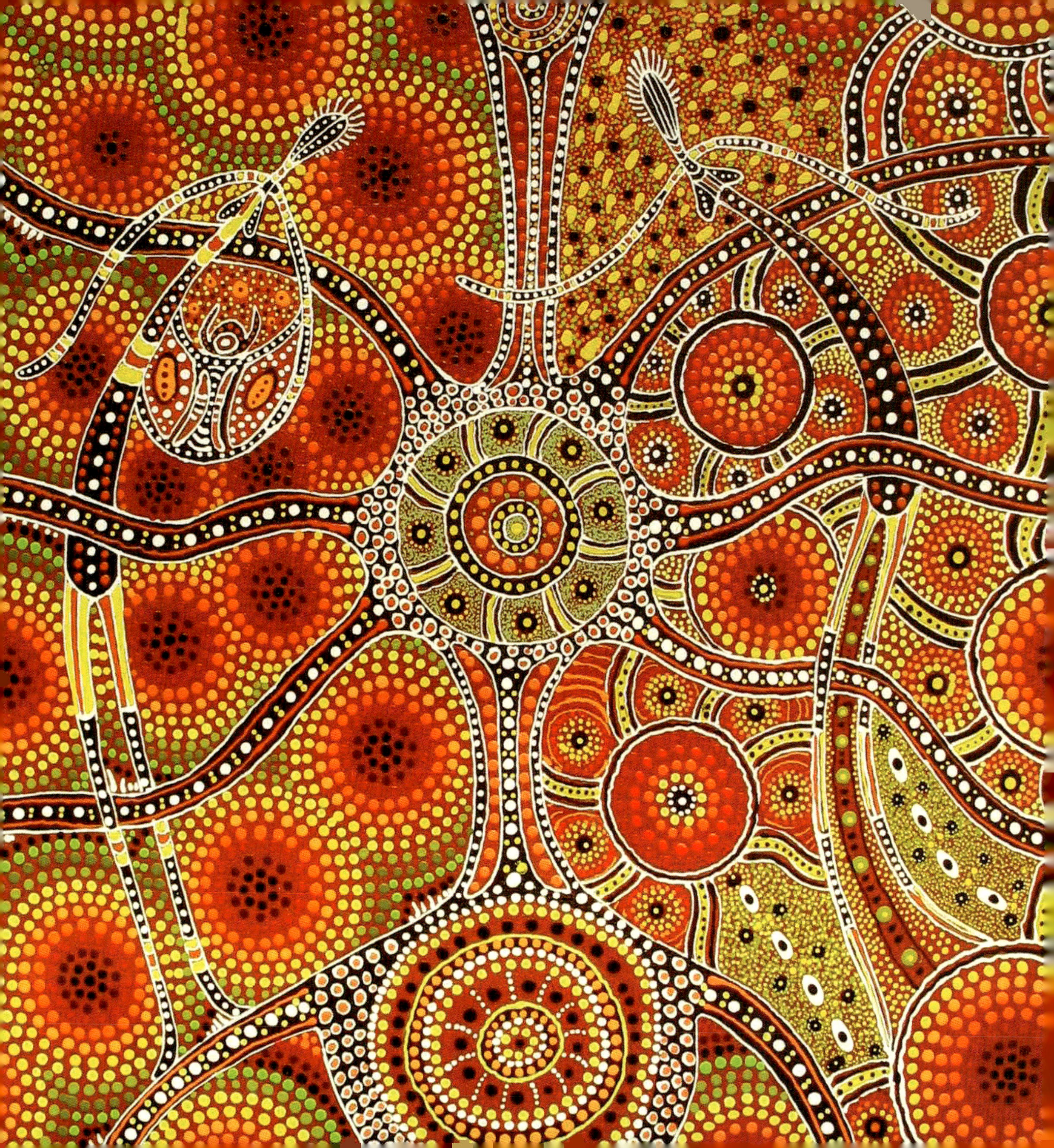

Mother tree

This is a story about a special tree, a tree which existed in the ancestor days at a time when the *altyerre* beings still roamed freely across the land, while they were bringing our world into being. The place where this tree grew is called Arrkernke and this story is about a tree, a baby who grew to be a young man called Tyangkertangkerte, and a family of puppies.

The story begins when two spirits in the *altyerrenge* were looking for *awenke*, a young woman of the right age to have a baby. They had the spirit of the little baby with them and it needed a mother to be placed in. We call this small spirit *arremparrenge*. The spirits guiding *arremparrenge* were travelling around looking for an appropriate young woman but they were having no luck. At Arrkernke were little girls with their families, none of them old enough to be a mother. They went to the next place where families would be camping and which was not too far away. That was Uyetye, but no one there was the right age. No *awenke*. They took that little spirit, the *arremparrenge*, to the next spring looking for a young woman. In this way the spirits carried the *arremparrenge* with them all across our country. They stopped at each spring where families were camping. They visited Itnewerrenge, then Mparnwenge, but still nothing for the *arremparrenge*, so they went to Irlkerteye, then Ltyentye Apurte. From there they visited Arterrke, before travelling to Therirrerte.

The spirits carrying the *arremparrenge* had travelled a long way. It was taking them many days and nights. They needed to continue until they could find a mother to put *arremparrenge* into, so it could grow inside her and become a human baby. After they left Therirrerte they decided to try Ulerarrlkwe so they travelled there and found it was just like at the other springs – there was no one the right age to have the little baby spirit. The spirits kept going, travelling to Inteye Arrkwe, but found nothing. Still nothing!

They came back to Alyapere, which is next to Salt Bore. They went around that round rock we call Ulyerperre Ampetye – it means kangaroo leg. Then past that little round hill we call Alyathenge, on the other side from Werirrte.

The spirits were worried now. They had travelled for a long time, and the *arremparrenge* needed a place to grow and be born a person. They went to Werirrte but there was still no luck for the *arremparrenge*. There were no girls there at all. They tried Alyathenge again and from there they went back to Arrkernke.

What shall we do now, who will we give this little spirit to? they wondered. It was then that the spirits carrying the *arremparrenge* noticed some wonderful big trees called *ankerre*, coolibah, at Arrkernke. One tree in particular took their attention. It had a very round hollow in its trunk which presented itself with a little hole as an opening. By now they had become quite tired of carrying this little baby spirit, so they decided to put it inside that tree and give the tree *ngangkere*, enabling it to look after a growing baby.

This is how the baby found itself being grown by a mother tree. While that baby formed in the big tree, the *arremparrenge* spirit grew in the baby, living in the safe hollow inside the mother tree. When it was old enough the little baby began to crawl out from the safe hollow in her trunk to explore the world around the tree. After crawling about this way and that he went back inside the hollow to be held and protected. This was how the days went on at Arrkernke. The baby boy grew.

One day a pregnant dog travelled to Arrkernke looking for a place to have her puppies. She saw this very same tree. You see, the mother tree had roots which made a nice dark cave on the ground. It was flat, cool and soft in the sand among her roots. The dog had her puppies in there. They too started growing up in the shelter of the mother tree.

As the baby grew into a boy child, the puppies grew too. The mother tree used to talk to the little boy, telling him what to try next, suggesting things he needed to do so he could grow into a fine, healthy man. As he and the little dogs got bigger the pups sometimes got rough with him – you know how little puppies are, they bite with little sharp teeth. When this happened the little boy crawled into the mother tree's hollow. She closed up around him, only leaving the hole opened for air to come in so he could breathe.

That is how his life was for many years as he grew with his mother tree protecting him in her hollow, giving him a place to sleep safely. He would wake up from his rest and learn through his playing the many things he needed to know for survival. As he started to walk she couldn't help him, he had to learn to do things for himself from an early age. She talked to him, explaining that he was a human being and that he needed to learn and do many different things in order to look after himself as he grew older and bigger. So that's what he did.

He needed to eat as he grew so he had to learn to hunt for himself. First of all he started

Tree and Puppies, 2006, acrylic on canvas, 60 x 46 cm

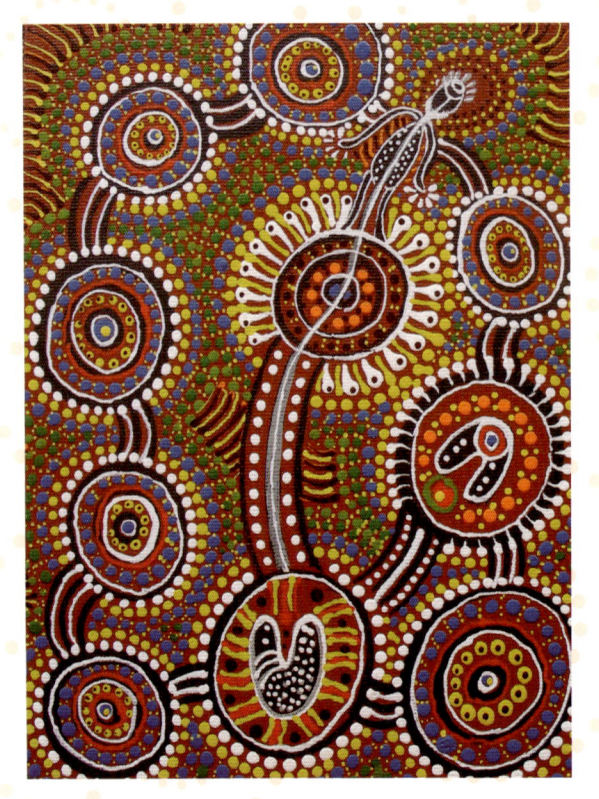

Mother Tree, 2007, acrylic on canvas, 20 x 15 cm

catching and eating little lizards, tender grass shoots and *inmartwe*. It is a really nice, soft green plant that people still eat today. Then the boy began to catch and eat bigger animals and other bush foods. The mother tree told him to go and look for bigger things, "you need to get your belly really full, so look for a perentie and some *alangkwe*, bush banana. *Atwakeye*, bush oranges, are good for you too. You look for those as well". The boy started eating these bush foods and many more. She named her son Tyangkertangkerte.

Naturally, the dogs would follow him as they too were hungry and needed to hunt and catch food. Sometimes the boy used to be naughty and tease those dogs until they chased him. He was quick on his feet and clever enough to look for the fastest way to race back to the shelter of his mother's hollow where she protected him from the angry dogs.

As time passed he grew up tall and, naturally, the dogs grew bigger too. Because this happened in the *altyerrenge*, these dogs were much larger than the ones we have today. They grew to about half his height, capable of being fierce and menacing, but still he kept teasing them. By the time he was twenty, he was prepared to travel out a long way away from his mother tree to look for the best kangaroo to hunt. Even still, he would tease the dogs, who got so wildly angry with him that they tried to attack him again and again. The young man could run so fast he would beat the dogs back to the safety of his mother's hollow and she would always close around him to stop the big dogs from jumping up and getting at him.

One day he was hunting further away from his mother *ankerre* tree than usual and he had caught not only one but two kangaroos for himself. Carrying them up on his shoulders, he looked towards his mother tree, lined her up from where he was and then started to tease the dogs. The hungry dogs became angry and vicious as usual. He started to run from the dogs, but the boomerangs and spears he had made for himself felt too heavy. He threw them off, and set off again. This time the kangaroos he carried weighed him down. The dogs were catching up fast so he threw the kangaroos aside too. He lined up the tree and he sped off as fast as he could run towards her. Reaching the tree he leapt at the trunk where her hollow should have been. He had made a mistake. He had lined up and run towards the wrong tree. It was not his mother tree. The tree he leapt up to offered him no protection. The angry dogs caught hold of him and they killed him right there.

In the days when I was first taught this story, everyone was aware that it was important to behave respectfully. Living together and protecting one another was the only way we could survive. We were taught that our elders couldn't protect us if we kept putting ourselves in danger, so it was important to respect what they told us and behave as they taught us.

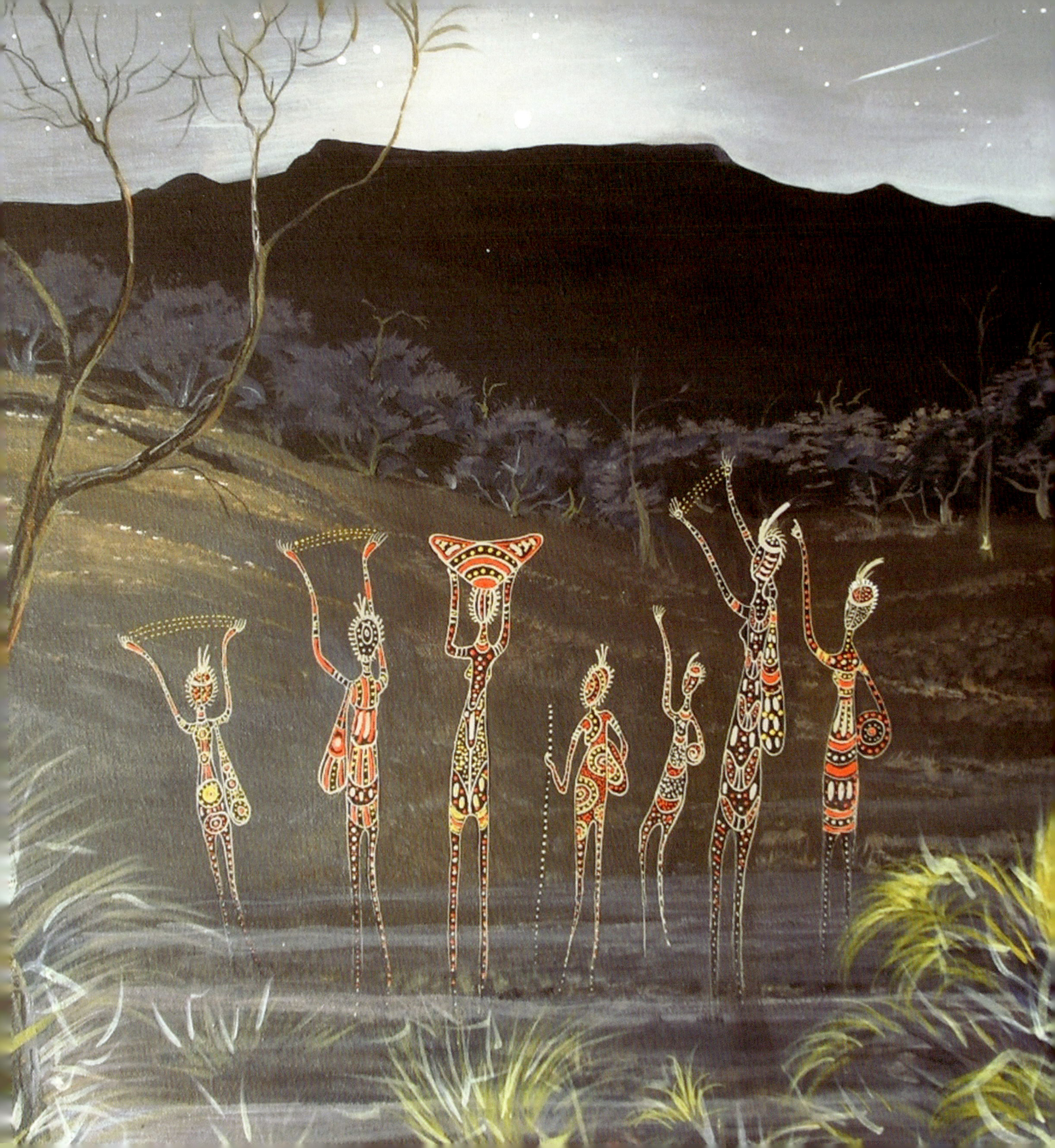

Akngartiweme, What's happening now?

After my husband and I had lived together at Santa Teresa for a year or two we went to Inteye Arrkwe, Ross River homestead. Auntie Aggie is from over near there and so was my grandfather Werirrte. At this time Aggie was staying at Santa Teresa, with Janey Young, her daughter. We were all moving in and out of the mission in those days, trying different places to work, or to live. Inteye Arrkwe and Ulerarrlkwe, Loves Creek, are part of Aggie's homelands, and mine too.

My husband spent lots of time around Inteye Arrkwe when he was growing up, and his homelands and my homelands were overlapping. Our families all used to work together. His homelands were a little bit to the north, and our families made connections in the Aboriginal way. His traditional homelands were towards Garden station – Unamarre, they call that country. He was an Anmatyerr man, from north of Arrernte country, but his father had worked around Inteye Arrkwe, Ulerarrlkwe and Atnarpa stations for many, many years, so this is where he mostly grew up.

When my husband and I went to Inteye Arrkwe in about 1969, it was to work for two men called the Green brothers who ran a tourist venture for the visitors coming out from Alice Springs. I worked in the house with my cousin who's passed away now. Every day tourists came, so there were heaps of plates to wash in the kitchen, all the little cabins to clean, all the sheets to wash. It was hard work. That was the work my cousin and I did every

OPPOSITE: *Irrernte-arenye at Dawn*, 1996, acrylic on canvas, 60.5 x 45.5 cm (detail)

RIGHT: *Irrernte-arenye at Dawn*, 1996, acrylic on canvas, 60.5 x 45.5 cm

OPPOSITE: View down the gully at Therirrerte.

day and it took us hours and hours. There were only two of us in the house to do all the domestic work. One washed the sheets and cleaned the bungalows. The other washed up the plates and cleaned the kitchen area. Three times a day we set up the table for the tourists. They would come in, have something to eat, then we would wash it all up and set it all out again for the next meal. Tourists often stayed for a few days at a time, so we prepared everything for them – every cabin they stayed in and every meal they ate.

My cousin and I got on really well together and we worked well together. While we were inside doing this domestic work, my husband was outside. He used to get the horses ready to take the tourists. He packed flour, salt, tea and milk to carry to N'Dhala Gorge, Alkwerture, Arlengarrkerle and Alyapere. Some tourists rode with him on horses, others travelled on the bus. My husband would get big *tyape* and sometimes he showed the tourists how to get them from the tree trunk. He cooked the *tyape* and made a damper and a cup of tea while the tourists looked around at the gorges or the bluff. At lunch time he had everything ready on the table, including the *tyape*, for the tourists to enjoy. There were sometimes forty people in the group.

My husband took them to Alkwerture first where fresh water comes up from underground. In the rocks above the spring you can still see what is left of the shield of a brave ancestor who fought a mighty battle there. It is not far from the homestead and he told them a bit about the spring. Next he took them to Arlengarrkerle which is a big straight cliff and then to a place called Arlirntarlpe to see the beautiful patterns on the rocks where the seven sisters danced for joy, thinking themselves free of the trickster man who was chasing them. When the tourists reached N'Dhala Gorge there was a bower bird nest and they always took a picture of it. Moving on a bit further they went to Alyapere where there is big creek. This is where he used to get the biggest *tyape*. In the afternoon he would ride back with the tourists to Inteye Arrkwe.

My husband's pay packet was combined with mine, although I think he got paid a

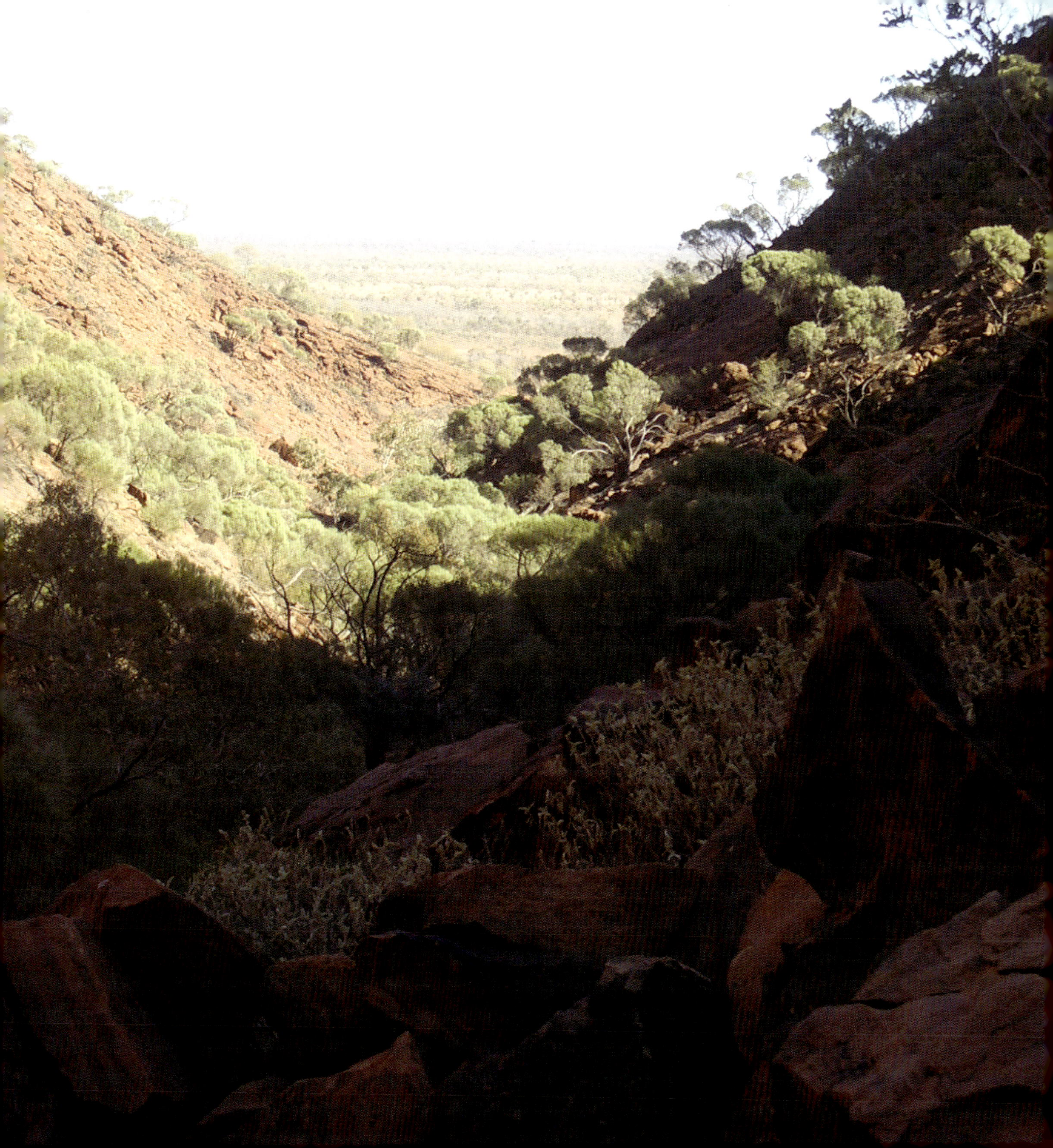

bit more than me. I didn't think money was important to me so I gave it to my husband because he knew how to spend it. The money we were paid we often just spent at the station buying our food. After a year at Inteye Arrkwe, working with the tourists, we went back to Santa Teresa mission. Before we left we were given our tax papers, but didn't understand what they were about. We didn't know what to do with them, so we threw them away. We never claimed back the tax we should have received from that job because there was no way to understand the system and no one to sort it out with. We had worked very hard for those bosses at Inteye Arrkwe.

During this time we still hunted for goanna, kangaroo, emu and bush food at the weekends but to take part in family or Aboriginal business we had to go back to Ltyentye Apurte. Our traditional business was usually in the summer and other times we still did some traditional things on our land, hunting mainly. But the other bit was getting lost: culture, singing, dancing, family gatherings. I used to think: What's happening now? No dancing! Because I had been at the mission, where not much cultural activity or business went on in the 60s and 70s, I was missing it all very much. So was my husband.

For the old men who had been forced into the mission by the drought, things were a bit freer now. They were still taking off and wandering around doing their own thing when they could. They still had boomerangs and spears, no guns. They still kept to their springs and travelled a bit around their homelands. But the other things, the big group things, huge ceremonies, large gatherings, travelling dances, *urrwempele* – they were all finished for us. No more. It was a strange and difficult time.

LEFT: *Ancestors of Therirrerte*, 2008, acrylic on linen, 24 x 34 cm (a study for the subsequent larger painting)

RIGHT AND OPPOSITE (detail): *Ancestors of Therirrerte*, 2008, acrylic on linen, 90 x 46 cm

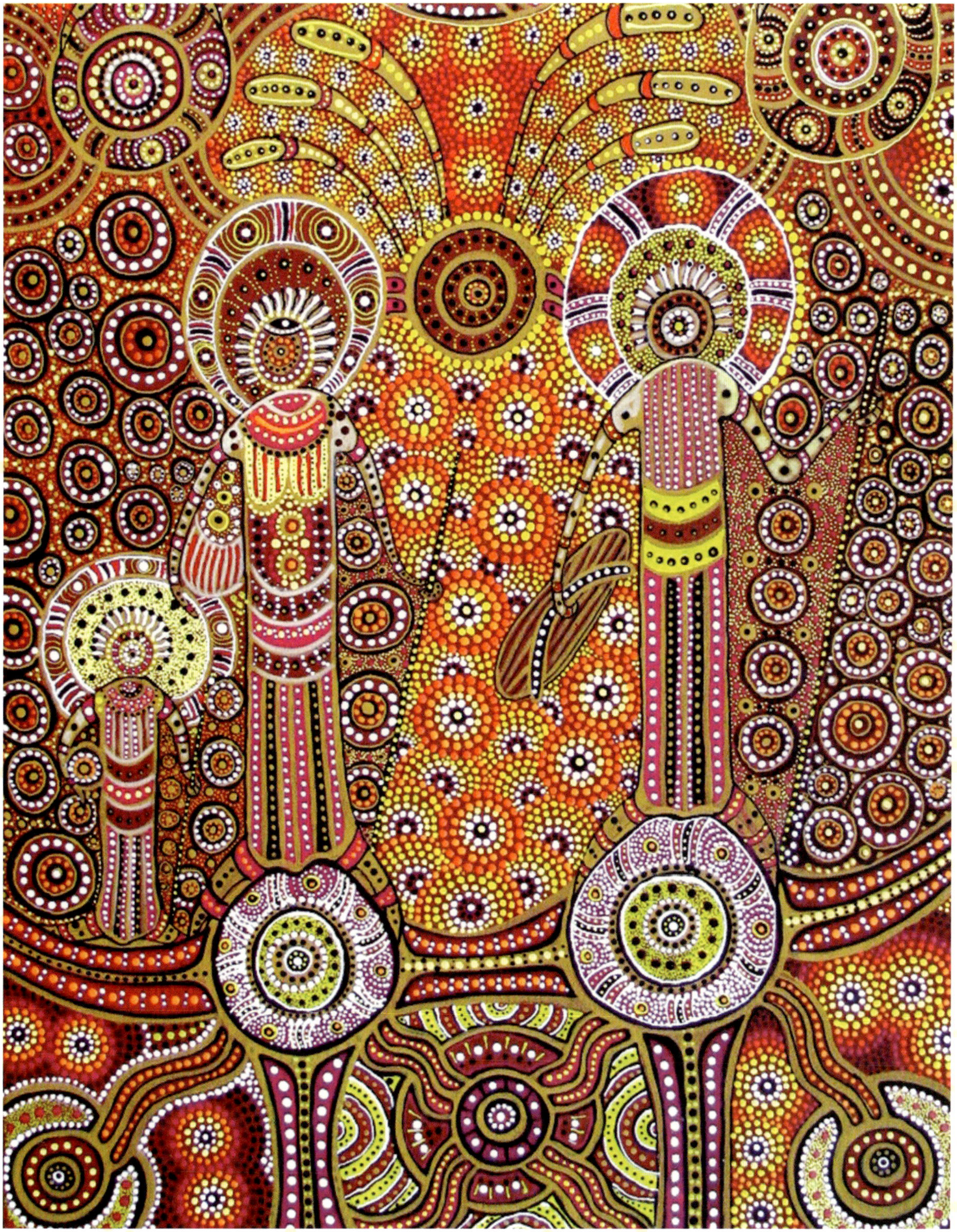

Alantye-akerte

Alantye apele artwe akngerre-apenhe anthurre-arle aneke. Arrenge-arrenge atyinhele ileke ayeye nhenhe. Arrurle anthurre artwe nhenhe untherle-apetye-ame akwele. Ikngerre-iperre re aneke. Artwe atningkeke artweye re aneke. Renhe artwe atningke apentewerretyarte. Itne apeke angkerreke apmere arrpenhe aretyeke, "atwetyeke alhetyekaye!"

Alantye apetyeke akenhe mape apele apale anerlte-anerlenge, akunye-areye.

Re kwenhe nterte ware apetyeke artwe atningke-akerte. Nterte-nterte ware itne apetyeke. Hale River thayetenge-ntyele itne ularre apetyeke, Inteye Arrkwenge irntwarre. Alyathenge itne arlengenge arenheke. Keringke-werne itne arrernelhetyerte-alheke ingwele-ingwele. Akenhe akunye-areye itne apale ware interrirreke. Atwerlenge ante ware itne arelheke. Untetyakenhe anthurre itne aneke. Akwete-ilemele atweke yanhe ikwere. Atwekawe itnenhe! Anhelhemele ware!

Kele atwerle-alhekiperre itne apmere arrpenhe ikwere-werne alheke, Apmere Inannge-werne, Therrirte itweke. Yanhe ikwere itne artwe ampwe anyente-arle aretyerte-alheke. Kele itne imernte angkerreke, "kele, ipmentye-arle impaye! Rarle ingwenthe ware ilweme, artwe ampwe-arle re." Kele renhe ipmentye impeke inteyele anerle-anetyeke.

Kele itne akarelheke Therirrerte-nge angathele aneme. Atningke-arle itne areke arltele. Ingweke itne akarelheke artwe itne. Nhakwe akenhe mpwarirrerlenge itelaretyakenhe, itnekenhe akwetethe mpwarirrepirreme mape itne mpwarerlte-aneke, ntange-arlke athemele, kere-arlke itemele. Ankweke iwelpe-iwelheke.

Ingweleme anthurre apele itne atweke urreke akeme-irreyeke, interlenge akwete. Arrpenhe-arle untetyakenhe arrangkwe. Ingkerrenyeke anthurre atweke. Artwe ampwe atyelpe apeke alheke akenhe ikwereke artweye-areye ingkerne-arle atweke. Atweke-arle-iperre aketheke ware itne impeke tyerrtye ilweke-arle-areye. Ampe apeke akwintyeke kweneke itnarle atyerremele atwerlenge arneke arlpere arrernemele.

Ikwerengentyele itne, atweke-arle-iperre, Alerarrlkwe-werne anteme alheke. Urrpetye itne aretyerte-alheke. Akare kine itne alheke ingwe-irretyenhenge. Ingwele-ingwele iknge itne atwetyarte. Itne yanheke aneme atweke akenhe itne marle anyente ineke apmere arrpenhe imernetyeke. "Irlkernalheke" arritnye marle re aneke. Itne renhe arrerneke arne atnartenge kele atweke-arle-iperre itne apurrke kwenhe aneke. Artwe akngerre-apenhe arelhe ikwere-werne apetyeke. "Iwenhe arritnye unte?" Re renhe apaye-utnheke. Arelhe re ilelheke "'Irlkernalheke' kwenhe ayenge." Akenhe artwe re ilelheke, "Ayenge-arle 'Alantye' arritnye, atwentye-akngerre!"

"Urreke! The antyeltye akeme ngenhe atwetyenhenge 'Irlkernalheke' mpwaretyeke!"

"Atyenge ilaye apmere nthenhe-nthenhe awethe-ame-arle aneme!" Arelhe re akenhe arrewemele akwele aneke Alantyele apele arne renhe akekenge.

Artwe itne akenhe atningke re kere-arlke itemele itne nhenge atwek-arle-iperre akunye-areye ilweke-arle interrirrerlenge akethe ware. Arelhe re apele itirreke, "Iyete ayenge untetyenhenge." Re akwele arelheke kele akeme-irremele unteke. Artwe mape renhe alwerneke akenhe re akenhe akwele tyerre-anthurre-alhelenge. Artwe-arle renhe alwernekaye arelhe re apele untentye-arrpenhe kwenhe arle aneke. Uyarne alwernemele akwele artwe itne apetye-alpeke, "kele impaye! Anyente-arle re."

Arelhe re Uyetye-werne unteke. Uyetyele apele urrpetye-arrpe kine-arle aneke. Irrtyarteke itne ilyernpenye anthurre-arle aneke. Arelhe re Uyetyeke apwerte atwatyeke alheke imerte akayele artnemele irrpenheke. Akenhe ampwe itne renhe awerrirreke, "aye arelhe-arle akayele artnintyeme," kwenhe. Artwe ampwe-areye apwerte atwatye lherele apetyeke arneke-arnare. Artwe arrpenheme apwerte akertneke antyeke kweneke-arle aretyeke. Irrtyarte arraweye anthurre itne tnerrirreke.

Kele artwe ampwe urrpetye, arelhe ampwe urrpetye lherele apetyerlenge arelhe renhe aretyeke, "iwenhe-iperre-aye?!" kwenhe. Kele arelhe rawerne akengentye ware tnyeke, ilelheke, "anwerneke artweye mape," kwenhe, "'Alantye' arritnye-arle atweke." Rawerne ileke, "Alantyele awerre anwerneke artweye atweke. Arrangkwe ingkerreke aneme kwenhe". Kele itne artnerrirreke ikwere-arle. Kele artwe anyente, Urlamparenye, angkeke, "awe, atyewelatye atweke?!" (Alantye uthene Urlamparenye uthene atyewenhenge aneke.) "Atyewelatye kwenhe atweke!" Kele re tyerrelheke, artwe irrtyarteke ilyernpenye itnenhe re ineke. Urrpetye ware itne aneke. Itneke-akerte nterteke-irreke.

Alantye akenhe itelareke Irlkernalheke artwe arrpenhe-areye, Uyetye-arenye, alkngarre-iletyenhenge. Itne apeke ikwereke akarelhetyenhe. Kele re itirreke alpetyeke. Itne-arle apetyeke rarle itne alpeke.

Kele artwe ampwe, Urlamparenye-arle, nterteke-irreke. Rarle itelareke ingweleme-ingweleme atwentye-akngerre.

Wale, Alantyele mpwarerte-alheke kele re akenhe ikwerenhe mape yerne-arle-irtneke, apmere itwe-arle anekenge, "kele, alperle-iwaye! Ayenge ingkerne alpeyemenge". Artwe akngerre-apenhe apele angkeke. Re akenhe atnyeneke ampe urreye ikwerenhe, arelhe ikwere anewe atherr, untherle-apetyeke.

Itne intetyerte-alpeke apwerte akertnele, Hale River side-le, arrpenhe mape yernirtnekiperre. Ingwele intetye-ame akenhe Uyetye-arenye-areye-arle aretyeke-arle alheke, apertemele aretyeke itwenge. Wale, arrpenhe-arle irrtyarteke inkerrelhe-ileke

Akenhe Alantyele aweke. "Ure yanhe ilwernaye!" Kwenhe. "Irrtyarte the awernenge inkerrerlenge." Kele ure renhe ilwerneke. Ure-kwenye ware re intetye-ame, arelheme, "ilengare apeke arratintyeye?" Akenhe Uyetye-arenye-areye ingwelemeke akarelhelenge.

135

Arlte aneme-arle ikngerre irrintyemele, atetheke, ikwereke apele itne atwerreke. Irrtyartele nterneke Uyetye-arenye itne Alantye renhe. Kele re akelpe-akeme-irrerlenge akenhe atningke anthurre re akwete renhe irrtyartele nternewerreke. Re akenhe atyerre-arlke-lhilerlenge irrtyarte itnekenhe mpepele ultakirtnemele, arrpenheme akenhe itnekenhe irrtyarte akenhe ware ilertnetye-alperlenge ikwerenge-arlenge. Alantyele Uyetye-arenye arrpenheme itnenhe irrtyartele akngerre-apenhe ikwerenhele nterneke, ilwetyeke-ante.

Alernnge akertne-irreke Alantye apele akngerre re alhwe unteke arrernelhartneke akwele. Re angkeke, "apetye-alherle-iwaye! Nthenhe-arenye mape-arle arlkwemeyaye?"

Apetyeke, rarle alhengke-anteme-areke, "atyewatye!" Akenhe atyewikwe Uyetye-arenye-arle angkeke, "iwenheke unte apmere anwernekenhe-werne apetyeke atwetyeke?" Alantye-arle angketyakenhe aneke kele imernte anteme, "ware, anhelemele atwetyeke," re ileke. Akenge akngerre rlkanyele iwelheke imernte irrketye ikwerenhe atyewikwe nthemele. Arelhe ikwere anewe atherre ntheke-arle atyewikwe, ampe urreye ikwerenhe uthene. "Nhenhe-areye ngkwenge aneye, akngirtnaye, ayenge nhenhe ikwere ilwemenge." Kele itne alperle-iweke atweke-arle-iperre. Alantye-arle akenhe akenge akngerre ware aneke. Akenhe artwe anyente untetye-alpeke angkerlenge, "akunye, ayenge untetye-alpeye arerle-iwetyeke." Akenhe re akenhe renhe atnerte alterremele anthurre akeke, ilwetyeke anthurre aneme.

Lyete ulkere ngkwerne ikwerenhe yanhe ikwere akwete inteme.

Arrenge-arrenge-arle ileke re aretyeke alheke ayeye aweke-arle-iperre. Arratye renhe ngkwerne areke. Akngerre-apenhe anthurreyaye, angkerralye. Yanhele aneme re akwele.

Arrurle arrpenhe ngkwerne akethe ware inteke Therirrertele atweke-arle-iperre. Therreyelawe (Strehlow) urreke apetyenhenge ngkwerne yanhe-areye inerleke arrernetyeke Tarte-tarte mapele. Anwerne-arlke ampe mape aneke ngkwerne itnenhe aretyarte. Anwerne-arle Therirrerte-werne akwetethe alhetyarte ane Kurlpe inteye aretyarte ngkwerne mape.

Giant

Arrernte families have faced difficult times in the past too. This is a history story which happened around the time of my great, great grandfathers. As children, we were told this story and shown the remains from the battle.

Sometime in the past, maybe even before the white men came here, there used to be many, many more Arrernte people than there are today. At the time when this event took place we all spoke our own old dialects, but interacted as part of a larger group, connected as family through our skin names and our culture. In those times we were like those big groups today – Warlpiri, Pitjantjatjara and Pintupi, there were many more of us than are left now. We were a really big group with relations all over the place, from Aputula up to Utopia, and through the big Simpson Desert. But then, many of my family were killed in our homelands by a great big, giant man from another tribe to the north.

The way my grandfathers told me this story, which their grandfathers had told them, was that a man from another tribe came through the country from the north and he attacked our people at Therirrerte then set off to return to his country through the Hale River area. As he travelled through our homelands, he would sneak up on our family camps at night and kill everyone, before they could wake up to run away or to fight him properly. Not many of our people escaped the giant, only a few got away to alert other people about what was happening.

A woman who escaped from Therirrerte ran all the way across to Uyetye with the giant and his warriors chasing her. They had captured her at Therirrerte to take her along with them, trying to make her show the giant where other families lived. She escaped and ran towards Ulerarrlkwe, then across to Uyetye. She was a strong brave one, that woman, and she got away from her captors, who chased her half way to Uyetye. Luckily for all of us, she was a really fast runner.

My ancestors were at Uyetye when she came running towards the cave, following the river bed, and crying out all the time for our old people – crying out to warn them, to ask for help and protection from them. They were peaceful people, our Arrernte people – always – but they were good hunters and they were very

View from the ranges near Therirrerte.

strong in law and business, so they knew what had to be done.

As the woman came closer to Uyetye, the people heard her crying from the creek, so some old men went straight down in front of the cave, but other old men went on either side. One thing about Uyetye that made it such a safe place is that the cave is entirely hidden from view unless you stand in front of it, and it's under a huge flat slab of rock, so you can't tell if anyone is around when you stand above it either. At the sides of the cave it's steep, rocky and craggy – quite dark enough for a clever hunter to disappear into the side of the rocks and never be seen by other people. The creek that runs from the front of the cave down to the river and the river flats is quite full of trees and boulders too, so you can't see straight up to the cave from that side either. Our families always felt safe there because no one could just come upon the cave without first being seen.

The brave runner from Therirrerte knew where Uyetye was and who might be there. She told some of the older women and the warrior men from Uyetye exactly what had happened and who was killing our people. The men from Uyetye went after that big giant man, and they fought him and finished him off. This was towards Hale River, somewhere out there. He really was a giant-sized man and it took them all day to kill him. The men's spears were like little pins to him and it took many, many attacks to weaken him, but in the middle of the day he started to go down. He had murdered many of our people. They had to spear him all over; even though their spears were like pins, they fought him like that all day to make him die. In the afternoon, finally, they finished with him. Towards Hale River you may still see his bones on a hill. They are probably covered with sand now. One day my grandfather showed me those bones, and told me this story – when I was a child.

We know this giant was from the north-east, a long way away. One of the men from Uyetye who was responsible for killing the giant was my grandfather's grandfather. He and the giant had gone through initiation together and so they were *atyewe* to each other. It was not until the giant was dying that he realised that he was being killed by his *atyewe*. He would certainly have known that he should not have come this way to kill our people. They were minding their own business – they were not any threat to his people or to him. We were always peaceful people, but that giant killed so many anyway, and then our men killed him.

This was a long time ago, but we still talk about it, even today. I was told all about this by my grandfather and all my aunties and uncles know of this giant as well. Perhaps it was Utitjuta, my grandfather's grandfather, who fought that giant.

OPPOSITE: Looking out from the cave, Therirrerte.

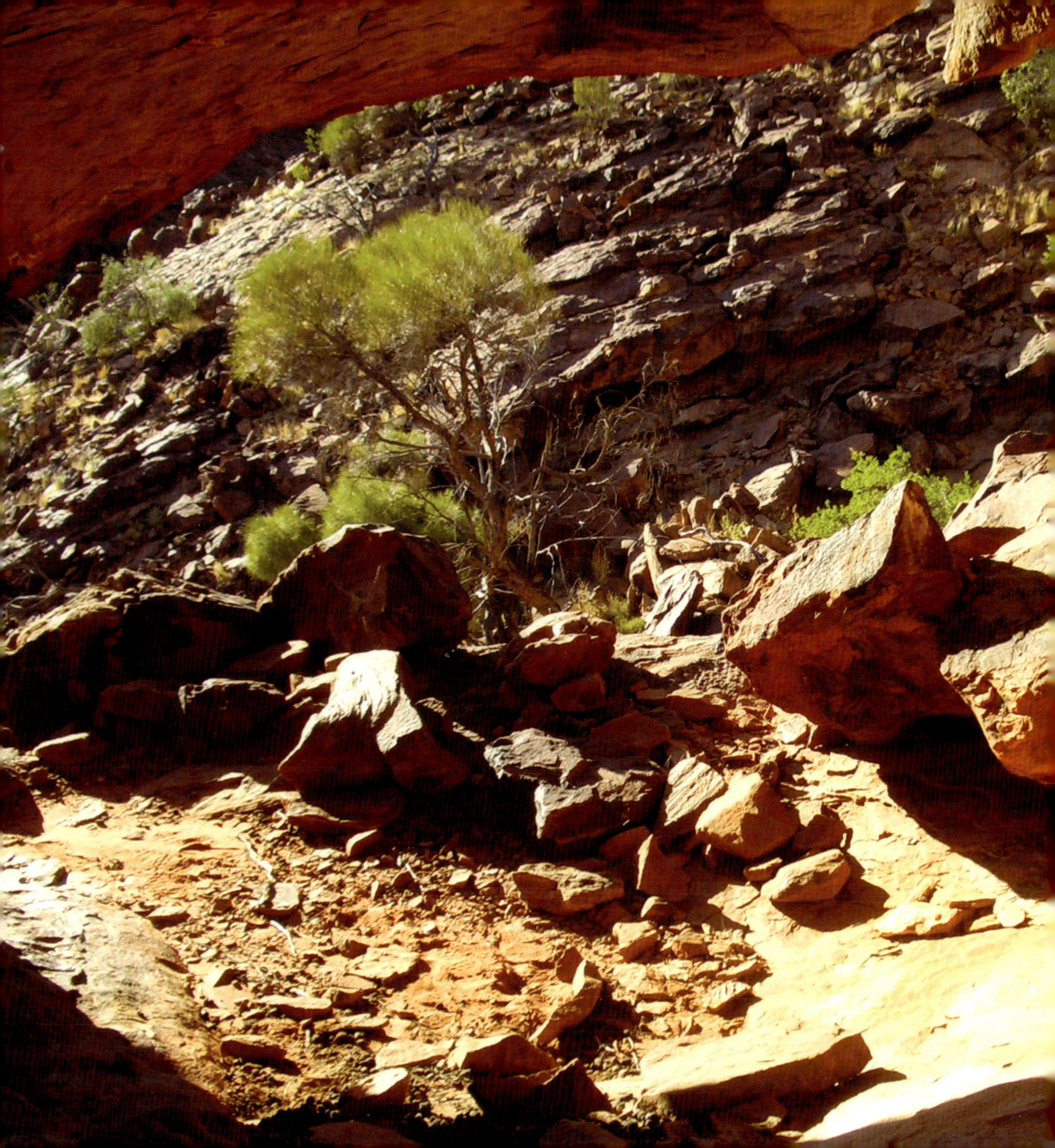

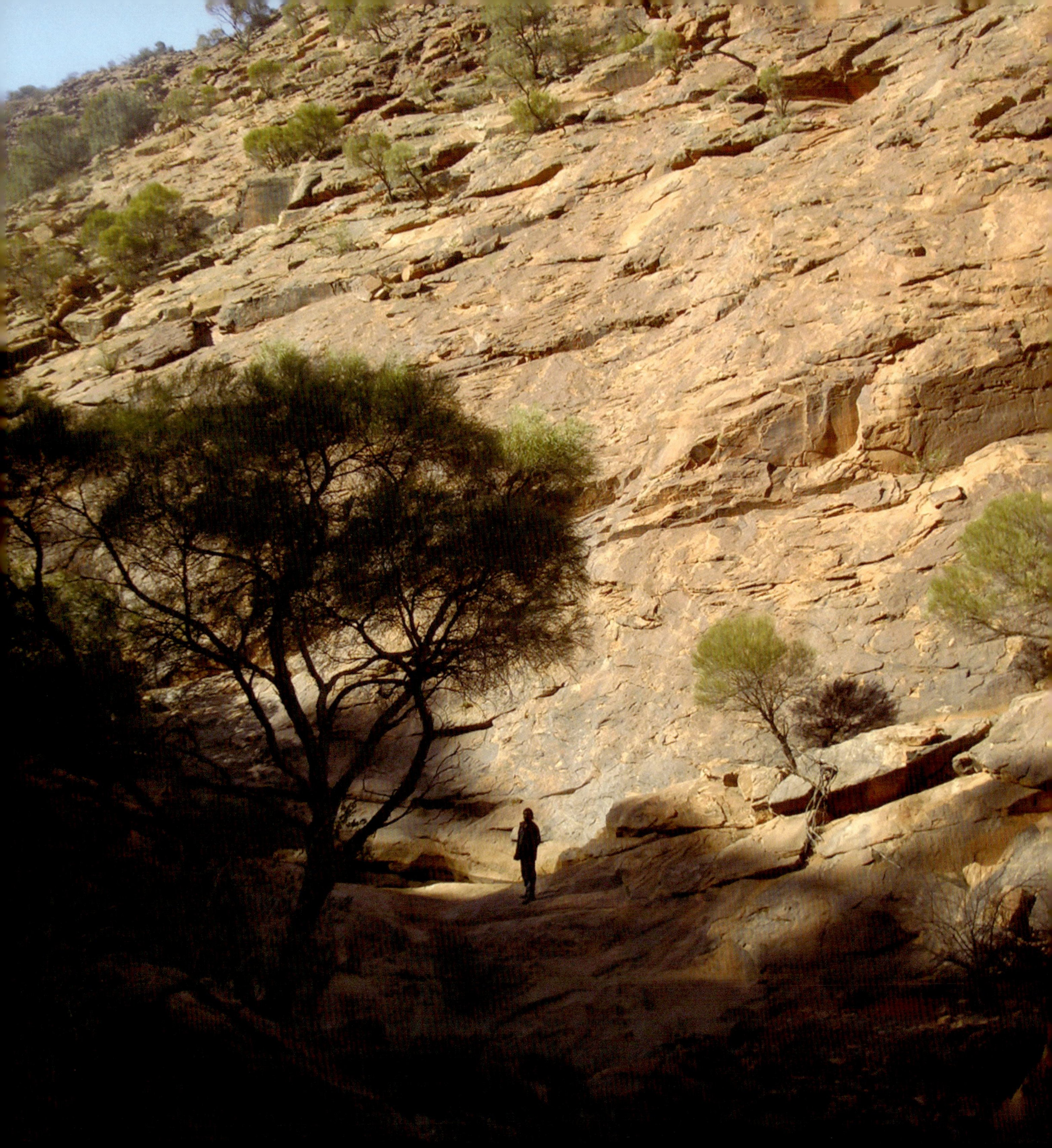

Therirrerte

We call this place Therirrerte because that means running straight along, and the range is really straight here. My mother's father and grandfather are both from here. Our family has many generations of ancestors from this place. They are a part of Therirrerte – they still have a strong spirit in that place. Those men, they were *Therirrerte-arenye*, the incarnated ancestors from the *altyerrenge*, from here. So you see, it has always been our homeland.

Therirrerte was a large, comfortable camping ground with space for everyone and access to hunting, food and water. Whole tribes came and camped there together. It was a really good camping spot because they could get water from the rockhole up the gully, and sometimes water was held lower down the gully, nearer the camp area at smaller rockholes, too. The one near the fig tree is the main one – it's quite a deep rockhole. People camping at Therirrerte could do everything from there, including holding big ceremonies for rain and other things. The families could grind seeds, hunt, and cook, and look after their frail old people. It was a peaceful, safe place.

Therirrerte is a sacred and protected place, and women and children are still not permitted to go above the main rockhole. In our culture, old women and widows are allowed to be shown the men's sacred places, told the business; however, I can't do that now because there is no one left to take me there – it has to be done in the right way and there are

OPPOSITE: Stanley Wallace near Therirrerte rockhole.

no old men left to show me or my aunties in the right way. So that business is also finished now.

My grandfather's totem was the *atyelpe*, native cat. It had a white tail, but they are not found here anymore, and you don't see them around anywhere else either. Those *atyelpe* were a very big and strong group of our ancestors from the *altyerrenge*, and Therirrerte holds many powers associated with *atyelpe*. Many of my ancestors were of *urlampe* totems, involved in the sacred sites and business of water and rain and, at Therirrerte, associated with the native cat totem.

Therirrerte has two good rockholes up the gully. Women and children only visit the first one because the second one is a men's site. Next to the first rockhole is a big fig tree and past the fig tree is another waterhole and the men's site. Our old people would stay at Therirrerte for quite a while, until the water ran out, then they would come back towards Uyetye. Water was always especially important for us – life saving. It was the water that always brought people back from Therirrerte to Uyetye – another special homeland – because water was always to be found nearby at Uyetye. There are plenty of springs around that area and the creek water flows under the sand.

If you look at the rock art at the rockholes, you can see that many of my painting designs come from Therirrerte. The circles

LEFT: *Athere*, grinding stone.

RIGHT: Kathleen relaxing at Therirrerte after the climb up the gully and the story recording.

142

are sometimes for waterholes, or ceremony grounds or rockholes. I always feel excited when I see the circles which I think represent sacred ceremony sites, drawn on the rocks by our ancestors a long time ago. These other circles with the little dots in them are the birds' nests and eggs. You see birds' footprints and the eggs. Sometimes I don't put the birds' prints into the painting; I just paint eggs lying in their nest, just like on those rock carvings. Some tiny little dots represent grass, seeds, flowers and trees. There are many figures, representing all kinds of spirit ancestors carved on the rocks too. I was first shown these carvings on the rocks as a young girl. I also think about the designs from sand drawings and from ceremonial body paint as well as from those rock carving designs. Wherever they come from, I have taken them into myself and formed them into paintings in my own way. I do this with the permission of my grandparents.

Because my ancestors have lived here for so many generations, back into the ancestor days, there are a great many events and stories connected to Therirrerte, and even though Therirrerte is a peaceful, safe place for us, the two stories I want to tell you from this place are about journeys in the *altyerrenge*, the ancestor days when things were very different and unusual activities took place quite often. I will tell you a big story which was told to us as children, and which I never forgot. The other story is one which we were always told about a young woman at Therirrerte. It is a story which we see illustrated around us in the rock carvings in the gully, as the figure of this woman was carved there many times.

Rock carving of bird's eggs in a nest.

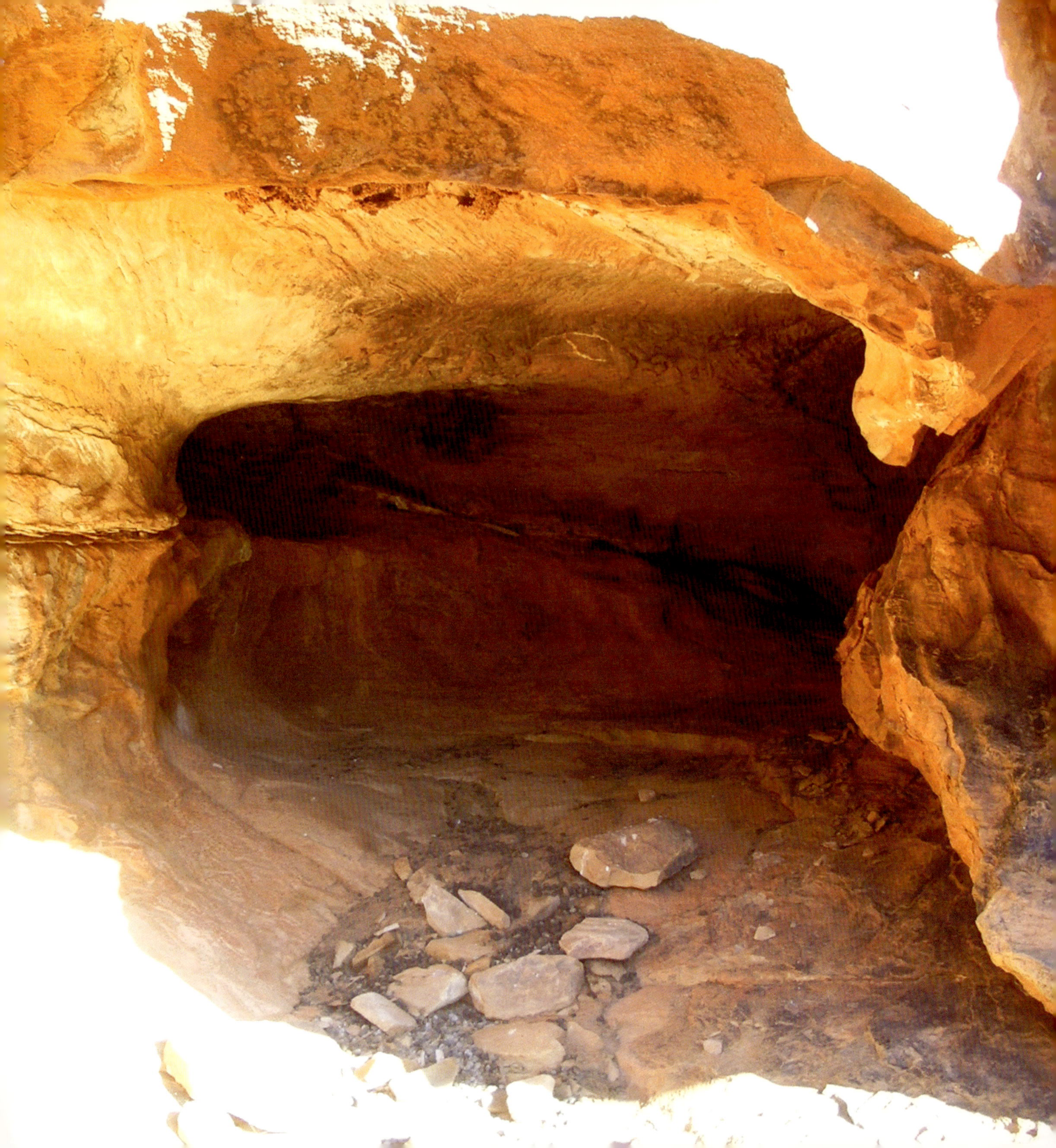

Apmere Arturte-akerte

Apmere Arturte apele Therirrertenge irntwarre. Altyerrenge aneke ayeye nhenhe antyipere mape-akerte. Antyipere arrpenhe-areye antekerrenge-ntyele, ayerrerenge-ntyele apetyeke, arrpenhe-areye-arle arlturlenge-ntyele apetyeke. Arrpenhe-areye akenhe ikngerrenge-ntyele apetyeke apmere anyente yanhe ikwere-werne. Itne anyenteke-irreke yanhe ikwere apwerte akweke akertneke. Yanhe ikwere aneme itne atwerreke. Atwerreke-atwerreke rarle itne.

Akenhe arlenge ulkere akenhe arelhe mape, artwe-arlke arerrirrerlenge, "angwenhe re aneme utnherreme?" kwenhe. Itwe ulkere aremele itne areke irlpe-akerte mape atwerrerlenge re, prape tnyante re, arlkwerlenge-arlke arrpenhe mapele. Prape arlenge arlentye re itne atwerreke. Mape akenhe apatemele arerlenge, "iwenheke arrkngele itne atwerreme?" Itne apaye-utnherreke.

Itne atwerreke-atwerreke akenhe antyipere arrpenhe akertneke antyeke alkereke-irreke kweneke-arle imernte aremele artwe ampwe anyente ampe urreye akweke-akerte tnerle-anerrerlenge areke.

Antyipere re akenhe irrtyarte-akerte-arle aneke. Akertnenge-ntyele nterneke ampe urreye akweke renhe atnerte atanthemele irrtyartele. Ikwere antime re ilweke urreye akweke re. Arrengikwe ahele anthurre irreke, "iwenhenge-arle re areke antyiperele nterneke apelaye?!"

Re aneme irrtyarte ikwerenhe ineke alkere-werne-atheke nterneke antyipere ikwere. Akenhe antyipere rarle arlpelhe-akerte aneke arlenge-ame-arlenge aneme irreke. Arratye aneme antyipere renhe atweke. Irrtyarte ikwerenhe re alyeke aneme arratye aneme atwetyeke. Alkere ikwere re nterneke, akertne aneme, kweneke-arle tnyeke re. Akenhe itne atwerreperreme akwete ure-arlke itemele, ureke-arlke atyerreme. Apmere akwetethe-arenye mape akwete arnterre arerrirrerlenge, arlengenge ware.

Artwe ampwe re iletyakenhe ampe akweke renhe nterneke arrentyele, antyiperele. Rarle antyipere renhe atweke. Atwerrentye-iperre antyipere mape apmere itne-arle apetyeke ikwere-werne alperlenge akenhe antyipere arrpenhe-areye-arle Therirrerte-werne-atheke apetyeke, atwerreke-arle-iperre. Akenhe mape-arle itweke apetyemele areke ilweke-arle mape, intenhepenherlenge, antyipere mape. Inngirre prape arrpenhe re, "Eee! Inngirre irntirte mape-arle atwerreperreme apmere anwernekenhele," akwenhe, "nthenhe-arlke-iperre mape-arle atwerreke?"

Akenhe antyipere arrpenhe mape Therirrertenge irrenhewerreke apwerte atwatyenge. Kele itne aretyakenhe artwe anyente, Therirrerte-arenye, inteyele intetye-ame. Inteye kwenele atyakwerte inteme alyelhetye-ame, artelhemele arteke. Inteye arriwele tnerrirretyame irrtyarte ikwerenhe. Antyipere itne-arle renhe awetyakenhe re. Itne anpere alheke.

Akenhe tyerrtye yanhe-arenye apetyeke aretyeke iwenheke antyipere-arle atwerreke. Apwerte urlkere mape-ante itne areke

OPPOSITE: Cave at Therirrerte.

interrirrerlenge. Yanhe apele alhwe-arlke, tyelke-arlke itnekenhe rarle apwerte yanhe-areye. Apwerte anteme itne akngarte-iwelheke, akweke anthurre mape-arlke, urlkere ingkerreke. Apwerte arturte anteme itne irreke. Yanhele itne aneme akwete, Pintyeyenge irntwarre.

RIGHT AND OPPOSITE: *Bat Chair*, 1996, acrylic on wood, 89 x 44 x 44 cm

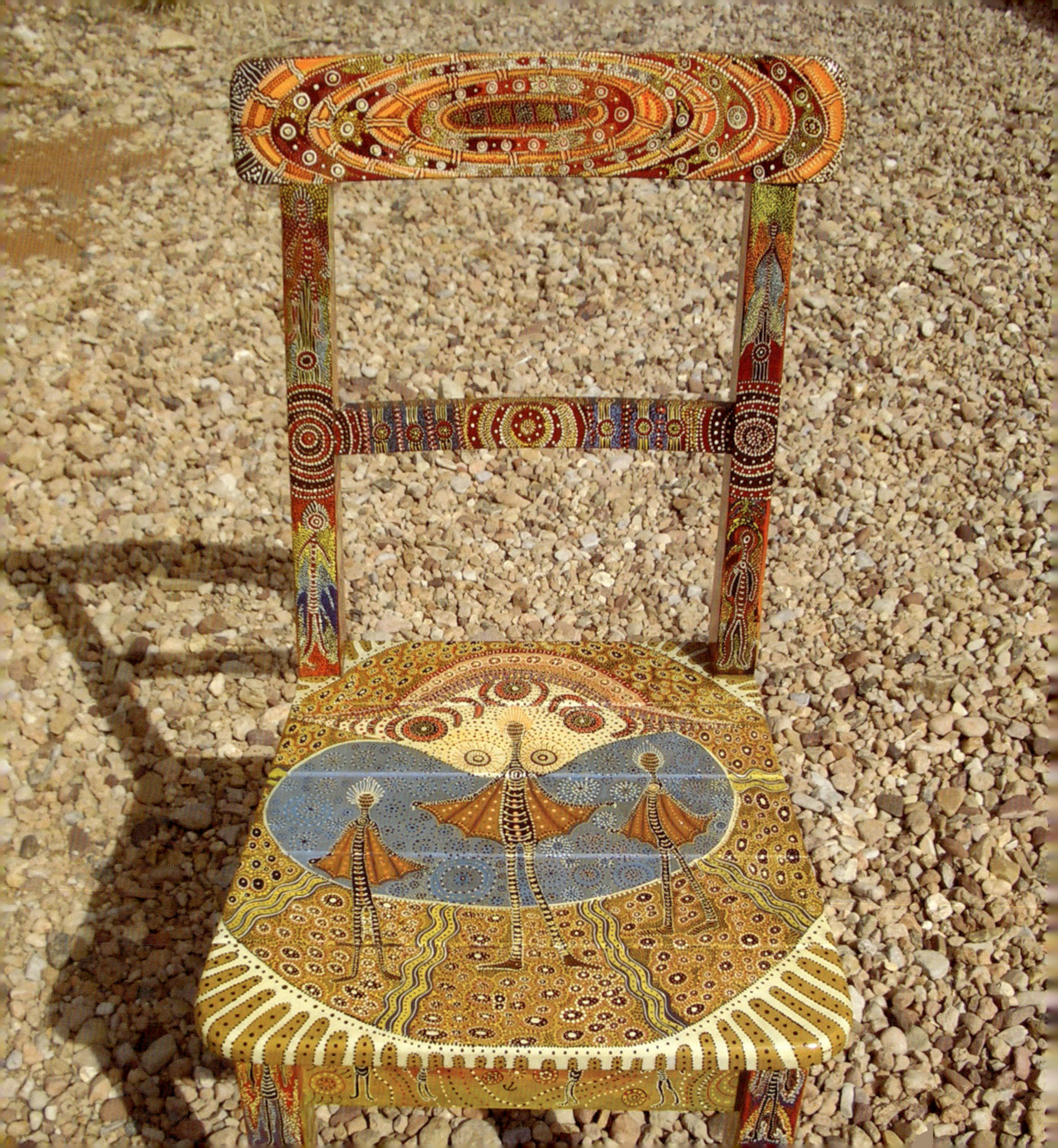

Bat ancestors

The events in this story took place at Arturte, which is a site not far from Therirrerte. Arturte is in the Simpson Desert. Today it stands as two little hills in the desert sand, hills piled up with shiny, rounded, smooth rocks. These two little hills are the only place we know of where you can get such strong, smooth, round rocks. We use those rocks for grinding seeds, bush tobacco and bush medicine, and they have been carried quite far and wide for these purposes, we have found them at Therirrerte, Uyetye, Keringke, and further out around the homelands. The way these rocks were formed is a story told to me since I was young. It is a violent and bloody story that happened a long, long time ago when *altyerre* beings moved around the country,

View from one of the Arturte hills.

changing their forms as they went, and creating things as we know them today.

The story is about some fierce bat ancestors who came from Therirrerte. One evening they were drawn out into the desert to fight other bats who came across from the south-east. This battle went all night. We know this story because our old people were watching the fight from a distant part of the range, thinking: what sort of creatures are these who are fighting one another so viciously and so long over there?

Some old men went closer to the fight until they saw the bat creatures. Those men stopped away over on the range; they didn't want to go any closer because the bats were fighting savagely, tearing each other's flesh apart. The old men thought they might get eaten too if they got too close to the fighting ancestors! They could see that the creatures were a bit like men, but their long arms had wings, their hands had claws and they had bat's heads.

The bats fought viciously into the night, savagely tearing each other to pieces. Sometimes, lumps of their flesh fell on the ground as they cut at each other. As the flesh fell to the ground, it burst into flames. Some bats ate the flesh and the rest of it melted into big lumps, piling up higher and higher. Through the night the big flames burnt high in the air.

Our old people watched from a safe distance until they judged the fighting was finished. Then they came closer, to see what was left after the fight. They saw bits of the bats lying around, their blood on the ground everywhere. Some had been eaten, maimed and burnt, but some survived and they flew away towards Therirrerte.

The bats flew right back through the gully at Therirrerte. It may have been Inkiljaku, my ancestor, who was in a cave at Therirrerte that day, lying on his back with one leg on his other knee, singing and singing away, when the fierce, angry bats went through the gully. But they didn't hear him or see him; they went right past the cave as he was singing. Inkiljaku must have protected himself with his song, becoming part of the *apmere*, so he couldn't be seen; he was safe. He saw the bat ancestors fly past, and he had his spears, boomerangs and everything ready; his spears were all standing up in front of his cave. Inkiljaku too had very strong powers – he is part of Therirrerte.

We don't know where the *altyerre* bats went next, what they became, or what happened after that, we just know what happened to make the special, smooth, shiny rocks from the melted flesh of the ancestor bats at Arturte.

Antethe-akerte Therirrertele Itwe

Therirrerte Woman, 2007,
acrylic on canvas, 60 x 44 cm

Apmere arelhe atniwetyakenhe rarle yanhe re Therirrertenge angathe, ayeye nhenhe. Yanhe ikwere-arenye arelhe atherre aneke. Mape yanhe re anetyarte. Mikwe ilwekenge apeke amangke-arle-ileke. Ratherre akwete anetyarte Altyerrenge. Mape-arle arlenge ratherre anetyarte. Ratherre-arrpe rarle alherretyarte. Arrpenhe mapenge-arlenge alherretyakenhe ratherre anetyarte. Arelhe awenke atherre ratherre aneke, arrpenhe akngerrepate-arle aneke. Ratherre merne alangkweke-arlke, merne arlpeke unthetyarte, merne urrkenngeke-arlke. Yanhe ulkere ratherre arlkwetyarte, alewatyerre-arlke.

Ratherre urlpe apernelhetyarte akenhe atnerte urrperle-arle, aperrke-arle apernelherle. Iwenhe apeke rarle ratherre yanhe apernelheke, urlpe atetheke apernelhelenge inngerre-arlke re, ngkwerne-arlke. Mapele arerrirretyarte, "yanhe atherre akwetethe re! Urlpele apernelheme, atnerte ante urrperle ilelhemele," kwenhe.

Arelhe ratherre apeke ankwe-ipenhe angkerretyarte aye, "ilerne alakenhe apernelhe," kwenhe, "aperrkele, urlpele apernelherle". Mapele ntertele arerrirretyarte.

Apernelhe-alherrerle alewatyerre-arlke, merne-arlke unthetyeke. Apurte re apmerele anerrirretyarte imernte alhelenge atherre-arrpe unthetyeke, artepeke ratherre anetyarte. Mape alherle apurte, apmere arrpenhe-werne alherle kwatyeke akenhe ratherre anyente ikwere apmerele anetyarte kwatyeke imernte alhemele Therirrerte-werne. Kwatye antywemele alperle apmere anyente ikwere-werne. Wale, arlte arrpenhe-arle aneme ratherre unthetye-ame alewatyerreke, arne-artnele akenhe artwele renhe-atherrenhe aretye-ame. Ratherre apale re. Wale, akngerrapate awelheke, "angwenhele-ame ilernenhe arepe-areme," kwenhe, "nthenhe-ame arepe-areme?" kwenhe.

Artwele akenhe arne-artnenge aretye-ame. Artwe re apele itirreke, "awe, arrweketye prape anewe-anewenge akwenhe yanhe atherre. Atyenge arntwirrketyenhe," kwenhe. Artwe

150

Therirrerte-arenye re alhirreke. Alhirremele aretye-ame.

Akwetethe re artwe re arltele apetyarte ikwere atherreke. Akenhe arelhe akngerre akenhe, "angwenhele-ame ilernenhe arepe-areme?" kwenhe, "ayenge akwenhe awelhe-apelheme arerlenge," kwenhe, marle akweke renhe ileke. Re akenhe awenke-arle aneke itelaretyakenhe artwe. Ikwere-atherreke-anteye artwe alhirretyarte. Arelhe re arrpenhe mape iletyakenhe anetyarte.

Wale, artwe anyentele Therirrerte-arenye renhe areke, apaye-utnheke, "iwenhe ikwere unte nhakwe-atheke alhepe-alheme?" kwenhe. Kele ilelheke anteme, "arelhe mwerre akngerre atherre the arepe-areme," kwenhe. "Arelhe ikwere atherre uyarne the ikngwepe-ikngweme," kwenhe, "arelhe akngerre-awerne-arle mwernte iknge-irreme," kwenhe.

Arratye re anteme arntwirrketyeke aneke akenhe ratherre unterreke arne-artneke irremele. Uyarne re imernte artwe unthetye-ame, impatyeke-arlke arrangkwe. Impatye ware uyerrenheke. "Nthenhe-ame ratherre irreke? Utyaknge re impatye nhenhe," kwenhe.

Unteke-arle ante ware ratherre. Ratherre irrkaye-arle-irreke ikwerengentyele. Arlte arrpenhele ratherre arratetyarte artwe nhenge unthetyarte, re imernte itwe-irremele akenhe ratherre irrkaye-arle-irremele.

Arlte anyentele kwatye akngerre urnteke arelhe ikwere-atherre arrangkwe-arle anerleke.

Antethe atetheke lyape-arle-irreke. Artwe re imernte arerlenge, "araye, antethe arrpenhe ulkere nhenhe lyapeme!" Arelhe ratherre antethe aneke.

Ankweye-anteme-irreke akenhe renhe-atherrenhe aretyarte yanhe ikwere, arelhe awenke renhe-atherrenhe antethe anteme, atnerte urrperle tyerrtye atetheke. Lyete ratherre aneme irrernte-arenye apmere yanhele. Artwele arntwirrketyakenhe artwele apanetyakenhe akwete.

Blood stains left on the rocks.

Young woman

This is a story that women always told us at Therirrerte. The place where this story happened is a very powerful place for us, and has many stories. This is just one part of one story. It teaches us the importance of family for survival.

Therirrerte was a very important site for our men and for large gatherings of several language groups. There are many petroglyphs, rock carvings, here and this is the story we were told about one of those carvings. Many of the stories we learnt were for a particular place, and we don't know what happened to the *altyerre* being before or after our part of the story. This is another story like that.

A long time ago, a beautiful young woman came to Therirrerte from across the desert, a long way away. She was not an Arrernte woman, but she was a very beautiful girl and all the men from her tribe had wanted to marry her. There were so many men; all of them had asked her at some time or other to go with him. For her own reasons she kept saying no to each man. They must have become quite angry with her because eventually they all ganged together against her and they kept on and on asking her. This is when she must have decided to run from them.

She ran really far, all the way across the Simpson Desert, into this gully at Therirrerte. Those men seemed determined too, and they pursued her right across the desert. It was a long, long way and as she ran she must have felt really scared and very alone. When she found herself in this gully, our homeland, she must have thought she could hide and be safe.

The escape had been too hard on her body, racing the men across the desert, and half way up the gully she felt very sick. Being both scared and very sick, she struggled back down the gully, but the entrance to the gully was too exposed and she was still afraid of being caught by the men. She climbed back up the gully again. By now she was bleeding profusely, losing a lot of blood into the gully – you can see where it is still left on those rocks.

She had been pregnant, and since her hard run across the desert she was too weak and sick and she miscarried the baby, just behind the fig tree.

The young woman made it back up to the rockhole, and she bathed herself next to where her baby had miscarried. But she had lost too much blood, and she died there too. Our old people found her body, and her baby's body, by the fig tree. They carved pictures of her, on the rocks here, and told her sad story. She was young, and she must have thought she was going to be safe. It is a sad story.

OPPOSITE: The large rockhole at Therirrerte.

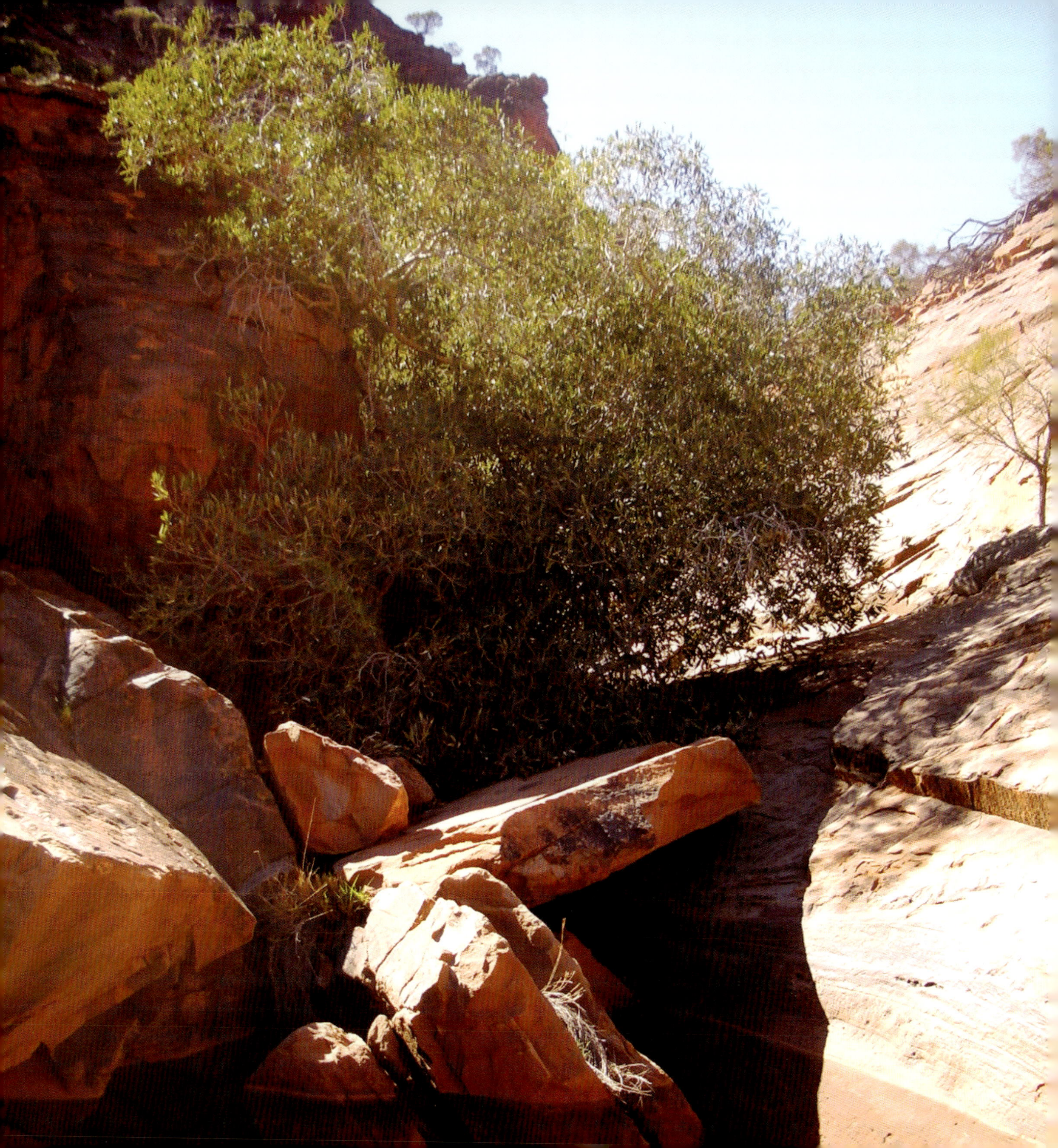

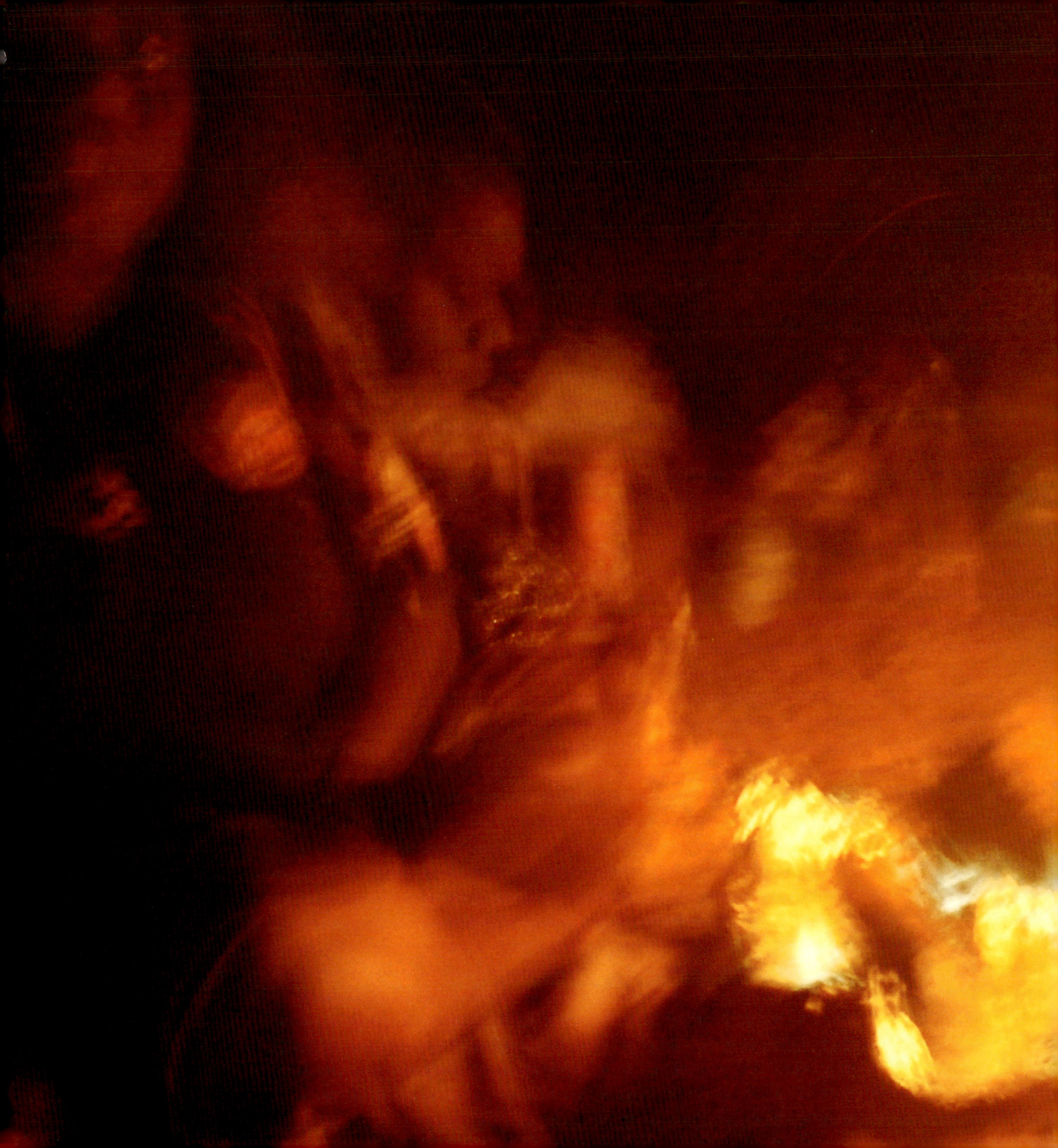

Itelarentye, Knowing our culture

The changes, from when I was a baby living in our homelands to today, were made quickly, under pressure, and have entirely altered our lives. Many Arrernte people had been born at the missions at Charles Creek in Alice Springs, or at Arltengke, or at Santa Teresa mission. This movement away from homelands prevented a lot of cultural activity and business from taking place. As young people, we did not learn all our Aboriginal business while we lived in the missions, we did not have the access to our homelands, our elders or the knowledge of our people.

The few old ones who were still out in the bush tried to keep the culture going as well as possible and we tried hard to learn as much as possible from them. Strong culture had depended on having everyone looking after their own homelands and their business, but then people were sent off their land. Children were born far away from their country. All any of us could do was to keep going with the bits we could manage, but nothing came together anymore for the whole larger group, no more *urrwempele*. The missionary people didn't like us to go off travelling for our own reasons, some station owners didn't want us on our homelands visiting our sites, but in the summer we could still hold some ceremonies. Slowly that has decreased too.

OPPOSITE: Patricia Ellis preparing roo tails on the campfire at Therirrerte.

RIGHT AND OPPOSITE (detail):
Evil Spirit Eagles, 2009,
acrylic on linen, 48 x 40 cm

Evil spirit eagles

In the *altyerrenge* there were two big eagles. They used to hunt for meat. One day they couldn't find any and at that time there was a ceremony going on to make young men. They saw the young men left by themselves. It was in the evening. They couldn't find any kangaroos so they came down and took two young men and ate their hearts out.

The men came back from hunting but there were no young men there. They looked and they saw tracks of birds, big birds, so they talked: "what sort of bird is this?" The birds had only eaten the young man's hearts and not their bodies. The men wanted to find out what the big birds were and where they were living, so they looked everywhere but couldn't find them. The birds were up in the sky.

There was one *ngangkere*; he saw them coming back down in the evening: "They are looking for more young men," he said. The men speared the eagles but couldn't kill them. Then the women rushed up. They had fire sticks and they were making a lot of noise which made the birds go away back up into the sky. They are still up there, as two white clouds up in the sky. When there is ceremony going on the birds' spirits come out, and even today the women rush up and make the noise to make them go away. They are *irretye*, eaglehawks.

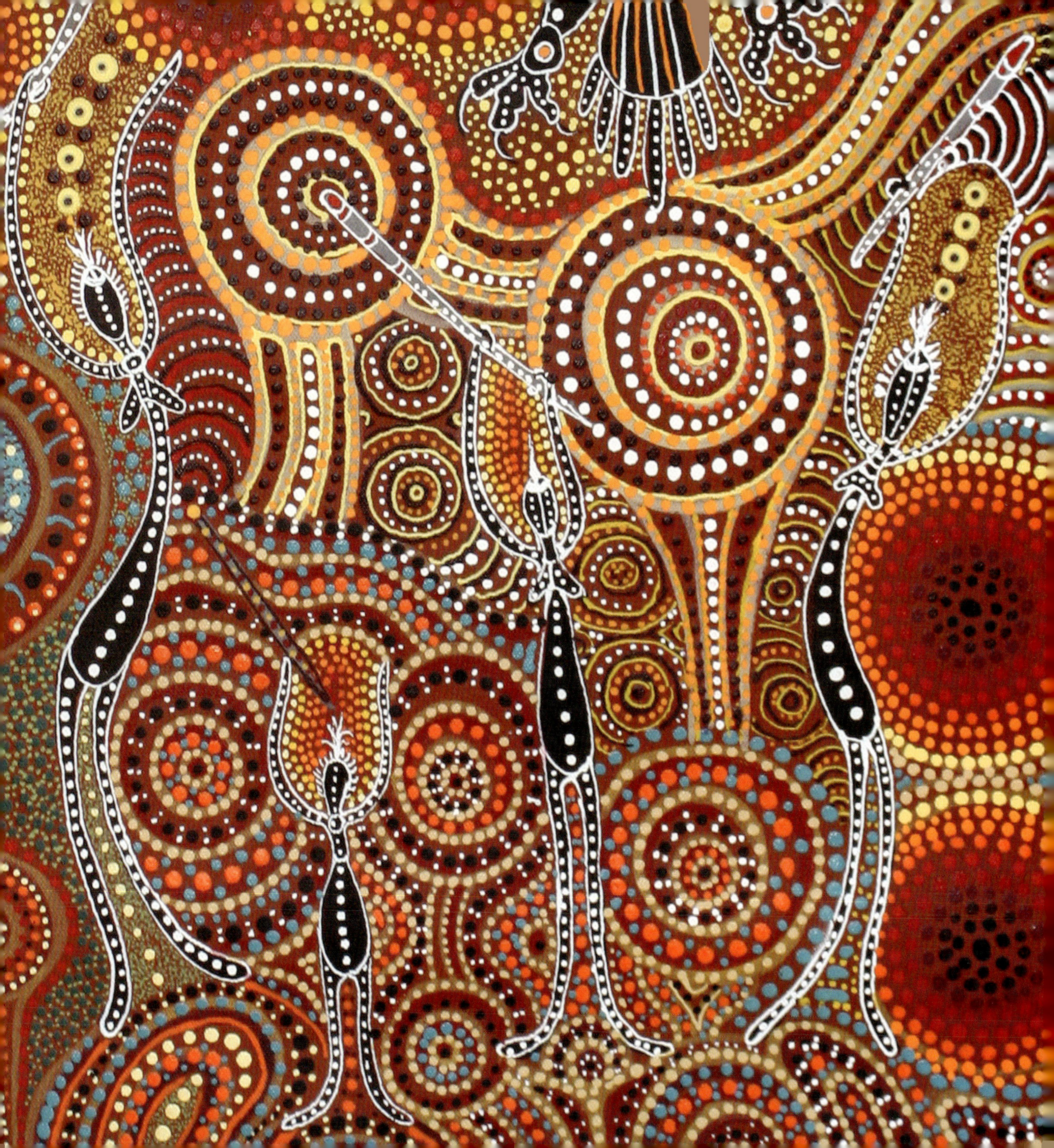

When my grandfather Atyelpe died in 1984, many people were very, very sad. The elders were very sad. They felt his death symbolised the end of our knowledge and our cultural practices. The changes to our culture and our way of life had been happening so fast and Atyelpe was one of the last who represented the old ways, one who had held ancient knowledge from the ancestors. The family he left behind was deeply sad and some of them did not want to pass on our cultural knowledge anymore. They didn't want to teach me or other younger people about the old days, the culture, stories, songs or dances. They wanted to forget what we had all lost. There was so much grieving, we were always in sadness thinking about the past.

When Atyelpe died, it was like a symbol of the end of our culture. The younger ones at Ltyentye Apurte don't seem to maintain their sites as well. They know their country – they know that really well – but they are not practicing much traditional business, or maintaining their sites. Some of our younger ones don't even know the stories of their country, they have forgotten their totems, and they don't know the special country of their grandparents. That is a sad thing. It needs to change.

When my Auntie Aggie lost her mum, she felt that way too. She didn't want to show anybody the songs and dances for their land anymore. From Therirrerte to Uyetye, and all the springs along the way, Aggie remembers the homelands song. I didn't want her to leave the songs closed, though. She was really so sad that the old people were finishing up, that her mum was gone.

Just after Atyelpe had passed away, I began teacher training up near Darwin. As part of the teacher's training we had a choice of what to research. I wanted to research my culture.

Tyepetye-ileme, sand drawing.

158

Therirrerte for the first time for many, many years. It was the end of the 1980s, before Aggie's mum died. Magelena was there, Aggie, her mum, my grandfather's sister, and old Mrs Ryder. We cried when we got there. We felt so sad; my grandfather's sister grieved because being in that homeland brought back all the memories of her life with her family. They were already finished up when we went back there that time. This sadness is part of the whole experience. The sadness and the loss we feel is part of our past and our memory. We were grieving for people who had died but also for what knowledge we were losing, what culture we had lost. But we go past that sorrow and grief.

Doing that research project with my elders helped me remember more of the stories I had been told. It made our songs and stories seem important and valuable again. I don't ever want that to be lost. I remember all the names of places in our country because I started learning those when I was still little. My husband also taught culture and was proud about me doing teacher training. He used to tell stories. He was really strong in his culture; we had the same mind about it. He let me study and when I went away, up near Darwin for teacher's college, I left him to look after all the little children at home by himself! He didn't mind, he knew what I was learning was important.

In the research I wrote about visiting Therirrerte and remembering our songs.

Ancient figure of woman and butterflies at Therirrerte.

I think I always knew that if we didn't do something it would all be lost and forgotten. I feel the same way now too. In order to keep holding our *altyerrenge* and their songs which are part of our culture, it became important then, as it still is now, to learn and to know our culture.

I went to Auntie Aggie and other family members and after a while they agreed to visit

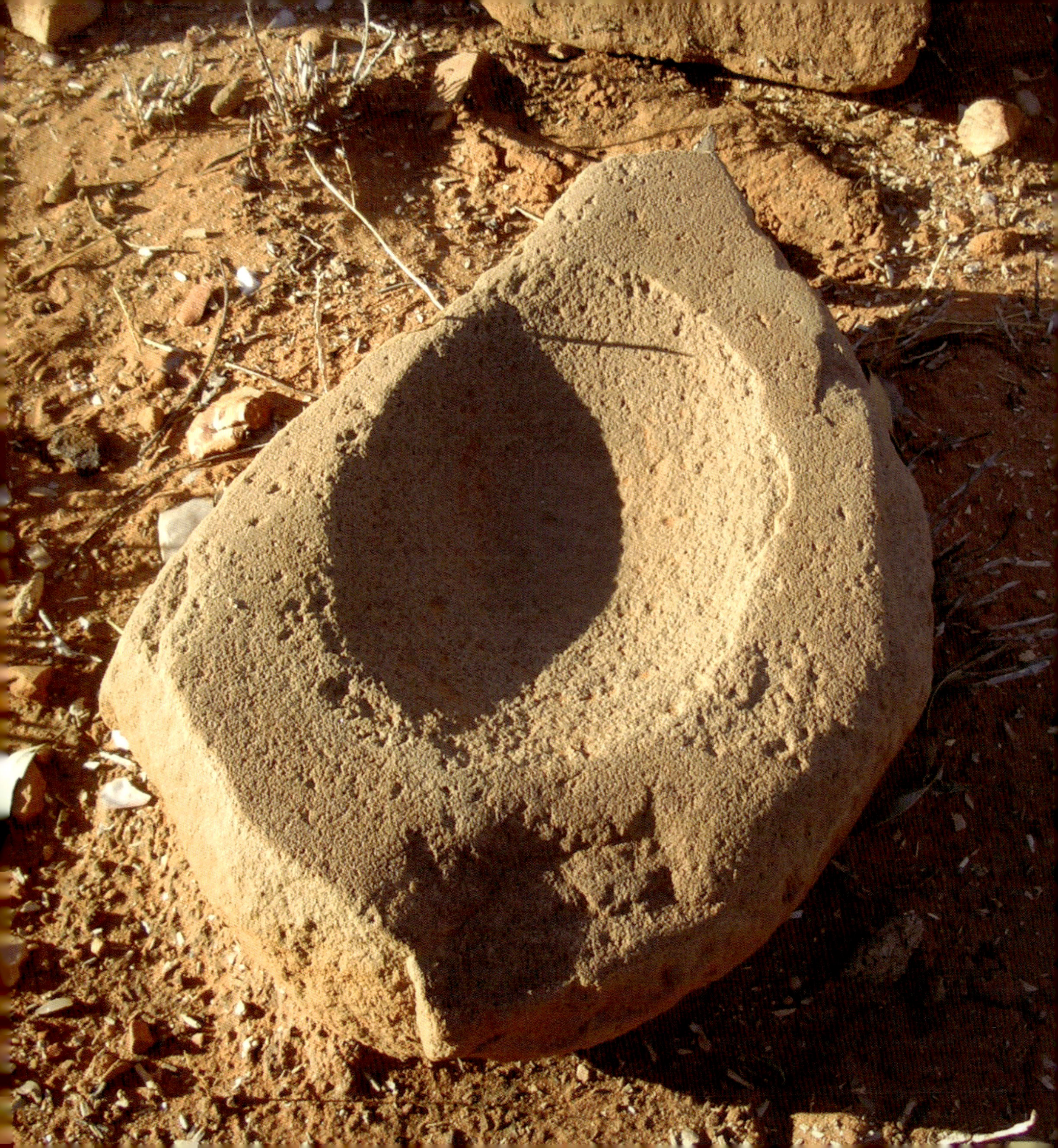

I brought all my writing back with me from Batchelor in a big box but I don't know where it is now. Even at the time I was doing teacher training I thought about making a book.

At Therirrerte I asked Aggie and the others to teach us younger ones the song. At first they all just wanted to leave it alone. Never teach us anymore, never teach our young ones. But I remember my childhood, living in a traditional way with my grandparents. I knew it was still important and I didn't want to lose my culture, that's why I went back to the old people left in my family. They felt it was finished when the old people finished. But parts of that homelands song were still in my mind. We had nearly forgotten how to sing it, but when all my aunties started singing together they remembered the whole thing – little by little. We sang the homelands song.

That song is celebrating, it is about the beautiful journey through our homelands, guided by the ancestors and the country itself. It's not a love song, but the homelands song is for everyone. It is about a journey that all the family share. It tells us about the journey our ancestors took through our land.

Auntie Aggie had sung little bits of other songs to us, but some bits she never sang until we started doing this book. My cousin sister Sharon and I had to really keep on at her. We are two of her nieces, and these are the songs of our mothers, her sisters. They are very private and special songs belonging to particular women in our family. She did sing them to us, and we have them to keep now.

So, you see I have to keep on asking my elders to teach me too, even though I am an elder now. I want all the young ones to know their culture, and their country. My sisters and my cousins are the same, we all want to try and preserve the bits and pieces that are left with us, before we too are gone. Our job is to look after the knowledge we are given and to pass it on properly, to the correct people, but not to own it. Our job is to look after it and with it our *apmere*.

Our grandfathers always told us not to lose our culture, always encouraged us to learn it from them. Aggie knows that too. Her elders told her that when she was growing up. I had lost some of it when I was sent to school at Santa Teresa mission. It was our elders then who kept it going – Aggie and other aunties and uncles – and I have always asked them to keep teaching me.

OPPOSITE: *Athere,* grinding stone.

Tapping stick song

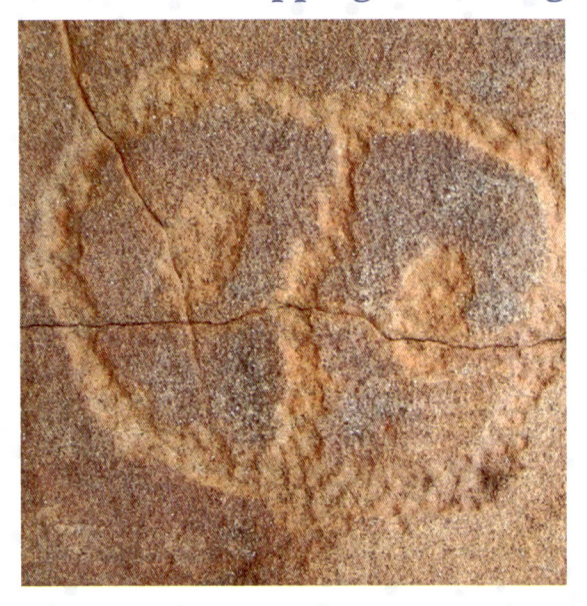

The Tapping stick song is about a journey our ancestors made from Therirrerte to Antewerle. It celebrates the *apmere* and the world we knew so well. When I hear this song, it makes me remember how we too walked from one camp to another, across our homelands, and how we were taught so many things – the names of the birds, trees, snakes, stars, of all the places in our country we needed to look after, where the soaks and rockholes are and when and how to clean them out – things my grandparents taught me as I grew up.

In the old days, our ancestors spent time watching the world around them, watching things like the butterflies. They would watch from the start, first the little eggs, then the caterpillars, then larvae and finally beautiful butterflies. The butterfly would die after laying the eggs and then the cycle would start again. People loved to look around and spent much of their time watching the life around them. The butterflies and their cycle of life were important to our ancestors. Sometimes the ancestors would find a butterfly that was missing a wing or nearing the end of its life. They would feel sad that such a beautiful thing would end up that way, but they knew that the cycle would continue with the laying of more eggs and the growth of the butterfly through its life stages.

In this song we talk a lot about water and lightning, and a bit about butterflies. The old people would have seen lightning many times and sometimes, when rain comes, the lightning is magnificent – I think that is why they started singing about it. Because the lightning is so exceptional when it lights the sky – and it's connected to *kwatye* which is life giving – everything was compared to lightning in the Tapping stick song! Movement is like lightning, tapping sticks sound like lightning, leaves sparkle like lightning, girls eyes flash like lightning, water ripples like lightning, butterfly's wings shimmer and move like lightning.

The story in the song began with everyone leaving Therirrerte to move to another camp. They knew they must leave because the food and water were running low, but they still needed to be guided on their journey. As they prepared to leave, the children saw pretty little yellow and blue butterflies underneath the low bushes. The children called out to tell the others and soon everyone started to notice them. That is how the dance starts: the beautiful butterflies are fluttering their wings like little bits of lightning. The dancers swing little sticks and leaves around while they dance – the leaves shimmer like lightning. We sing about the sweet perfume from the flowers the women pick and how very beautiful they look; when the women dance, they have soft, flashing eyes. The perfume from the flowers is sweet and the women are very beautiful.

Soon, the butterflies are left behind, and the women in the group all see a rainbow, indicating the next camping place they must walk to. The rainbow they can see spreads from behind Atyenhenge Atherre at Ltyentye Apurte, which is a sacred site with a little spring on one side

LEFT TO RIGHT: Rock carving of butterfly.

Butterfly, 2003, acrylic on ceramic, 20 x 20 cm

Butterfly, 2004, acrylic on ceramic, 43 cm diameter

Butterflies, 2004, acrylic on ceramic, 50 x 30 cm

Tapping Sticks, 2006, acrylic on canvas, 60 x 46 cm

of the Urlampe-arenye Range. From there the rainbow arcs across the sky to Antewerle. From that rainbow the women know which direction the group needs to travel to find their next good camp.

As they all walk towards this rainbow they see big, bright lightning, but no clouds. They ask one another, "where are the clouds? Why is there lightning without rain clouds?" Suddenly, a pair of tapping sticks fly out of the ground and up into the sky. The tapping sticks are a strong guide – they appear so that they can show people which way to go, to bring them home from a long way away or to lead them forward to the next camp. The people know they can follow the sticks and they will be led towards a good camp area with food and water close by. These two tapping sticks often flew up from the ground into the sky to guide people when there was a need. The same sticks could be sent after someone if they ran away, to turn them around and bring them back home. So when people saw them they thought, this is the sign for us to move on. It is all finished here – nothing will be left to hunt for or to drink. We will walk towards the rainbow, following the tapping sticks.

In this way everyone followed the sticks from Therirrerte towards Ltyentye Apurte spring. In my grandfathers' grandfathers' days everyone walked everywhere, slowly, and in the song the two tapping sticks never left them until they had all arrived at the next camp.

The hill behind Ltyentye Apurte community, near Keringke Art Centre, is part of the Urlampe-arenye Range. The community which is called Ltyentye Apurte does not actually stand where the Ltyentye Apurte spring was. That was a special spring on the other side of Atyenhenge Atherre, Grandfather and Grandson. It is a water Dreaming place, but now that sacred site, where

Dancing Women, 2004, acrylic on canvas, 35 x 25 cm

ABOVE: *Irrarnte*, c. 1990, glazed ceramic, 34 x 18 cm

RIGHT: *Landscape*, c. 1970, acrylic on canvas, 38 x 50 cm

the ground-water spring was, is all covered up with sand. Those two, Atyenhenge Atherre, are still sitting there though. In the ancestor days they had travelled all around our homelands bringing rain to make rock pools, springs and creeks. Although Grandson had wanted to keep travelling, Grandfather was too tired. He said to that young man, "I can't go any more; I am too tired and I am stopping here". So, that's right where they stopped and they're still there, in those two big rocks. That is what we were taught.

After a while, Atyenhenge Atherre became two large clouds that moved off that hill. Their rock form stayed there, as we see today, but as *altyerre* beings these old ones changed shape from one place to another. Coming from that hill the two big clouds moved around until they stopped over Irrarnte-Kenhe, Black Cockatoo Bore. In the song, the old people sing about the rain they made there all falling in that one place. The people didn't know why that rain was just in one place and all coming from just two big clouds – it must have been Atyenhenge Atherre, as those big clouds. There was lightning then too, but only where Atyenhenge Atherre was.

From the Therirrerte side of Urlampe-arenye country, the people walking could see the big rain falling in one place. When they got there they found it had drowned everything but the black cockatoos. Those cockatoos were everywhere! Water remained there and even today we still stop and drink water from there. These days there is a little creek, and a windmill, but it is still named after the little black cockatoos, Irrarnte-Kenhe – Black Cockatoo Bore.

Our song ends when they have reached Antewerle, passing the springs at Irrarnte-Kenhe and Ltyentye Apurte, going around Urlampe-arenye Ranges and passing Atyenhenge Atherre there.

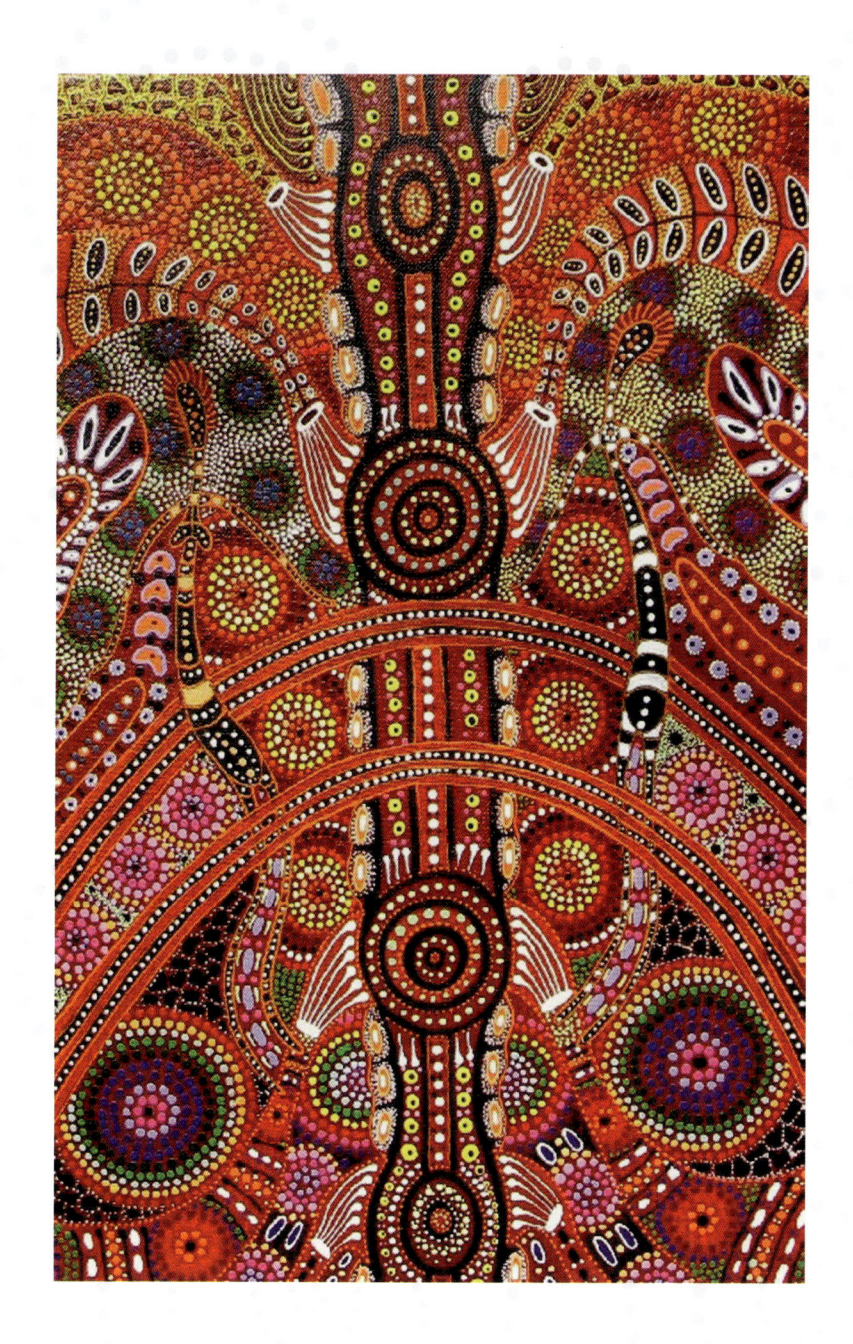

Mpwelarre, 2003, acrylic on linen, 46 x 30 cm

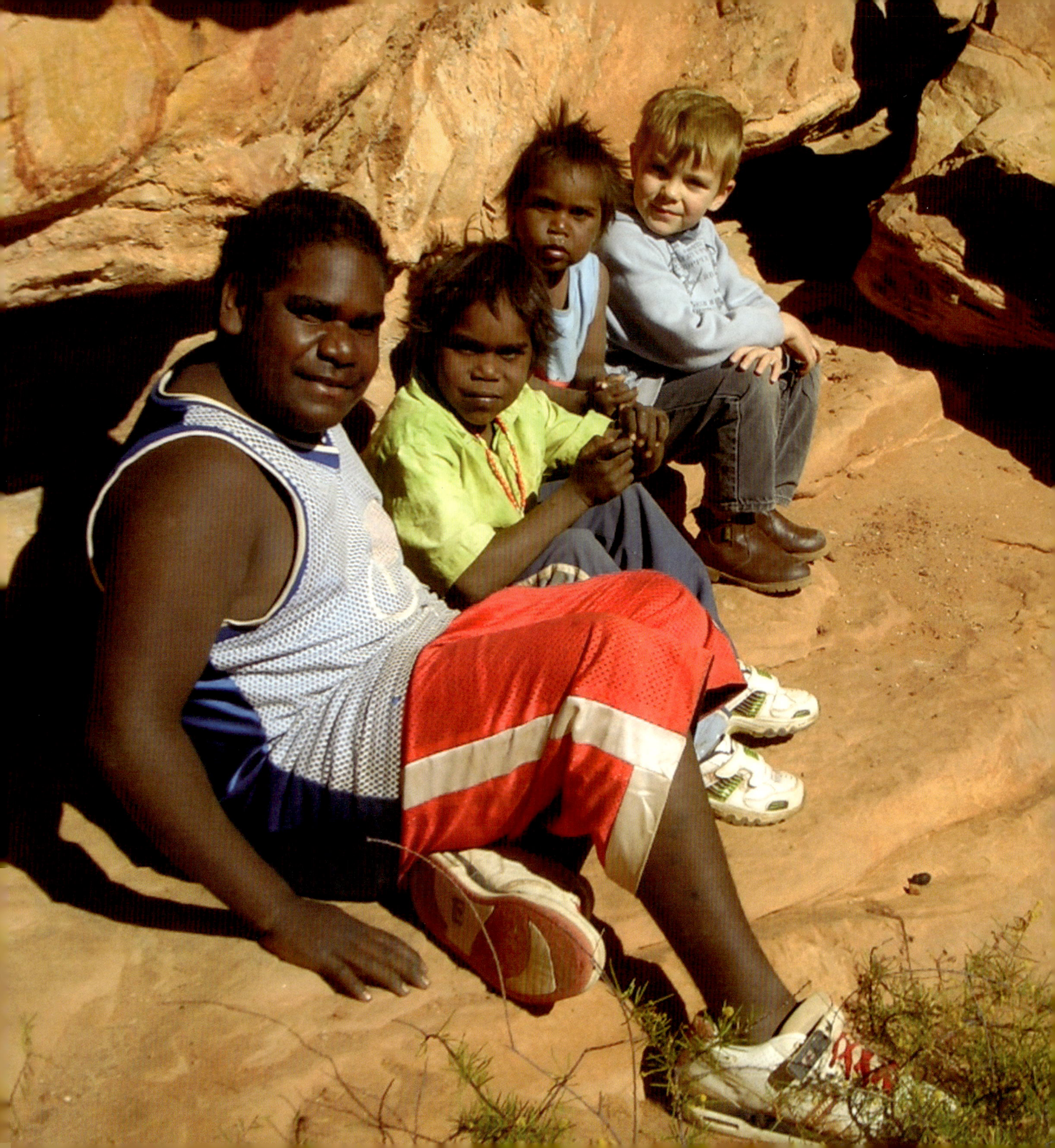

Akangkwirreme, Listen deeply

Through this book, my painting, our trips out bush, I am trying to help us see ourselves properly again. I want Arrernte to find their totem, their culture and their songs. I want them to learn these things for themselves and to keep them, teaching them to the young ones, for the future. I want them to know and understand their country. I want them to ask their elders, ask us to tell you the stories, sing you the songs and teach you the dances, the designs and the paintings.

We all need to learn and to keep learning. I keep asking my elders to give me information. My two aunties and my uncle, they are the last ones who can teach me. I have learned many things from my grandparents, my parents and others who have passed away. Most of this I was taught in the bush. That was my best schooling. I had to learn everything: name the trees, birds, animals, places, people, everything. I am sad that a lot of those animals and plants are all finished now, but I still don't want to forget them. The spirits are still here, in our country. Our way of life has all changed, but we can still listen to our ancestors, our elders, our country and our culture.

Our homelands country has slipped away from us now, and we can't get it back to how it was before. There have been too many cattle, and some station owners don't let us get through to our own sites. They don't even protect our sites from their cattle with fences. Out there, it's like we don't own anything anymore. The waterholes are choked up, or

OPPOSITE: Boys listen to Kathleen at Itnewerrenge (left to right): Randy Wallace, Jacob Doolan, Bart Doolan and Noah Tyley.

dirtied by the cattle, camels, wild horses. Some of our country is now just like a dream to us. When we drive through that country I just look at it. I look at the places where we don't live anymore. We can only look because it belongs to somebody else. The cattle money seems more important to many of them than us or our culture or our sites. It makes me really sad. We know how to look after this country, but no one even talks to us about that knowledge, or about our history and traditions.

All of us have been affected and most got sickness from the way things changed for us. First, it was just some old people going to look for easy food on the mission. Then they stopped hunting altogether, had nothing to do anymore, no country to look after. That started something which wasn't good. The younger people saw and thought: what are our old people doing? They are just drinking. So then they started to do the same thing. When the old people lose their culture, the children don't ever learn it. That is what has happened to too many Arrernte. They have lost something very important and special to them: They have lost identity in their culture, their songs, their Dreaming, even their totems. They don't know anything about who they are, or where their country is in our way. It is not good for them, not good for the land, not good for the children.

The strongest thing I want to say to our children today is: don't forget our culture. It is important. Listen to the old people, don't just turn away. Listen respectfully to what they say, and go forward.

To teach children we must tell the stories, take them out bush, move around out there with them. Go out hunting, look for what you want to find, talk to them about what you're looking for. It is survival. Teach children not to go hungry, but where to look for good food. Teach them to dance and sing in their country, explain to them the way our lives changed as we moved on to the missions and away from the homelands. They should still learn about the country and survival. Teach them about the trees, the wood and its uses. Water, where to find water and how to clean it up for drinking. Which trees to get witchetty from the trunk and which from the root. Think deeply, tell stories, talk about what you do – that is how our children learn best, by doing things. It is also a way to teach other people from outside our culture – show them our country.

My great grandparents always lived out bush. They never went into town; they didn't know what town was like. All they knew about white people was what they found at the stations where they used to get food from time to time. As it got harder and harder for them to find bush food the stations became unavoidable. Many younger relatives had taken work on stations, then later the boys from the Alice Springs Bungalow worked on the stations too. Gradually we all had to learn to live in the European world, but it is our world too. Both worlds are here now. Let's make it all work together.

To all the other children and people I would say: Come, listen to us, we will tell you our culture. Learn from us. That way we will all survive. We share this country. We need to work together and learn from each other. We must do things together: respecting, listening and thinking, doing things together, not just talking all the time. Sometimes think, just let there be silence. You must learn to wait, let your thoughts come back to you. Understand how the other person might be feeling too, appreciate you might not know the answer or understand the question. That's what it means to work in a cross cultural way. Respect has to flow both ways, learning too.

Together we have worked hard on this book. I hope you really like it, that you let the stories and the paintings teach you something new every time you look. I hope you listen deeply and let these stories in. These stories are for all time, for the old days, to help remember the old people, but also for the future and for young people now. In return for the stories from our elders, we had to give the food we had hunted – it was what we had to do to learn, sharing means our survival.

Emu man ancestor

Everyone can learn from stories; this one is about listening, learning and respecting the culture we share. It is about the knowledge of our ancestors, speaking to us through *apmere*, art, dance, song and stories. This story used to be told to us by our grandparents. It shows us the importance of respecting our culture and its laws – especially about trying to break up other people's family. It is a story of endeavour, trust and good faith.

The place where this story happened is somewhere over towards Deep Well, but where it happened is not as important as what happened. When they told us, our grandparents would stop every little while and sing a special song, which makes this a really long story. It is a story about a man from the emu *altyerre* called Pintaherraherre who had two human wives. We would usually be going to sleep as it ended.

In the beginning of his life, Pintaherraherre took the form of a man who could change into the form of an emu. An evil woman spirit, an *arrentye*, saw him and wanted him for herself. He was already happy with the two wives he lived with and they were happy with him. Politely he told the evil spirit, "I am very sorry, but I already have two wives". The spirit woman got very angry and turned him into an emu who could not change back into the form of a man. She made him *arrentye* too, as punishment for refusing to become her husband. He stayed in the form of an emu for a long, long time. His human wives stayed with him although he

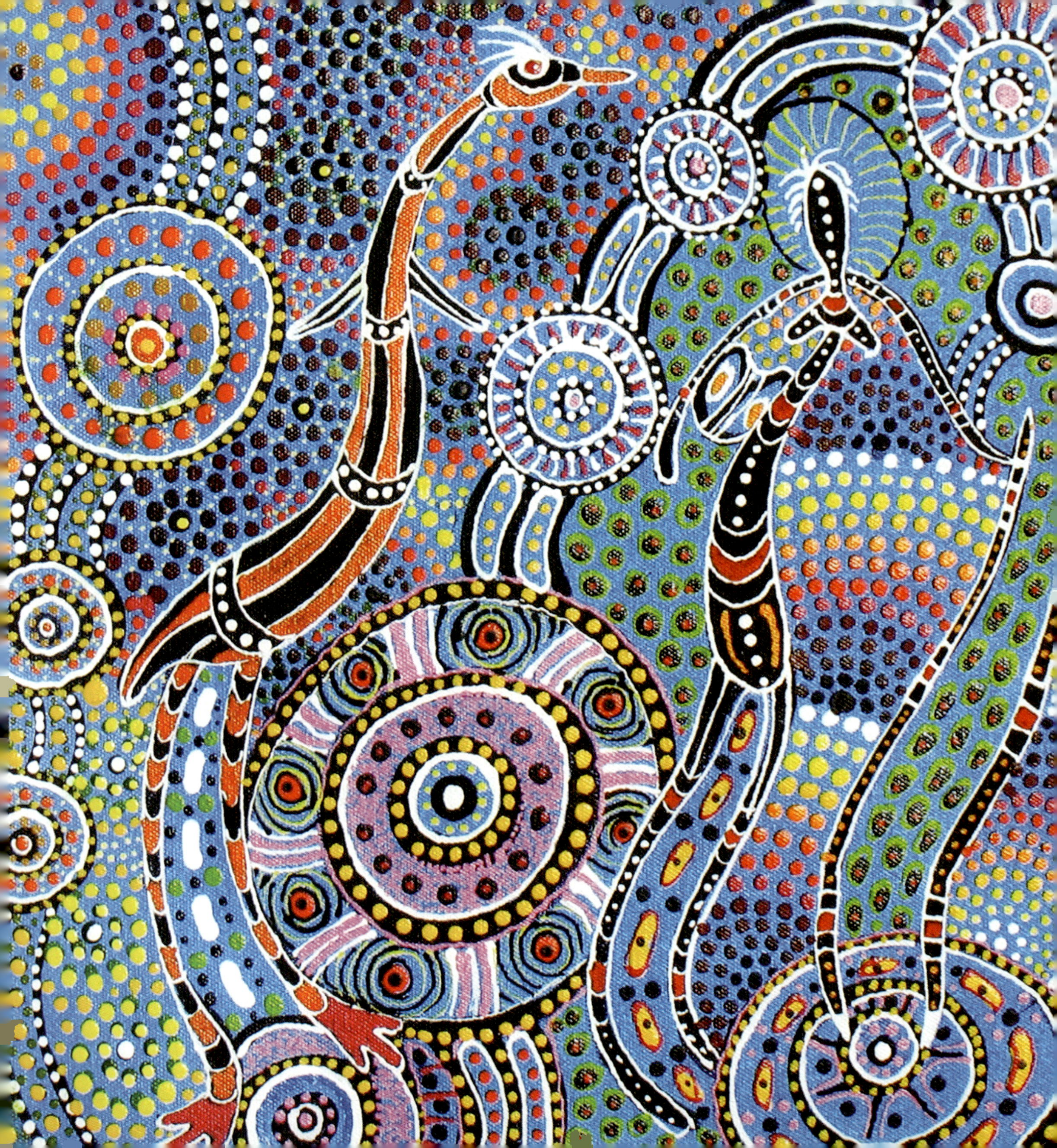

was now an emu and held powers of *arrentye*. They walked around everywhere together. Pintaherraherre used to gather *awele-awele*, bush tomatoes, for them and the women still gathered food for him. Like all emu, he found he especially liked *alyawe* seeds, and *ngkwernelyerre* berries.

This part of the story was often drawn for us in the sand as our elders sung the story. They scooped out the sand to form the holes, drew the wurley shape and the fire. Sometimes they added gum leaves and sticks to indicate the wurley, or the movement of the people. We used to follow the story as they drew it out in the sand.

Together, the family set up a proper camp with a wurley, a windbreak, and some holes next to it to sleep in. One wife made a hole to put the seeds in for Pintaherraherre to eat from, and another hole for him to sit down in. The other wife made two holes for the two wives. Pintaherraherre sat in the hole his wives prepared for him and ate his seeds from the other hole. The women made another hole for the *awele-awele* they would share. The family had a fire the women used to cook beside their holes and their wurley. It was a good bush camp.

Pintaherraherre sat in a hole on one side of the wurley, eating what the women gathered for him, and they sat on the other side eating what he gathered for them. As a man he had carried a bag on a string around his neck. You will notice that to this day the emu has a sack in front of his neck called a crop, with his food in. As a real man, he used to take food from the bag around his neck and give it to his wives. As an emu he ate it first and then brought it up from his crop to feed his wives.

The family slept in the windbreak at night and each day they would go out hunting. Pintaherraherre used to go a long, long way away to look for food, but the women stayed closer to the camp. Before he went far away he would tell his two wives, "you look after yourselves or someone might try to take you away from here".

LEFT AND OPPOSITE (detail):
Pintaherraherre, 2008,
acrylic on linen, 25 x 35 cm

"Oh," the women would say, "we'll look after ourselves". "I am going to pick some seeds," he would say. And his wives would say, "we're just going over there to pick some *awele-awele* and some berries".

Pintaherraherre had a strange power which helped him when he was away from his wives. His beak was very sensitive and sometimes it would twitch. He had learnt to pay attention to

Tyepetye, sand drawing of emu footprint.

the twitching and so he knew that a little twitch alerted him that something was happening out of the ordinary, so he would come back quietly and see if the women were safe. After reassuring himself they were safe and happy he would continue his hunting. Each day they all did the same things. They were all happy enough like this.

One day, they all went further than usual. Pintaherraherre went a long way further away, leaving the women entirely unprotected. Usually he came back before the sun went down, but this day Pintaherraherre was too far away to get back before darkness.

Two young men had come past earlier that day and spied on the women from behind some bushes. The young men followed the women but didn't want to come into the camp straight away because they thought the women would run away. They hid themselves carefully, watching and waiting. They liked the look of the women and said to each other, "oh, we'll take them away for ourselves".

They jumped out from the bushes to grab the women, who shouted at them, "leave us alone, we have already got a good man, we've got *atyeperre*, special one. He's an *arleye*, emu, and he is *arrentye*, so he will really hurt you!" But those young men wouldn't listen at all to the women. They dragged Pintaherraherre's wives away from the family's camp. As they did so the women told them, "oh leave us alone! We got one *atyeperre arleye*. He will come after you".

While all this was occurring Pintaherraherre – who was still far, far away – felt his beak twitch violently. Oh, something big is happening back there at camp, he thought. He was picking all the *awele-awele*, but not very carefully anymore. He was distracted, thinking about what might be happening back at camp and how far away he was. However, he still went further away, picking more *awele-awele*. It was not until early morning that he finally returned to their camp to find that his wives had been dragged away by the two men!

That morning when he first approached their camp he noticed that there were crows flying around everywhere. He looked very carefully around and saw the tracks from the women being dragged along the ground. He started to follow them. He was very, very angry by then. He felt his head spinning, which made his eyes get very large. "Someone took my wives!" He looked like a really fierce *arrentye* by this time.

Pintaherraherre followed their tracks for four days. The women could see the dust cloud made by his feet as he came running closer. He was kicking up lots of dust because he was running very fast. His wives said to the two young men, "look, see over there! That is the dust flying from the feet of our *atyeperre arleye*. He is coming to get us back. He is *arrentye* and he is really angry with you two!" The men and women began to hear Pintaherraherre's footsteps drumming across the ground as he ran. Those two young men started to be really, really frightened. They realised that they had made a very big mistake; they should have listened to the two wives and left them alone. The women had never wanted to run off from their husband, even if he was an emu man! The two men quickly climbed up a big desert oak tree in the *arlpe*, sandhills, in an attempt to escape the angry *arrentye* husband.

As he sped towards them his wives jumped to one side, getting out of the way for Pintaherraherre so he could see the men climbing up the tree. He went straight for the tree the men were in. With his foot slashing from side to side, he sliced that tree trunk until the tree fell over. Then he stamped all over the young men, killing them, stamping all over them and the fallen-down tree.

Pintaherraherre turned to set off home again with his two wives, jumping over a few dry sticks as they went. As soon as he had jumped over those dry sticks his form changed back into that of a man. He was no longer *arrentye*, nor held in the form of an emu. Once again, Pintaherraherre was a proud young man.

Rock carving of emu footprint.

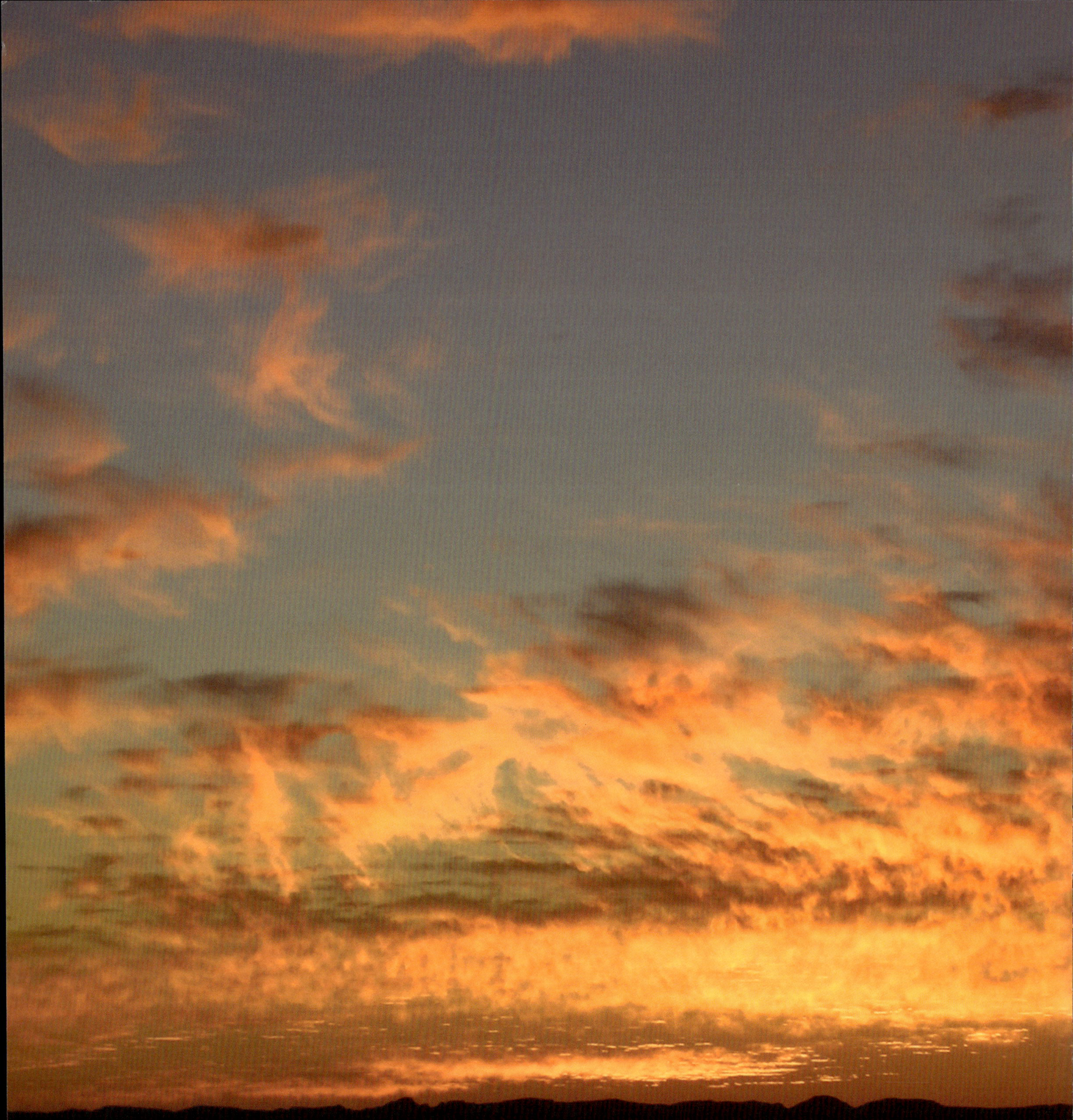

About *Listen deeply*...

This book is a journey into Kathleen Wallace's Eastern Arrernte world, a place with rich meaning and deep, strong cultural knowing. Through Kathleen's words and paintings we visit her country and its people, and through her life experiences and understated honesty we gain insight into some of the changes being experienced in her Arrernte world.

We hope that this book is inspiring and enriching to Eastern and Central Arrernte and to people from other places and cultures. Making it has been an exciting process.

In the first instance the stories in the book were recorded, in English, at the places where they belong. When we were camping out collecting stories, Kathleen, her aunt Aggie and some of her extended family performed songs and dances associated with the stories and their places. Seeing and hearing them in their country brought to life the images, gestures, people, colours and movement of Kathleen's art and her storytelling.

When the English was translated into Eastern Arrernte, we found that the stories didn't include enough Arrernte references to make sense when written in that language. We are very grateful to the women who undertook this initial translation – their hard work is the foundation of the Arrernte manuscript which has been reviewed through a further process of recording and transcription. Kathleen retold the stories in Arrernte especially for this book, so that they reflect her voice and her style of narration. They contain words which do not appear in any published Eastern Arrernte language resource. For example, there are many terms for a stone knife in the *Eastern and Central Arrernte to English Dictionary* (IAD Press, 1994), but the knife Kathleen calls *thurle* is not there. Not having a written record of Kathleen's dialect to refer to required writing down some terms for the first time. This has been done based largely on the current orthographic conventions of Eastern and Central Arrernte, but with ultimate deference to capturing the social context and purpose in Kathleen's spoken voice.

LEFT AND OPPOSITE: Sunset clouds at Therirrerte.

There are always gaps between oral traditions and their written forms. In Kathleen's childhood, the storytelling was often performance of a story: *tyepetye-ileme*, women's sand drawings using leaves and twigs, or singing and dancing together while decorated with particular ochre body paint designs. Some of the words written here are the narratives of those stories. The paintings are from the same Arrernte world as the narratives and show powerful events taking place within that world. Kathleen's use of both traditional and personal symbols makes the connection from her art form to its roots: the knowledge given by her ancestors. It is her responsibility to pass that knowledge on. By placing her stories and paintings side by side in this book Kathleen is revealing the complexities of this Arrernte world.

We have chosen our words carefully. We have used Arrernte words in some places in the English text to help you to understand the Arrernte ideas, or at least their connection deep into the Arrernte world. If we had tried to explain these ideas using English words, the meaning conveyed would have been deficient. For example, *altyerrenge* has commonly been translated as 'dreamtime'. But *altyerre* is not a dream and it is much more multifaceted than the English word 'dreamtime' suggests. As you will have found while you were reading, *altyerrenge* and *altyerre* name the events and beings from the beginning of the Arrernte world whose essence continues on in their land and its people. The term 'dreamtime' does not relay this perpetuality.

The potency of the oral narration in print is only captured when the essential voice that is Kathleen's is truly represented, as we have aspired to, in both languages. Her voice can be clearly heard on the CD, and by seeing her paintings and listening deeply to these stories, the complex, rich, deep Eastern Arrernte world is made more real and important to you.

Kele mwerre, urreke aretyenhenge!

Judy Lovell with Kathleen Wallace

LEFT: Judy and Kathleen working together at Uyetye. Photographer Andrew West

OPPOSITE: Kathleen painting.

About the paintings...

Kathleen Wallace's paintings are easily recognisable. Within a contemporary survey of Aboriginal art, her style and palette are singular. The painting surface is stippled with intricate, fine dotting and line, broken into colours which may either resonate or jar one's visual perception. This field of energy and intricate detail resides within brush strokes that provide strong compositional design.

Kathleen's paintings are full of different spaces and overlapping focal planes. Some spaces open out or close in around the viewer, leading the eye over an aerial, horizontal plane. This view of a kind of landscape is inhabited by figures which hang in a vertical space, having ethereal qualities that nevertheless leave them barely separate from the landscape. Within and around these spirits and landscape forms identifiable Arrernte symbols can be found: clearly marked bird tracks, nests with eggs, or kangaroo, emu and other animal tracks. These often traverse and delineate their particular space within the painting in ways which are metaphoric of journeys taken by Kathleen's ancestors in their various forms.

Many of the marks made on the painting surface represent details which may not be readily interpreted until the viewer has some familiarity with the Arrernte world that they represent. As you listen deeply and let the stories in, learning something of this Arrernte world, you may see more deeply into the painted layers that inform the cultural events and activities within these paintings.

Judy Lovell

IAD Press
PO Box 2531
Alice Springs NT 0871
PHONE: +61 8 8951 1334
FAX: +61 8 8951 1381
sales@iad.edu.au
www.iadpress.com

Proudly sponsored by
Northern Territory Government

Australian Government
Department of the Environment, Water, Heritage and the Arts

Australia Council for the Arts

Published by IAD Press in 2009

© Arrernte language and cultural information: Arrernte people
© Text: Kathleen Wallace and Judy Lovell 2008
© Artworks: Kathleen Wallace
© Photographs: Judy Lovell, unless otherwise indicated in captions
© Audio stories: Kathleen Wallace
© Audio recording: Judy Lovell

This book is copyright. Apart from any fair dealings for the purpose of private study, research, criticism or review as permitted under the *Copyright Act 1968* and subsequent amendments, no part of this book may be reproduced, stored in a retrieval system, or transmitted in any form or by any means electronic, mechanical, photocopying, recording or otherwise, without prior permission. Please forward all enquiries to IAD Press at the address above.

National Library of Australia Cataloguing-in-Publication data:

Wallace, Kathleen (Kathleen Kemarre), 1948–
Listen deeply: let these stories in / Kathleen Wallace, Judy Lovell.
ISBN 978 1 86465 094 5 (pbk.).

Painters, Aboriginal Australian – Northern Territory – Biography.
Women, Aboriginal Australian – Northern Territory – Biography.
Eastern Arrernte (Australian people) – Religion.
Eastern Arrernte (Australian people) – Social life and customs.
Other Authors/Contributors: Lovell, Judy.

759.994

Cover photographs: Judy Lovell
Book design: Darren Pfitzner, A4Art
Map image: TGH Strehlow
Printing: Hyde Park Press, Australia

This activity is supported by the Australian Government under the Indigenous Culture Support Program of the Department of Environment, Water, Heritage and the Arts.

The Institute for Aboriginal Development is assisted by the Commonwealth Government through the Australia Council, its arts funding and advisory body.

Acknowledgements...

Many people have contributed to the journey which became this book and we are grateful to them all. There is not enough room without writing another book to say thank you in full, but we will list them here:

Thank you to Douglas Peltharre Wallace (dec.), Veronica Perrurle Dobson, Mia Mulladad, and Agnes Perrurle Abbott, for their assistance in matters of language and culture.

Thank you to Anita Gorey, Elaine Gorey, Agnes Mary Palmer (dec.), Sally Ulamari, Barry McDonald and, again, Veronica Dobson, for their work with translation. Thank you to Mary Flynn for her work on the transcriptions.

We thank Keringke Arts Aboriginal Corporation, Waltja Tjutangku Palyapayi, IAD Press and A4Art for their unwavering support for our travels and for recognising, valuing and supporting this process.

We are grateful for assistance from the NT Government History Grants scheme, the Aboriginal and Torres Strait Islander Arts Board of the Australia Council, and Arts NT.

To our families we are especially grateful and we thank our friends without whose constant support the book would not have been completed. So, in alphabetical order, thank you to:

Katie Allen
Bart Doolan
Jacob Doolan
Bo Doolan
Kerry Doolan
Neville Doolan
Dorothea Cambell
Kwementyaye Cambell
Maureen Ellis
Sacara Ellis
Patricia Ellis
Amber Hammill
Michael Hayes
Rosalie Hayes
Carole Kayrooz
Shorty Mulladad
Noah Tyley
Jess Tyley
Alan Tyley
Luke Wallace
Deandra Wallace
Treahna Wallace
Randy Wallace
Stanley Wallace
John Wallace
Tania Whyte